ACCOUNTING FOR NONPROFIT ORGANIZATIONS

FOURTH EDITION

EMERSON O. HENKE
J. E. Bush Professor of Accounting
Hankamer School of Business
Baylor University

KENT PUBLISHING COMPANY
 A Division of Wadsworth, Inc.
Boston, Massachusetts

Senior Editor: John B. McHugh
Assistant Editor: Katherine B. Murray
Production Editor: Eve B. Mendelsohn
Interior Designer: Nancy Blodget
Cover Designer: Glenna Lange
Production Coordinator: Marcia Stanczyk

Kent Publishing Company
A Division of Wadsworth, Inc.

Printed in the United States of America

1 2 3 4 5 6 7 8 9—90 89 88 87 86

Material from the Uniform CPA Examination Questions and Unofficial Answers for the years 1951 through 1984, copyright © (1983 and 1984) by the American Institute of Certified Public Accountants, Inc., is reprinted or adapted with permission.

Portions of this text have appeared in *Introduction to Nonprofit Organization Accounting,* Second Edition, by Emerson Henke, Kent Publishing Company, 1985. Copyright © 1985, 1980 by Wadsworth, Inc.

Library of Congress Cataloging-in-Publication Data

Henke, Emerson O.
    Accounting for nonprofit organizations.

      Bibliography: p. 322
      Includes index.
      1. Corporations, Nonprofit—Accounting. I. Title.
HF5686.N56H448   1986   657′.98   85–23872
ISBN 0–534–06018–8

PREFACE

Accounting for Nonprofit Organizations, Fourth Edition is the twentieth anniversary edition of a book that was first published in 1966 as a 147-page paperback in the Wadsworth Accounting Series. This edition, like the others in its twenty-year life, is designed for upper-level undergraduate or graduate students in accounting. It can also be used as a supplementary text for part of an intermediate or advanced accounting course dealing with the accounting practices for this less frequently encountered area, as a reference text for a CPA review course, or as a text for part of a survey course in accounting theory.

The book introduces the student to the accounting practices of nonprofit organizations. It demonstrates similar fundamental accounting and recording problems faced by all the more important types of entities operating within the nonprofit area. Discussion of specific procedures is minimal except in Chapters 3 and 4, which cover basic fund accounting techniques. In those chapters the recording procedures recommended by the 1980 edition of Governmental Accounting, Auditing and Financial Reporting (GAAFR) are used. Users of the text should recognize that these recording *procedures* reflect that publication's *interpretation* of the concepts embodied in Statement 1 issued by the National Council of Governmental Accounting (NCGA).

Question, exercise, and problem materials have been expanded in this edition and are now provided for all chapters. They are designed to encourage the student to think creatively and to develop the ability to apply the concepts and techniques developed in the narrative part of each chapter. Questions and exercises should be especially useful in promoting class discussion.

One completely new feature of the Fourth Edition is the inclusion of a chapter on budgeting. This chapter is designed to show the student how budgetary data are developed and used by nonprofit organizations. Illustrative transactions for colleges and universities and health and welfare agencies have also been added (see Chapters 6 and 7).

Chapter 8, dealing with the analysis and interpretation of nonprofit organization financial statements, is designed to show students how externally interested parties can use the published financial data and other information in evaluating the activities of those organizations. These materials should be useful to all students as they become constitutents of or serve on governing boards of these organizations.

I wish to express my appreciation to the American Institute of Certified

Public Accountants, the National Council of Governmental Accounting, the National Association of College and University Business Officers, and the American Hospital Association for allowing me to quote from their publications. I am especially indebted to the American Institute of Certified Public Accountants for permitting me to use a number of nonprofit organization oriented problems from past CPA examinations. I would also like to thank the following reviewers for their helpful comments: Bernard Newman (Pace University), Walter A. Robbins (University of Alabama), and Charles R. Wagner (Mankato State University). Finally, I wish to express my appreciation to Mrs. Evelyn Hupp and Mrs. Cathy Talbert for their work in typing and retyping the manuscript as the book was being produced.

Emerson O. Henke

CONTENTS

---

5 ACCOUNTING FOR COLLEGES AND UNIVERSITIES   170

---

6 ACCOUNTING FOR HOSPITALS   216

CONCEPTS UNDERLYING ACCOUNTING PRACTICES FOR NONPROFIT ORGANIZATIONS

1

Accounting is the language of economic activities. Therefore, accounting procedures, records, and statements should be logically consistent with the operating objectives of an organization and should provide useful information for interested groups. This chapter deals with the operating philosophy of nonprofit enterprises as it relates to their accounting practices. We shall develop that relationship by first examining operational characteristics common to nonprofit organizations and then describing accounting practices designed to meet those observed characteristics.

THE ENVIRONMENT SURROUNDING NONPROFIT ORGANIZATIONS

A *nonprofit organization* is an economic entity providing *socially desirable services without the intention of realizing a profit. Nonprofit organizations have no ownership shares that can be sold or traded by individuals and any excess of revenues over expenses or expenditures is used to enlarge the service capability of the organization. They are financed, at least partially, by taxes and/or contributions based on some measure of ability to pay, and some or all of their services are distributed on the basis of need rather than effective demand for them.* Within this definition we can characterize governmental entities, colleges and universities, most hos-

1

pitals, health and welfare agencies, churches, and foundations as nonprofit enterprise units.

Nonprofit organizations are characteristically exempt from federal income tax. The Internal Revenue Code currently lists twenty-eight classifications of organizations that may qualify for such exemption. Ordinarily, a form must be filed with the Internal Revenue Service to claim tax exempt status.

Even beyond their tax exempt status, nonprofit organizations can be categorized in a number of different ways. First, they can be divided into voluntarily and involuntarily supported entities. Private colleges, hospitals, health and welfare agencies, and churches are examples of voluntarily supported nonprofit organizations. Governmental entities supported by tax assessments make up the involuntarily supported group. This group includes entities such as cities, political subdivisions, and public schools. Nonprofit organizations can also be divided into categories based on the nature of support from their constituencies. For example, some organizations, such as hospitals and private colleges, are often expected to sustain their own normal operations after receiving an initial capital contribution. In another group are organizations that require full or partial operating support indefinitely. This group includes governmental units supported by periodic tax assessments, as well as health and welfare agencies, churches, and other organizations supported by repetitive voluntary contributions.

Enterprise units can be divided into four categories on the basis of their sources of equity financing and operating objectives, ranging from pure profit entities through quasi-profit entities and quasi-nonprofit entities to pure nonprofit entities. These are briefly described and related to the logically desired content of their operating statements in Exhibit 1.1. In this section we will examine more closely the operating environments surrounding both quasi-nonprofit and pure nonprofit organizations by considering:

1. their operational characteristics

2. their organizational structures

3. the underlying economic and social considerations justifying the existence of these organizations

4. the groups interested in the financial data of these organizations.

Operational Characteristics

The primary objective of a business enterprise is to return tangible benefits, generally in the form of cash distributions, to its owners. In contrast, the objective of a nonprofit organization is to supply a socially desirable service without regard for financial gain. Within the constraint of this basic service

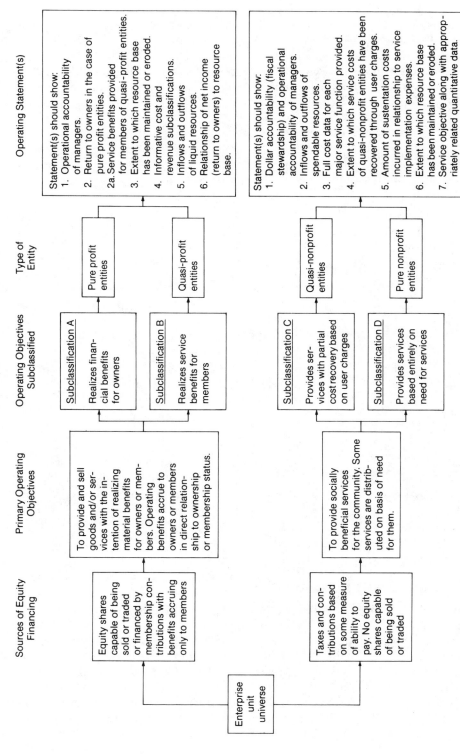

EXHIBIT 1.1 Elements of Enterprise Unit Universe

objective, however, some nonprofit organizations charge fees to cover some or all of the costs of their services. For example, colleges charge tuition and hospitals receive fees for their services. Generally, these charges are associated with those organizations expected to be more or less operationally self-sustaining after the initial input of capital by the constituency of the organization.

Organizational Structures

Within the limits imposed by our legal and economic environments, the operating requirements of an entity largely determine its organizational structure. This is especially observable as we examine the organizational characteristics of nonprofit organizations.

Individuals' rights to control the use of their property is a fundamental concept underlying the capitalistic system. As a person invests resources in the ownership shares of a business enterprise, he or she acquires a proportional voice in the management of the enterprise. As a result of this basic right, business enterprises are managed directly by their owners or indirectly through elected boards of directors.

Nonprofit organizations have no equity interests that can be owned, bought, or sold by individuals. Therefore, the rights to their management and control must be based on different relationships. Membership in a nonprofit organization may carry an equal voting privilege regardless of the amount paid or contributed. For example, a citizen has one vote on governmental affairs, and each church member typically has one vote on the affairs of his or her church. Control in these instances rests equally with each member regardless of the amount contributed in the form of taxes or church pledges.

Nonmembership organizations, such as colleges and hospitals, typically have *boards* elected or appointed in accordance with a charter or other legal document. In other instances, the constituency—those having an active interest in the entity—may select a board of trustees as the external management group. Either of the methods used to select the external management group is contrary to the basic arrangement—control being in proportion to ownership—used in profit-oriented enterprises.

Underlying Economic
and Social Considerations

Why do nonprofit organizations exist in the midst of our free enterprise system, which provides a standard of living far above that in any other country? Socially conscious people realize that dependence on profit motivation alone often fails to provide socially desirable services for those who most need them. Profit enterprises respond to the demands of the marketplace. These demands reflect not only needs for particular goods and services but also the purchasing power necessary to acquire them. Many persons lack the purchasing power for services that they need and desire. Therefore, if it is considered socially desirable for these persons to have such services, a governmental or other nonprofit agency will be established to meet those needs and desires. Thus, tax levies pay for the operations of a public school system, and voluntary contributions enable health and welfare agencies to provide socially desirable services for the less fortunate.

As we examine the operational activities, organizational characteristics, and underlying social and economic considerations of nonprofit organizations, we find that, to be logically consistent with such an environment, financial reports for nonprofit organizations should reflect the *service story* of the entity, rather than net income or net loss realized by the entity. In sharp contrast, accounting reports for profit enterprises must emphasize the extent of achievement of the profit objective and the ability of the entity to support itself.

Groups Interested in the Financial Data

As we have said, the service story should be emphasized in the financial reports for nonprofit organizations. The specific organization and content of financial statements should be determined by the needs of the groups expected to use them. The accountant should ascertain the kinds of information the users want and, within the limits of practicality, design the records and procedures necessary to provide the data. The principal groups using the financial data for nonprofit entities are:

1. external management groups such as boards of trustees

2. internal managers

3. the constituency

4. users of the entity's services

5. creditors

6. rating agencies

7. regulatory and accrediting agencies.

Having identified the environment within which nonprofit organizations operate and the principal groups using financial data for these enterprises, we next consider the accounting practices designed to meet those needs.

ACCOUNTING PRACTICES DESIGNED TO MEET THE ENVIRONMENTAL CHARACTERISTICS OF NONPROFIT ORGANIZATIONS

Accountants generally emphasize the fiduciary relationship of the entity to its constituency as a primary determinant of the information needed by user groups. Because nonprofit organizations have no profit objective by which the discharge of managerial responsibilities can be evaluated, accountants have turned to the concept of *dollar accountability* in defining the data to be included in the financial reports for some of these organizations.

As the term suggests, this concept of financial reporting requires an accounting system designed to produce data showing where the dollars of liquid (appropriable) resources originated and how they were used. These inflows and outflows of appropriable resources are reflected in a *statement of revenues and expenditures.* A *balance sheet* is prepared to show the amounts of appropriable resources available to the entity at the end of each period along with the short-term obligations to be met from those resources. The equity account in such a balance sheet is called *fund balance.*

As we analyze the operations of an entity using this concept of reporting, attention is focused on *judging whether resources have been acquired and used in desirable or prescribed ways, rather than on evaluating the results of their use.* The interested groups, therefore, receive details about the sources of assets and the ways they were used. This need for details about inflows and outflows naturally leads to a strong emphasis on item-by-item controls in the acquisitions and disposals of resources.

In this section we explain how these controls are implemented by:

1. describing techniques that can be used in controlling the uses of resources

2. citing the primary sources of prescribed nonprofit accounting principles

3. presenting the Summary Statement of Principles for Governmental Entities

4. developing and explaining the nonprofit organization accounting equation

5. listing the unique types of transactions typically found in dollar accountability accounting records.

Controlling the Uses of Resources

Managerial compliance with fiduciary responsibilities can be disclosed by three reporting techniques that are consistent with the concept of dollar accountability, some of which are also used in the profit area.

Fund Entities and Control.   The management of a nonprofit enterprise can exercise the most complete control over the flows of resources by using fund-accounting techniques. In this arrangement, the assets of the organization are divided among a number of self-balancing accounting entities called funds. A *fund* is defined as a fiscal and accounting entity with a self-balancing set of accounts recording cash and other financial resources, together with all related liabilities and residual equities or balances, and changes therein, which are segregated for the purpose of carrying on specific activities or attaining certain objectives in accordance with the special regulations, restrictions, or limitations.[1]

Each fund is treated as a separate operating entity when transactions are recorded that involve relationships either with outside enterprises or with other funds. These separate accounting entities can be beneficially classified into two categories: (1) source and disposition funds and (2) self-sustaining funds. In addition to funds, we may also have other accounting entities called *account groups.*

Source and disposition funds are accounting entities used to account for the inflows and outflows of liquid (appropriable) resources. The primary accounting objective for these funds is to show where appropriable resources originated (sources) and how those resources were used (dispositions). Therefore, we use *dollar accountability accounting procedures* designed to show inflows and outflows of dollars for source and disposition funds. These funds typically are used to account for spendable resources and short-term obligations associated with financing operations, improvements, and debt payments.

The term *resources* is often used as a synonym for *assets.* In accounting for source and disposition fund activities, however, *resources* means assets capable of being expended (liquid or appropriable) in achieving the operating objectives of the fund entity. Therefore, the balance sheets for such fund entities *will contain no long-term assets or long-term liabilities.*

We use the term *revenues* to reflect the flows of appropriable resources into source and disposition funds. These include cash received and short-term receivables realized in connection with such things as taxes, customs, and other sources. We recognize these inflows in the accounting records when they become *available* and *measurable.*

The outflows of appropriable sources from source and disposition funds are called *expenditures.* These are evidenced by the incurrence of a short-term liability or by the payment of cash for the purpose of acquiring an asset or a service. Expenditures are recognized when a *fund liability is incurred and measurable.*

These funds also use the *modified accrual basis* of accounting, which is consistent with the dollar accountability concept of reporting. With it, inflows of appropriable resources are recognized as revenues when they become available to be spent and are measurable. Outflows of appropriable resources are recognized as expenditures when a short-term liability is incurred that can be measured. Both revenues and expenditures include capital items as well as items earned or consumed during the reporting period.

[1] *Governmental Accounting, Auditing, and Financial Reporting* (Chicago: Municipal Finance Officers Association of the United States and Canada, 1980), p. 9.

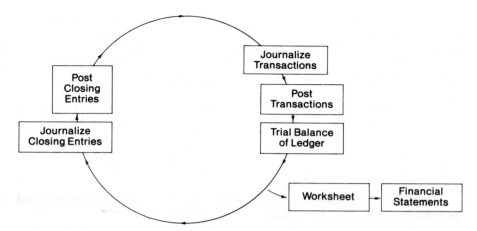

EXHIBIT 1.2   Accounting Cycle for Source and Disposition Funds

The accounting procedures for source and disposition funds call for the completion of the accounting cycle reflected in Exhibit 1.2. As you compare this accounting cycle with the one shown for self-sustaining funds, you will observe that adjusting entries are omitted from the items shown in the cycle for profit entities. These entries are used to record the amortization of fixed assets, the accrual of expenses, the accrual of revenues, the recognition of prepaid expenses, the recognition of unearned revenues, and the provision for uncollectible accounts. All except the last of these are designed to convert transaction data to full accrual basis data. Because source and disposition funds use the modified accrual basis of accounting, there is no need to recognize these changes in the accounts. Also, because of the emphasis placed on showing only the inflows of appropriable resources as revenues, the provision for uncollectible accounts (generally for taxes receivable) is recognized as part of the entry used to record the inflow of resources. Thus, instead of showing the provision as an expenditure it is reflected as a reduction of revenues.

Self-sustaining funds are reservoirs of resources expected to be used for specified purposes in such a way that the fund entity sustains itself from its operations. Because the operating objective of these funds is similar to that of profit enterprises, they follow accounting practices similar to those used in the profit area.

The record-keeping procedures for such funds call for the completion of the accounting cycle reflected in Exhibit 1.3 during each fiscal period. The only difference between the accounting procedures for businesses and self-sustaining funds is that the account fund balance is used to reflect the capital contributed to these funds. The excess of revenues over expenses will often be closed to a retained earnings account at the end of each period, just as is done for business enterprises.

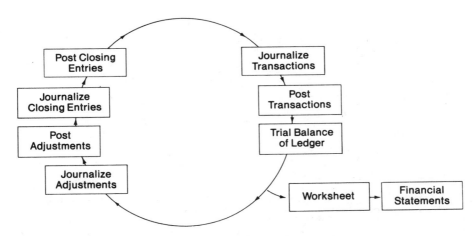

EXHIBIT 1.3   Accounting Cycle for Self-Sustaining Funds

As we observed earlier in this chapter, nonprofit organizations have no proprietary interests owned by individuals. Therefore, the primary equity account for both source and disposition and self-sustaining funds is an account called *fund balance.* This is the term used to describe the residual equities of source and disposition funds and the contributed equities of self-sustaining funds.

Account groups are accounting entities that cannot be classified as funds because they do not contain appropriable resources. They must be included in the accounting records of nonprofit organizations that have source and disposition funds because the modified accrual basis of accounting used by these funds does not distinguish between capital and revenue items. These accounting entities are used to provide records of general fixed assets and general long-term debt.

In deciding which accounting entities should be incorporated into the accounting records of a nonprofit organization, we can think of the resources and obligations as being divided into the types of accounting entities shown in Exhibit 1.4. As you can see from this exhibit, we should first think of those resources and obligations as being divided into *unrestricted* and *restricted* categories. Each of these categories should then be divided into spendable and nonspendable subcategories. These subcategories then cause us to originate the accounting entities designated Type A, Type B, Type C, and Type D accounting entities in Exhibit 1.4.

A Type A accounting entity would be the fund used to account for the spendable resources available to carry out the organization's general operations. In many instances, these will be source and disposition funds. Nonspendable, unrestricted resources and general long-term obligations of the organization would be accounted for in Type B accounting entities. These include the account groups described earlier in governmental ac-

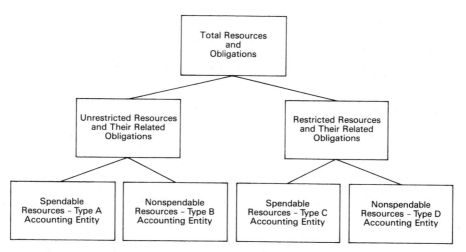

EXHIBIT 1.4   Types of Accounting Entities

counting records. In other instances, these resources may be accounted for in plant funds or similar accounting entities that include long-term assets and obligations as well as the resources designated to purchase such assets and retire long-term obligations.

Spendable restricted resources and their related obligations would be accounted for through use of a Type C accounting entity. These accounting entities typically are source and disposition funds used to account for resources designated for the acquisition of long-term assets or the retirement of long-term obligations. Nonspendable restricted resources would be accounted for in Type D accounting entities. These include such things as endowment funds and other self-sustaining funds, in which the operating procedures call for the maintenance of the original investment in the fund.

Accounting records can be unnecessarily fragmented by the use of too many fund entities, making it difficult to interpret the financial reports for the organization as a whole. Although this difficulty is now recognized more clearly than it was some years ago, we still find instances where new fund entities are created and used to account for the flows of resources when the use of designated claims accounts within already existing fund entities would achieve adequate control.

Control Through Designated Claims Accounts.   As noted previously, we can achieve control over the use of assets by designating specific claims against them within already existing fund entities. This is accomplished by setting up *internal restriction accounts* to specify that designated amounts of the general assets shown in the balance sheet are to be used for particular purposes. We frequently find this technique of control used in the profit area when amounts are appropriated from retained earnings for plant construction or some other purpose. This level of control can be further strengthened by setting aside certain assets in the balance sheet. For example, business enterprises frequently segregate in a sinking fund account the assets to be used for the retirement of long-term debt. When this occurs, we will also typically have an "appropriation for sinking fund" account shown in the capital section of the balance sheet. Similar arrangements can be used within existing fund entities for nonprofit organizations.

Appropriation Control.   Whereas separate fund entities are suitable to control the acquisitions and disposals of specially restricted resources, other techniques are used to disclose accountability for the acquisitions and uses of general operating resources within the general operating fund. Extension of the concept of dollar accountability suggests the need for an item-by-item control over the acquisitions and uses of resources. That need is met by the use of appropriation control techniques restricting the uses of these assets.

Appropriation control requires preparation of a detailed spending plan for operations before the beginning of each period. For example, the control process for a government entity begins with an item-by-item estimate of expenditures required for a proposed program of service covering a specified period. These estimates, presented in the form of a proposed budget, are then reviewed by a group representing citizens—a city council or a board of commissioners—that is responsible for approving, modifying, or rejecting the budget. When the budget has been approved, the amounts appropriated reflect the maximum expenditures that can be incurred for each item in the budget. Any increase in an appropriation requires action by the same governmental body that originally approved the budget. Periodically, the actual amount of each expenditure to date is compared with the appropriated amount to determine the remainder available for spending during the period.

The use of appropriation control over expenditures logically leads to the preparation of a statement of revenues and expenditures to show the inflows and outflows of appropriable resources during each reporting period. To be most effective, *this statement should disclose the relationship between the actual and budgeted amounts for each item.* Other statements include a balance sheet, which reflects residuals, and a statement of changes in fund balance, which shows the connections between the fund balance account balances in successive balance sheets.

Financial reports and budget practices vary from one kind of nonprofit organization to another. Quite logically, nonprofit organizations supported by voluntary contributions typically place less emphasis on control by appropriations than do governmental units. There is also a tendency for organizations that charge fees for their services to make more extensive use of the business type of formula-controlled budget data rather than line item appropriation control budgets.

Statements of Principles

The accounting practices we have just briefly described are codified in individual statements of principles, which cover four of the major types of nonprofit organizations. The statement developed by the National Council on Governmental Accounting (see pages 14–17) stipulates the principles of accounting practices for municipalities. Widely recognized statements have also been developed for colleges and universities (see Appendix A), for hospitals (see Appendix B), and for health and welfare agencies.

Recently, we have seen the public accounting profession take a stronger interest in the accounting practices for various types of nonprofit organizations. For example, *audit guides* for governmental entities, colleges and universities, health and welfare agencies, and hospitals have been issued by the American Institute of Certified Public Accountants (AICPA; see the bibliography). These publications include references to the following accounting practices.

Emphasis on Use of Fund-Accounting Techniques.   As noted earlier, the fiduciary relationship of nonprofit organizations to their constituencies, coupled with the dollar accountability concept of financial reporting, has led to the extensive use of fund-accounting techniques. Such techniques divide the accounting records for the organization's resources into a number of separate self-balancing fund entities. As a result, many unique account names appear in the accounting records of these organizations. Instead of being concerned with one ledger, the nonprofit organization accountant will have *a separate self-balancing group of ledger accounts for each fund entity*. The number of these funds will depend on the number of restrictions placed on the uses of individual resource units by law, by donors, or by the management of the organization. This fragmentation of the accounting records also means that transactions can occur between the fund entities, requiring reciprocal or complementary journal entries in more than one of those entities.

Accounting for the Flows of Resources.   Because nonprofit organizations have a service objective rather than a profit objective, the accounting records of most fund entities, except those for hospitals and health and welfare agencies, are generally organized to reflect dollar accountability rather than operational accountability. Instead of reflecting incomes, expenses, and net income, the operating statement of these funds entities emphasizes accountability for the flows of spendable resources. Revenue accounts show the inflows of those resources, and expenditure accounts reflect the outflows of those resources. Within this scheme, there is little distinction between capital and revenue items. Both are generally recorded in similar expenditure accounts, which are subsequently closed to a fund balance account. The *operating statement*, generally characterized as a statement of revenues and expenditures, emphasizes the sources from which resources were realized and the ways in which those resources were used. This statement should not be interpreted as reflecting operational accountability, as does the income statement for a profit enterprise.

Accounting for Capital Expenditures. As noted in the preceding paragraph, most nonprofit organizations, with the exception of hospitals and health and welfare agencies, do not distinguish between capital and revenue expenditures in accounting for their general operations. Consistent with this practice, most nonprofit organizations, again not including hospitals and health and welfare agencies, record depreciation only on the fixed assets of self-sustaining funds.

Emphasis on Appropriation Control. Another result of the concept of dollar accountability is the widespread use of the appropriation type of budget in the nonprofit area. In many instances, particularly in government, budgets are considered such an important control device that the budget data may be formally recorded in the accounts. In contrast, hospitals and other organizations that charge fees for their services usually use budget data based on formula relationships between outlays and the anticipated level of operations, in much the same way that profit organizations do.

Basis of Accounting. There are many different types of nonprofit organizations, and their accounting practices call for different degrees of adherence to the accrual basis of accounting. At one end of the spectrum we have some governmental fund entities that use the *modified accrual basis.* Hospitals and health and welfare agencies, on the other hand, use the full accrual basis. The official literature for colleges and universities (see Appendix A) calls for use of the accrual basis. The practices recommended in that literature, however, more closely resemble those followed for the modified accrual basis described in the governmental statement (see pages 14–17).

The National Council on Governmental Accounting, in its Statement 1 (1979), states that governmental (source and disposition) type funds should be accounted for by using the modified accrual basis. Under that basis, *revenues are recognized when they become both "measurable" and "available to finance expenditures of the current period."* Also, under this basis of accounting, *expenditures are generally recognized when a fund liability is incurred.* This means that no distinction is made between capital and revenue items in accounting for the activities of governmental type funds. Also, consistent with that provision, no depreciation of general fixed assets is recognized as an expense or expenditure. On the other hand, proprietary (self-sustaining) funds follow the same full accrual basis accounting procedures used by profit enterprises.

The National Council on Governmental Accounting, in considering the objectives of governmental accounting and the needs of perceived users of financial information described earlier, has developed the following Summary Statement of Principles setting out the various elements of generally accepted accounting principles for governmental units. Although it is called a Statement of Principles, it is more realistically a statement defining accounting practices for governmental units.[2]

Summary Statement of Principles

Accounting and Reporting Capabilities

1. A governmental accounting system must make it possible both: (a) to present fairly and with full disclosure the financial position and results of financial operations of the funds and account groups of the governmental unit in conformity with generally accepted accounting principles; and (b) to determine and demonstrate compliance with finance-related legal and contractual provisions.

Fund Accounting Systems

2. Governmental accounting systems should be organized and operated on a fund basis. A fund is defined as a fiscal and accounting entity with a self-balancing set of accounts recording cash and other financial resources, together with all related liabilities and residual equities or balances, and changes therein, which are segregated for the purpose of carrying on specific activities or attaining certain objectives in accordance with special regulations, restrictions, or limitations.

Types of Funds

3. The following types of funds should be used by state and local governments:

Governmental funds

a. *The General Fund*—to account for all financial resources except those required to be accounted for in another fund.

b. *Special Revenue Funds*—to account for the proceeds of specific revenue sources (other than special assessments, expendable trusts, or for major capital projects) that are legally restricted to expenditure for specified purposes.

c. *Capital Projects Funds*—to account for financial resources to be used for the acquisition or construction of major capital facilities (other than those financed by proprietary funds, Special Assessment Funds, and Trust Funds).

d. *Debt Service Funds*—to account for the accumulation of resources for, and the payment of, general long-term debt principal and interest.

e. *Special Assessment Funds*—to account for the financing of public improvements or services deemed to benefit the properties against which special assessments are levied.

[2] Reproduced with permission from National Council on Governmental Accounting, Statement 1, *Governmental Accounting and Financial Reporting Principles* (Chicago: Municipal Finance Officers Association of the United States and Canada—now Government Finance Officers Association, 1979). Copyright © 1979 by the Municipal Finance Officers Association of the United States and Canada—now Government Finance Officers Association.

Proprietary Funds

f. *Enterprise Funds*—to account for operations (a) that are financed and operated in a manner similar to private business enterprises—where the intent of the governing body is that the costs (expenses, including depreciation) of providing goods or services to the general public on a continuing basis be financed or recovered primarily through user charges; or (b) where the governing body has decided that periodic determination of revenues earned, expenses incurred, and/or net income is appropriate for capital maintenance, public policy, management control, accountability, or other purposes.

g. *Internal Service Funds*—to account for the financing of goods or services provided by one department or agency to other departments or agencies of the governmental unit, or to other governmental units, on a cost-reimbursement basis.

Fiduciary Funds

h. *Trust and Agency Funds*—to account for assets held by a governmental unit in a trustee capacity or as an agent for individuals, private organizations, other governmental units, and/or other funds. These include (a) Expendable Trust Funds, (b) Nonexpendable Trust Funds, (c) Pension Trust Funds, and (d) Agency Funds.

Number of Funds

4. Governmental units should establish and maintain those funds required by law and sound financial administration. Only the minimum number of funds consistent with legal and operating requirements should be established, however, since unnecessary funds result in inflexibility, undue complexity, and inefficient financial administration.

Accounting for Fixed Assets and Long-Term Liabilities

5. A clear distinction should be made between (a) fund fixed assets and general fixed assets and (b) fund long-term liabilities and general long-term debt.

a. Fixed assets related to specific proprietary funds or Trust Funds should be accounted for through those funds. All other fixed assets of a governmental unit should be accounted for through the General Fixed Assets Account Group.

b. Long-term liabilities of proprietary funds, Special Assessment Funds, and Trust Funds should be accounted for through those funds. All other unmatured general long-term liabilities of the governmental unit should be accounted for through the General Long-Term Debt Account Group.

Valuation of Fixed Assets

6. Fixed assets should be accounted for at cost or, if the cost is not practicably determinable, at estimated cost. Donated fixed assets should be recorded at their estimated fair value at the time received.

Depreciation of Fixed Assets

7. a. Depreciation of general fixed assets should not be recorded in the accounts of governmental funds. Depreciation of general fixed assets may be recorded in cost accounting systems or calculated for cost finding analyses; and accumulated depreciation may be recorded in the General Fixed Assets Account Group.

b. Depreciation of fixed assets accounted for in a proprietary fund should be recorded in the accounts of that fund. Depreciation is also recognized in those Trust Funds where expenses, net income, and/or capital maintenance are measured.

Accrual Basis in Governmental Accounting

8. The modified accrual or accrual basis of accounting, as appropriate, should be utilized in measuring financial position and operating results.

a. *Governmental fund* revenues and expenditures should be recognized on the modified accrual basis. Revenues should be recognized in the accounting period in which they become available and measurable. Expenditures should be recognized in the accounting period in which the fund liability is incurred, if measurable, except for unmatured interest on general long-term debt and on special assessment indebtedness secured by interest-bearing special assessment levies, which should be recognized when due.

b. *Proprietary fund* revenues and expenses should be recognized on the accrual basis. Revenues should be recognized in the accounting period in which they are earned and become measurable; expenses should be recognized in the period incurred, if measurable.

c. *Fiduciary fund* revenues and expenses or expenditures (as appropriate) should be recognized on the basis consistent with the fund's accounting measurement objective. Nonexpendable Trust and Pension Trust Funds should be accounted for on the accrual basis; Expendable Trust Funds should be accounted for on the modified accrual basis. Agency Fund assets and liabilities should be accounted for on the modified accrual basis.

d. *Transfers* should be recognized in the accounting period in which the interfund receivable and payable arise.

Budgeting, Budgetary Control, and Budgetary Reporting

9. a. An annual budget(s) should be adopted by every governmental unit.

b. The accounting system should provide the basis for appropriate budgetary control.

c. Budgetary comparisons should be included in the appropriate financial statements and schedules for governmental funds for which an annual budget has been adopted.

Transfer, Revenue, Expenditure, and Expense Account Classification

10. a. Interfund transfers and proceeds of general long-term debt issues should be classified separately from fund revenues and expenditures or expenses.

b. Governmental fund revenues should be classified by fund and source. Expenditures should be classified by fund, function (or program), organization unit, activity, character, and principal classes of objects.

c. Proprietary fund revenues and expenses should be classified in essentially the same manner as those of similar business organizations, functions, or activities.

Common Terminology and Classification

11. A common terminology and classification should be used consistently throughout the budget, the accounts, and the financial reports of each fund.

Interim and Annual Financial Reports

12. a. Appropriate interim financial statements and reports of financial position, operating results, and other pertinent information should be prepared to facilitate management control of financial operations, legislative oversight, and, where necessary or desired, for external reporting purposes.

    b. A comprehensive annual financial report covering all funds and account groups of the governmental unit—including appropriate combined, combining, and individual fund statements; notes to the financial statements; schedules; narrative explanations; and statistical tables—should be prepared and published.

    c. General purpose financial statements may be issued separately from the comprehensive annual financial report. Such statements should include the basic financial statements and notes to the financial statements that are essential to fair presentation of financial position and operating results (and changes in financial position of proprietary funds and similar Trust Funds).

Official Pronouncements. For many years, the National Council on Governmental Accounting (NCGA) was the body charged with the responsibility of issuing official pronouncements relating to governmental accounting. That council, in cooperation with the Municipal Finance Officers Association (now Government Finance Officers Association), published the 1968 edition of Governmental Accounting Auditing and Financial Reporting (GAAFR). In March 1979, the NCGA released Statement 1, *Governmental Accounting and Financial Reporting Principles.* The principles portion of that statement is part of the 1980 edition of GAAFR and is also included in this book (see pages 14–17). Since that time, the NCGA has issued a number of interpretations of Statement 1 and six other statements dealing with various issues of governmental accounting. The issues covered by the more important of these statements can be summarized as follows:

• Statement 2, *Grant Entitlement and Shared Revenue Accounting and Reporting by State and Local Governments,* provides guidelines for recording and reporting such items. This statement recognizes that resources received by governmental units from other governments are frequently accompanied by legal or conceptual requirements that govern their use and therefore require special accounting and reporting procedures.

• Statement 3, *Defining the Governmental Reporting Entity,* provides criteria to be used in identifying the subentities that should be included in the comprehensive annual financial report for a governmental entity.

• Statement 4, *Accounting and Financial Reporting Principles for Claims and Judgements and Compensated Absences,* provides authoritative guidance relating to accounting and financial reporting procedures to be followed by governmental entities for FASB 5 and FASB 43 type items.

• Statement 5, *Accounting and Financial Reporting Principles for Lease Agreements of State and Local Governments,* explains how FASB 13 and other pronouncements relating to long-term leases should be applied to the accounting practices of governmental entities. It requires that financing type leases should be recognized by recording the assets and their related liabilities in the accounting records.

In 1984, the five-member Governmental Accounting Standards Board (GASB) was established to assume the responsibility of issuing official pronouncements relating to governmental accounting practices. One of its first actions was to issue Statement 1, giving authoritative status to NCGA pronouncements and the AICPA Industry Audit Guide. It also placed three issues on its working agenda, including basis of accounting, financial reporting, and pension accounting. One important issue under consideration when this book was written is the basis of accounting that should be used for source and disposition (governmental) type funds. Currently accepted practice (see page 16) calls for use of the modified accrual basis.

Nonprofit Organization Accounting Equations

Profit area accounting techniques are developed from the basic equation stating that assets are equal to liabilities plus proprietorship claims. Expanded to include nominal account classifications, the equation is stated as follows:

Assets = liabilities + proprietorship + revenues − expenses

The rule of debit and credit is developed by rewriting the equation with all elements stated positively. The equation then becomes:

Assets + expenses = liabilities + proprietorship + revenues

Accounts falling within the left-side (assets or expenses) classifications are debited to record increases in them. Decreases are reflected by credits. The opposite rule applies to the classifications on the right side (liabilities, proprietorship, and revenues). *Because self-sustaining funds operate essentially as profit enterprises, this accounting equation also applies to those fund entities.*

A similar approach for source and disposition fund entities that emphasize dollar accountability suggests the following accounting equation:

Assets + interfund claims + expenditures + transfers to other funds
  = liabilities + fund balance + interfund obligations
  + revenues + transfers from other funds

Accounts on the left side of the equation are increased by debits and decreased by credits. The opposite rule applies to the accounts on the right side of this equation.

If budgetary data are to be incorporated into the accounting records of the fund entity, you can add *estimated revenue accounts* to the left side of the equation and *appropriation accounts* to the right side. As a result, in recording budgetary data, estimated revenue accounts are debited to reflect the amounts expected to be collected and appropriations are credited for budgeted expenditures.

Because of the strong emphasis on controlling expenditures within appropriation limits, *encumbrance accounts* are also used to show the amounts of *resources committed to be used* for specified expenditure items. To do this, we add an account category, *encumbrances,* to the left side of the equation and another account, called *reverse for encumbrances,* to the right side of the equation. When a fund entity commits itself to use resources for a specified purpose, encumbrances is debited and reserve for encumbrances is credited. That entry is reversed when the expenditure relating to the encumbrance is recognized.

Types of Transactions

The operations of source and disposition funds, which are primarily concerned with accounting for the acquisitions and uses of resources within the limits of a specified plan, include the following five unique types of transactions:

1. *authorization to acquire and use certain resources* (budgetary and authorization entries)

2. *acquisition of resources,* including transfers from other funds not to be repaid (revenue recognition entries)

3. *disposition of resources,* including transfers to other funds for use by those funds (expenditure recognition entries)

4. *earmarking of resources* for a particular use (encumbrances)

5. *reclassification of encumbered resources* to an expenditure category (This transfer is accomplished by reversing the encumbrance entry and recording the related expenditure.)

Recording the authorization to acquire and use resources is best illustrated by the budgetary entry typically found in the general funds of governmental entities. These entries are recorded as follows:

Debit	Estimated revenues
Credit	Appropriations
Debit or Credit	Fund balance for the difference between estimated revenues and appropriations

Acquisitions of resources from entities outside the governmental unit will be recorded as follows:

Debit	Cash or receivables
Credit	Revenues

If resources are received from another fund that are not payments for goods received or services rendered or do not need to be repaid, those acquisitions would be recorded as follows:

Debit	Cash or other assets
Credit	Transfer from other fund

Dispositions of resources that go to entities outside the organization should be recorded as follows:

Debit	Expenditures
Credit	Vouchers payable or cash

If resources are transferred to another fund that are not payments for goods or services and without the stipulation that they be repaid, that transfer would be recorded as follows:

Debit	Transfer to other fund
Credit	Cash or other assets

We earmark source and disposition fund resources when a contractual obligation to use resources for future expenditures is created. This type of transaction can occur, for example, when a source and disposition fund contracts to buy equipment or other assets to be delivered some time in the future. When the contract is negotiated, the following entry should be made in the accounting records of the fund:

Debit	Encumbrances
Credit	Reserve for encumbrances

The encumbrances described in the preceding paragraph will be eliminated when the equipment or other items included in the contract are delivered to the organization. That action in effect converts the emcumbrance into an expenditure requiring the following entries:

Debit	Reserve for encumbrances
Credit	Encumbrances
Debit	Expenditures
Credit	Vouchers payable or cash

At the end of each fiscal period, the nominal account balances created by the preceding transactions must be closed. If we view as important the comparison of budgetary and actual revenue and expenditure data, it would seem logical to close revenues against estimated revenues and expenditures against appropriations. The 1980 publication of *Governmental Accounting, Auditing, and Financial Reporting* (GAAFR), however, suggests that the budgetary accounts be closed against each other. This in effect reverses the entry originally used to record the budgetary data. When this practice is followed, a second closing entry must be recorded to close revenues against expenditures, with the difference between those two items being debited or credited to the unreserved fund balance account.

SUMMARY

Accounting is the language of economic activities. This chapter developed the conceptual foundation underlying the accounting procedures, records, and statements of nonprofit organizations. The identification of that foundation was begun by defining a nonprofit organization and exploring the environment surrounding the operations of these organizations. We observed that the enterprise unit universe can beneficially be thought of as being composed of profit entities, quasi-profit entities, quasi-nonprofit entities, and pure nonprofit entities for the purpose of identifying the accounting practices that nonprofit organizations should follow.

Because of the service objective of nonprofit organizations, their financial statements should be designed to reflect the service story rather than the amount of net income earned over a period of time. This difference in reporting objective has caused many nonprofit organizations to adopt a concept of dollar accountability rather than operational accountability financial reporting procedures. Within that concept, the accounting records are designed to reflect the sources from which appropriable resources have been received and the ways in which those resources have been used. That in turn requires the use of fund accounting and appropriation techniques.

Fund accounting practices call for the division of the accounts of an organization into a number of separate self-balancing accounting entities called funds and account groups. Funds can be subdivided into source and disposition funds, which are concerned primarily with dollar accountability reporting and self-sustaining funds that operate essentially as profit entities.

After the different types of accounting entities used by nonprofit organizations were described, the accounting equations for self-sustaining and source and disposition funds were developed. The accounting equation for source and disposition funds includes a number of different types of accounts peculiar to a dollar accountability–oriented accounting system.

Next, the journal entries used to record different types of transactions unique to source and disposition funds were examined. Finally, the literature describing generally accepted accounting practices for nonprofit organizations was discussed and the Summary Statement of Principles for governmental units was presented.

QUESTIONS FOR CLASS DISCUSSION

1.1. Contrast the primary operating objective of a profit enterprise with that of (a) a city. (b) a hospital.

1.2. Why are some goods and services not provided by profit-making businesses?

1.3. Explain how financial reporting should logically relate to the operating objective of an economic entity.

1.4. Who "owns" (a) a city? (b) a denominational college?

1.5. (a) What basic principle determines who will control the actions of a business enterprise? (b) How can this principle be applied in the nonprofit area?

1.6. (a) Explain what is meant by appropriation control. (b) Why is appropriation control important in the management of nonprofit enterprises?

1.7. (a) How are the concepts of appropriation control and dollar accountability related? (b) What reporting technique has been devised for disclosing dollar accountability in the nonprofit area?

1.8. What are some of the special limitations on the managements of nonprofit enterprises in using their resources?

1.9. Compare and contrast the operational characteristics of a municipality with those of a church-related university.

1.10. (a) What are some of the major differences between conventional business accounting practices and those recommended for a governmental unit? (b) How are these differences related to operational differences between the two kinds of entities?

1.11. (a) How does the basis of accounting recommended for governments differ from that followed by businesses? (b) Is there justification for this difference? Explain.

1.12. (a) What does the term *fund* mean as it is used in accounting for governmental units? (b) What is a fund entity?

1.13. Could a profit enterprise follow fund-accounting practices? Explain.

1.14. What determines whether certain resources should be accounted for by means of a separate fund entity?

1.15. Does a governmental unit always have a general-fund accounting entity within its accounting system? Explain.

1.16. What determines which funds will be included within a specific governmental accounting system?

1.17. Explain the difference between a fund and an account group.

1.18. What is the operating objective of the debt service fund? How is a debt service fund initiated?

1.19. At what point should revenues from sales taxes be recognized? Justify your answer.

1.20. At what point should revenues from property taxes be recognized? Justify your answer.

1.21. State the accounting equation for a pure nonprofit entity using the modified accrual basis of accounting. How does it relate to the rule of debit and credit followed in recording entity transactions?

EXERCISES

1.1. Two enterprise units each have ten constituents. One of the units, a pure profit entity, is organized as a corporation with ten stockholders that we shall label A through J. Stockholders A through E each own 100 shares of stock acquired at its par value of $100 per share. Stockholders F through J each own ten shares of stock also acquired at par value. In that way the ten stockholders have provided the corporation with a total resource base of $55,000. The second enterprise unit is a governmental entity with ten taxpayers also labeled A through J. Taxpayers A through E each pay $10,000 in taxes, and constituents F through J each pay $1,000, giving the governmental entity a total resource base of $55,000. A question of operating policy is to be settled by the constituents of both organizations. In both instances, Constituents A, B, and C favor implementation of the proposed policy while the other constituents vote against it.

Required:
Will the proposed operating policy be accepted by either of the two enterprise units? Discuss the general implications of the way this issue was resolved for each enterprise unit.

1.2. Record the following actions and transactions for a pure nonprofit organization relying on appropriation control and accounting for inflows and outflows on the modified accrual (expenditure-oriented) basis in T-accounts.

1. The controlling board approves a budget calling for estimated revenues in the amount of $100,000 and appropriations of $98,000.

2. Revenue in the amount of $60,000 is received.

3. The organization incurs obligations for the following items:
   - (a) salaries, $10,000
   - (b) equipment purchases, $5,000
   - (c) supplies, $5,000
   - (d) payment on long-term debt, $10,000
   - (e) miscellaneous operating outlays, $5,000

4. The organization places an order for equipment, expected to be received in approximately sixty days, amounting to $20,000.

5. One piece of equipment ordered in transaction d and previously estimated to cost $5,000 is received. The billed price is $4,800.

1.3. A business and a municipality each purchase five trucks at a cost of $8,000 each. The trucks are expected to have a useful life of five years, after which they should have a salvage value of $1,000 each. The business enterprise uses the generally accepted full accrual basis of accounting; the municipality follows the modified accrual (expenditure-oriented) basis of accounting.

1. Record the purchase of the fixed assets for each of the two enterprise units.

2. Record depreciation (as required) at the end of each of the five years over which the trucks are used.

3. Journalize the disposal of the trucks at the estimated salvage value for each enterprise unit at the end of the five-year period.

4. Comment regarding the effects of the accounting practices followed by each of the enterprise units on its respective operating statements for the five years over which the trucks were used. Which reflects the more appropriate allocation of trucking costs to specific operating periods? Explain.

1.4. A pure nonprofit organization that maintains its accounting records on the accrual basis shows the following end-of-the-period trial balance.

	Debit	Credit
Cash	$ 3,000	
Revenues receivable	4,000	
Fixed assets	40,000	
Allowance for depreciation of fixed assets		$ 15,000
Vouchers payable		6,000
Fund balance		20,000
Revenues from constituency		65,000
Revenues from restricted fund		1,000
Expenses incurred in rendering service Number 1	9,000	
Expenses incurred in rendering service Number 2	20,000	
Expenses incurred in rendering service Number 3	25,000	
Depreciation expense (to be allocated on the basis of relative direct expenses)	5,400	
Assets restricted to use as investments	10,000	
Accrued revenues	2,000	
Prepaid expenses	800	
Accrued expenses		1,000
Restricted fund balance		10,000
Prepaid revenues		1,200
Total	$119,200	$119,200

Required:

Prepare an operating statement, organized as suggested in Exhibit 1.1, for this pure nonprofit organization.

1.5. A quasi-nonprofit organization shows the following end-of-the-period trial balance. User charges are expected to cover 80 percent of operating expenses.

	Debit	Credit
Cash	$ 4,000	
User fees receivable	6,000	
Fixed assets	100,000	
Allowance for depreciation of fixed assets		$ 40,000
Vouchers payable		8,000
Revenue from user fees		90,000
Direct expenses for service Number 1	18,000	
Direct expenses for service Number 2	30,000	
Direct expenses for service Number 3	62,000	
Assets restricted to use as investments	20,000	
Depreciation expense to be allocated equally to services 2 and 3	6,000	
Revenue from contributions		26,000
Revenue from investments		2,000
Contributions receivable, net of allowances for uncollectible amounts	3,000	
Fund balance		62,000
Prepaid expenses	1,000	
Restricted fund balance		20,000
Accrued expenses		2,000
Total	$250,000	$250,000

Required:

Prepare an operating statement, organized as suggested in Exhibit 1.1, for this quasi-nonprofit organization.

PROBLEMS

1.1 (AICPA adapted.) Select the best answer for each of the following items:

1. Accounting for a governmental unit tends to be somewhat different from that for a business, but accounting for a business is most like accounting for:

   (a) a special revenue fund
   (b) a special assessment fund
   (c) an enterprise fund (utility fund)
   (d) a capital projects fund

2. Fixed and current assets are not accounted for in the same fund, with the exception of the:

   (a) general fund
   (b) internal service fund
   (c) special assessment fund
   (d) special revenue fund

3. Depreciation on the fixed assets of a municipality should be recorded as an expense in the:

   (a) enterprise (utility) fund
   (b) general fund
   (c) special assessment fund
   (d) special revenue fund

4. Rogers City should record depreciation as an expense in its:

   (a) enterprise fund and internal service fund
   (b) internal service fund and general fixed-assets group of accounts
   (c) general fund and enterprise fund
   (d) enterprise fund and capital projects fund

5. In municipal accounting, the accrual basis is recommended for:

   (a) only agency, debt service, enterprise, general, and special revenue funds
   (b) only capital projects, enterprise, internal service, special assessment, and trust funds
   (c) only enterprise and internal service funds
   (d) none of the funds

6. What financial statement is *not* recommended for the general fund?

   (a) analysis of changes in fund balance
   (b) statement of cash receipts and disbursements
   (c) statement of expenditures and encumbrances compared with authorizations
   (d) statement of revenue—actual and estimated

7. Which of the following types of governmental revenue would be susceptible to accrual using the modified accrual method of accounting?

   (a) state sales tax
   (b) property tax
   (c) income tax
   (d) business licenses

1.2. (AICPA adapted.)

1. Which of the following accounts of a governmental unit is (are) closed out at the end of the fiscal year?

	Estimated revenues	Fund balance
(a)	no	no
(b)	no	yes
(c)	yes	yes
(d)	yes	no

2. Which of the following funds of a governmental unit uses the modified accrual basis of accounting?

(a) general
(b) enterprise
(c) internal service
(d) nonexpendable trust

3. Which of the following requires the use of the encumbrance system?

(a) special assessment fund
(b) debt-service fund
(c) general fixed-assets group of accounts
(d) enterprise fund

4. Which of the following funds of a governmental unit would account for depreciation in the accounts of the fund?

(a) general
(b) internal service
(c) capital projects
(d) special assessment

5. Revenues of a special revenue fund of a governmental unit should be recognized in the period in which the:

(a) revenues become available and measurable
(b) revenues become available for appropriation
(c) revenues are billable
(d) cash is received

6. Which of the following funds of a governmental unit recognizes revenues and expenditures under the same basis of accounting as the general fund?

(a) debt service
(b) enterprise
(c) internal service (intragovernmental service)
(d) nonexpendable pension trust

7. Which of the following funds of a governmental unit uses the same basis of accounting as the special revenue fund?

(a) internal service
(b) expendable trust

(c) nonexpendable trust

(d) enterprise

8. Which of the following funds of a governmental unit uses the same basis of accounting as an enterprise fund?

   (a) special revenue
   (b) internal service
   (c) expendable trust
   (d) capital projects

9. Which of the following funds should use the modified accrual basis of accounting?

   (a) enterprise
   (b) internal service
   (c) special revenue
   (d) trust

10. What is *not* a major concern of governmental units?

    (a) budgets
    (b) funds
    (c) legal requirements
    (d) consolidated statements

11. For state and local governmental units, the full accrual basis of accounting should be used for what type of fund?

    (a) special revenue
    (b) general
    (c) debt service
    (d) internal service (intragovernmental service)

12. A state governmental unit should use which basis of accounting for each of the following types of funds?

	Governmental	*Proprietary*
(a)	cash	modified accrual
(b)	modified accrual	modified accrual
(c)	modified accrual	accrual
(d)	accrual	accrual

13. Revenues of a municipality should be recognized in the accounting period in which they become available and measurable for a:

	Governmental fund	*Proprietary fund*
(a)	yes	no
(b)	yes	yes
(c)	no	yes
(d)	no	no

DEVELOPMENT AND USE OF BUDGETARY DATA

2

The budgeting process is part of the "plan" portion of the plan-operate-evaluate-plan cycle followed by all types of economic entities. We can think of it as the initial step in achieving financial and managerial control over the operations of an enterprise unit. More specifically, the budget is an *operating plan for an enterprise unit projected in the form of financial measurements.* Budgets may cover varying periods of time ranging from one month to several years. In this chapter, we shall develop and describe the procedures followed in *originating and using an annual budget.* Although budgets are used for all types of enterprise units, we shall give our attention primarily to budgetary procedures for governmental entities.

NCGA Statement 1, in Principle 9, sets out the following guidelines for budgeting, budgetary control, and budgetary reporting:

1. An annual budget should be adopted by every governmental unit.

2. The accounting system should provide the basis for appropriate budgetary control.

3. Budgetary comparisons should be included in the appropriate financial statements and schedules for governmental funds for which an annual budget has been adopted.[1]

In developing budgetary data, individual outflows of resources will be governed either by *appropriation control* or by a *formula relationship* with some other operating item. For example, appropriation control is being

[1] NCGA Statement 1 (Chicago: Municipal Finance Officers Association, 1979), p. 3.

used by the chief executive officer of a business who states that the business will spend $50,000 on advertising regardless of the level of operations. Conversely, a formula relationship could be used to establish a budgetary allocation for sales commission expenses by applying the commission percentage to projected sales.

Since self-sustaining funds in the governmental area operate in much the same manner as business enterprises, we shall begin by briefly describing the budgetary process for those funds. After that, we shall give our attention to budgetary and financial control procedures normally associated with source and disposition fund operations. In doing that we shall:

1. develop the general philosophy of source and disposition fund budgeting

2. describe the budget development cycle

3. explain how the budgetary data are used in controlling expenditures

4. discuss program budgeting procedures

5. relate the budgetary process to the operations of project-oriented source and disposition funds

6. explain how budget-related cost data can be used in controlling operations.

BUDGETARY PRACTICES FOR SELF-SUSTAINING FUNDS

Self-sustaining funds operate in essentially the same manner as business enterprises, and the budgetary practices associated with the plan-operate-evaluate-plan cycle for these funds closely parallel those followed by businesses. This requires that the budgetary process begin with a projection of the estimated level of operations in the form of the amounts of sales, fees, or other primary sources of income expected to be realized. Operating outlays in the form of expenses are then projected on a *formula-related basis* to complete the operating budget. Since the sale prices of goods and services of self-sustaining funds are often based on the costs of providing them, the *anticipated level of operations is generally first projected in nondollar quantitative terms.* After that they can be converted to dollars based on the projected relationship between the expected level of services and the costs of providing those services. Exhibit 2.1 shows the relationships among the budgetary data and the flows of those data in developing projected end of period financial statements.

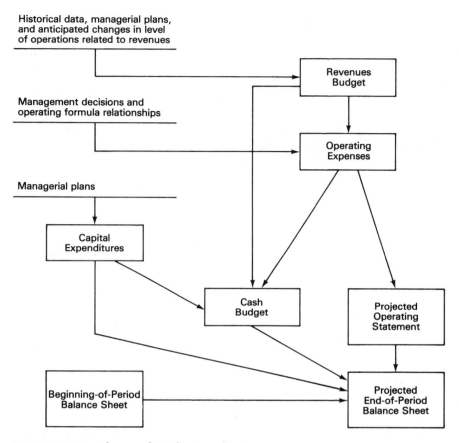

EXHIBIT 2.1   Flows of Budgetary Data

As we describe the budgetary practices for self-sustaining funds we will be concerned with:

1. procedures to be followed in projecting inflows of resources from operations

2. identifying formula relationships among the budgetary data

3. recognizing the points at which managerial decisions can be introduced to deliberately shape the budgetary plan

4. describing the budgetary summarization process.

Projecting Resource Inflows

The budgetary process for profit-seeking entities generally begins with a projection of anticipated sales or other revenues, because this is the primary factor constraining the overall level of operations. The revenue budget will be developed by reference to the past period data, managerial plans for pricing and selling goods or services, and various forecasts relating to the probable future level of operations. Generally speaking, this procedure should also be followed by nonprofit *enterprise funds.* In developing revenue projections for such funds, historical data, pricing and promotion plans, and the anticipated change in the volume of customers should be considered in arriving at revenue projections. These projections can also be presented more informatively by first estimating the quantity of units of service to be sold and converting that figure into dollars by applying projected sales prices to it.

For funds supplying only internally used services, however, the projected level of operations will be determined largely from some *measurement of the goods and services provided in prior periods to the units being served, adjusted for planned changes in their general levels of operations.* As an illustration of such an internal "customer-related" activity, let us assume that a municipal entity operates a vehicle maintenance center on a self-sustaining basis. If the city plans a 25 percent increase in the number of city vehicles, the maintenance center would, assuming other things are expected to remain the same, project a 25 percent increase in its volume of services for the next period. Initially this increase might be expressed in terms of service hours. Service hours, could then be converted to dollars by pricing them on the basis of an agreed-on relationship to operating costs.

Applying Formula Relationships

The revenue projections developed in the preceding paragraphs constitute the basic measurement of the anticipated level of operations for the budgetary period. In a profit entity, concerned with producing and selling units of product, the number of units to be produced or purchased can be calculated by using the following formula:

Beginning inventory + units to be produced or purchased
    − units projected to be sold = ending inventory

Historical data should provide the beginning inventory element of the equation, and managerial projections should establish an ending inventory target. When the revenue budget has been established projecting the anticipated number of units to be sold, the number of units to be purchased or produced can be calculated by entering the three known elements in the four-element equation.

Governmental self-sustaining funds often are involved in providing services rather than products. In that type of situation, the primary concern is with establishing formula relationships between the projected level of operations and the various operating expenses to be incurred in rendering the services. This involves the development and application of observed *cost-volume relationships* in projecting various operating expenses. In identify-

FIGURE 2.1 Self-Sustaining Fund Budgeted Operating Expenses for Next Period

	Prior Period Data	Programmed Increases	Other Adjustments	Budget for Next Period
Salaries (fixed)	$12,000	$ 720	$ –0–	$12,720
Wages (variable)	20,000	1,200	5,300	26,500
Other operating expenses (fixed)	15,000	–0–	750	15,750
Other operating expenses (variable)	30,000	–0–	9,375	39,375
Depreciation (fixed)	3,000	–0–	–0–	3,000
Total	$80,000	$1,920	$15,425	$97,345

ing cost-volume relationships we classify all items of expense into fixed and variable categories. Fixed expenses include those operating outlays that, in the aggregate, are expected to remain constant regardless of the level of operations. Variable expenses, on the other hand, are those items that are expected to change in direct relationship to changes in the level of operations. As a practical matter, many expenses are neither completely fixed nor completely variable. When working with such expenses we should try to identify and list separately the fixed and variable elements included in the "mixed" classification.

In addition to cost-volume relationships, it is also important to consider the effect that inflation and programmed increases in salaries and wages will have on the final budgeted amounts. In Figure 2.1 we demonstrate the procedures that can be followed in projecting selected operating

FIGURE 2.2 Analysis of Projected Changes in Operating Expenses Between Current Period and Next Period

Causes of Changes		Amount
Programmed salary increases		$ 1,920
Increases caused by anticipated increase in level of operations		
Variable wages ($21,200 × .25)	$5,300	
Other operating expenses (variable) ($30,000 × .25)	7,500	12,800
Increases caused by anticipated inflation		
Other operating expenses (fixed) (15,000 × .05)	750	
Other operating expenses (variable) (37,500 × .05)	1,875	2,625
Total increase		$17,345

expenses for the budget period. We have assumed that the self-sustaining fund in this illustration is projected to have a 25 percent increase in the volume of operations and that the inflation rate will be approximately 5 percent.

Figure 2.2 (on page 33) shows more specifically how the formula relationships are applied to prior period data to arrive at next period projections. It also explains why projected operating expenses are $17,345 greater for the next period than they were in the last period.

Changes Due to Managerial Decisions

Earlier in this section we noted that, in budgeting for profit enterprises, managers can make decisions that directly affect the budget data. Pricing, sales promotion, inventory, and research and development decisions are examples of managerial actions that will specifically affect certain segments of the budgetary projections. Any or all of these can enter into the budgetary process for enterprise fund operations, and some of them can enter into the budgetary process for internal service funds. The main point we want to make here is that, in addition to the formula type projections discussed in the preceding paragraphs, the accountant may be required to inject the anticipated results of certain management decisions relating to revenue and/or expense activities of self-sustaining funds.

Summarizing the Budgetary Data

Quite logically much of the emphasis in the budgetary process is on the projection of inflows and outflows in the forms of revenues and expenses. However, any enterprise unit charged with the responsibility of financing its own operations will also be concerned with its projected day-by-day cash position. This information can be provided through a cash-flow budget showing beginning-of-period cash balance adjusted for anticipated cash inflows and outflows in order to arrive at a projected end-of-period cash balance.

After the accountant has completed his or her projection of operating activities in the form of projected revenues and expenses, a projected operating statement can be prepared. Those data can then be combined with the beginning-of-the-period balance sheet figures, the cash budget projecting inflows and outflows of cash, and the capital expenditures budget to present a projected balance sheet for the end of the period. These data can best be combined by use of a worksheet showing beginning-of-period balances that are adjusted for transactions projected by the budgetary plans and for nonbudgetary items such as depreciation to arrive at a budgeted end-of-period balance sheet.

In developing budgetary plans for internal service funds, a billing price per unit of service must be established. If services are to be billed at cost, the billing rate per unit of service (such as per hour of mechanical service) can be established by dividing total budgeted costs by the units of service that the entity expects to provide. To illustrate this point let's assume that the self-sustaining fund, the operating expenses budget of which is shown in Figure 2.1, expects to provide 10,000 hours of service during the budget period. The billing rate would be $9.73 (rounded to the nearest cent). In such a situation services might actually be billed at $10 per hour to provide greater assurance of recovering total costs of operations.

Enterprise funds may also establish billing rates based on the projected operating expense for the period. Here again, the level of services to be provided must first be estimated. In such situations, however, estimating the probable level of services involves more variables than is the case for internal service funds. The estimation process typically will require consideration of such things as projected population change and any probable change in the level of business activity within the city during the next year. Nevertheless, when the probable level of activity has been determined, projected operating expense, or projected operating expenses plus the desired excess of revenues over expenses, should be divided by the number of units of services anticipated to be provided, to arrive at the billing rate per unit of service.

SOURCE AND DISPOSITION FUND BUDGETS

The budgeted figures for source and disposition (governmental) type fund expenditures must be established by appropriation. In other words, someone must be made responsible for deciding how many dollars may be spent for each item of expenditures. Those figures then constitute the expenditure budgetary data for the fund.

Philosophy Underlying the Budgetary Process

The general fund is the operating fund of governmental entities. Budgeting the activities of this fund involves allocating limited financial resources to the various programs and activities of the governmental entity financed by the fund. Although the final decisions relating to these allocations will be made by an elected representative group such as a city council, much of the work of developing the budgetary data will be done by a budget committee. This group, working in cooperation with city department heads and financial officers, takes the primary responsibility for developing an expenditures budget. The budget should reflect an expenditure plan that, within the constraints of available resources, the elected group believes will most appropriately meet the needs and desires of the voting citizens.

Because the representative group is elected by the citizens, such an arrangement allows the voters, over the long run, to have the last voice in shaping expenditure programs. That voice was forcefully demonstrated by the 1978 California election in which the famous "Proposition 13" was passed, limiting the amount of property taxes that could be assessed. The voters in that election were saying that too many services were being provided on the basis of need for them at the expense of property owners. This should lead directly to reduced expenditure budgets for the governmental units supported by those taxes.

In developing an expenditures plan, the budget committee *generally begins by considering changes that should be made to the prior year's program of services* because of population changes, because of observed deficiencies in services provided during that year, and because new services have been judged to be beneficial to community welfare. Beyond these considerations, the changes in the costs of providing a given level of services due to inflation and salary adjustments must be considered. Furthermore, since expenditures must be met by levying taxes. Proposition 13 and other taxpayer revolts have shown us that much attention must be given to the willingness of voters to accept a level of taxation sufficient to meet the projected program of expenditures.

Following the establishment of an expenditures plan, the elected group (city council or other similar body) is expected to develop a revenue budget that is appropriately synchronized with the resource requirements of the expenditures budget. The revenue plan may reflect a balanced budget if the governmental entity proposes to operate on a "pay as you go" basis. In that situation the revenues budget should provide for the levying of taxes and the realization of other revenues (excluding borrowing) approximately equal to the total of the expenditures budget. Alternatively, the proposed budgetary plan may call for either surplus or deficit financing. If a surplus-financing plan is projected, budgeted revenues will exceed budgeted expenditures (appropriations). The opposite would be true if the representative body chooses to operate temporarily with expenditures in excess of revenues. The revenues projected in this step of the budgeting process can be characterized as the revenue goal.

After the revenue budget has been approved, the elected body of the governmental unit establishes the tax rate required to produce the budgeted revenues. Most local governmental entities depend on such sources as property taxes, sales taxes, and income taxes, along with fines and fees to provide operating revenues. As a general rule, rates and allocation procedures for sales taxes and income taxes are established through other levels of management (generally the state) in the decision-making process. The local property tax rate, however, normally is established by the representative board. The tax rate required to meet the revenue goal can be calculated by using the following formula:

$$\frac{\text{total budgeted revenues} - \text{anticipated revenues from other sources}}{\text{the assessed valuation of property within the governmental jurisdiction}}$$
$$= \text{the tax rate per dollar of assessed valuation}$$

The tax rate calculated as described here must be approved by the city council or other elected body before tax assessment notices can be sent out to the citizens. The rate generally is expressed in terms of dollars per hundred or thousand dollars of assessed value. In other instances it may be stated in terms of mills per dollar of assessed value. A tax rate of $5 per $1,000 of assessed value, for example, could also be stated as fifty cents per $100 or as five mills per dollar. We should also observe that assessed value often bears only a fractional relationship to market value. *The important consideration, as far as the taxpayer is concerned, is the relationship between property taxes assessed and fair market value of the property.* The amount of taxes assessed against a particular piece of property can be increased by increasing either the tax rate or the ratio of assessed value to market value or by using a combination of these two changes.

Many jurisdictions also have some exemptions, such as the homestead exemption, that must be considered in calculating the tax rates and the obligations of individual taxpayers. For instance, in a taxing entity with a $5,000 homestead exemption, owner-occupied houses would be taxed on the assessed value less $5,000.

PPB and Zero-Base Budgeting

The budgeting process is supposed to allocate financial resources to various programs and activities with the objective of creating the best community environment that the limited resources available to the governmental entity can provide. Much attention has been given to the development of procedures designed to achieve that goal more effectively. Planning-programming-budgeting (PPB) systems have been adopted by some segments of the federal government to implement the allocation process. These systems were initially heralded as the best approach to a rational budget and improved management of governmental resources. Unfortunately, PPB has failed to fully meet the expectations of its proponents. Ideally it is intended to include:

1. a classification of the cost of government by programs with common goals or objectives

2. the development of qualitative and quantitative measures of program outputs

3. a projection of anticipated program cost inputs and the related service outputs over a period generally covering several years

4. the identification of special problem areas and the use of analytical techniques to appraise various possible solutions for them

5. an integration of this information into the budgetary process so that it becomes a part of governmental financial management.[2]

[2] *See* Ernest L. Enke, "The Accounting Preconditions of PPB," *Readings in Governmental and Nonprofit Accounting* (Belmont, CA: Wadsworth Publishing Company, 1977), pp. 27–39.

One of the principal problems associated with the implementation of PPB is the difficulty of developing objective dollar values for the service outputs. Viewed realistically, PPB may be seen as an ideal goal toward which managers of governmental entities may work in the development of budgetary allocations. It cannot be used for quantitatively relating the values of anticipated service outputs to anticipated expenditures. Nevertheless, the current emphasis on program budgeting (discussed later in this chapter) to some extent is an outgrowth of the PPB concept of budgeting.

Another philosophical approach to the budgetary allocation process is called *zero-base budgeting.* It is designed to achieve a more complete review of ongoing governmental programs and, as a result of that review, a more efficient allocation of resources. Conventional budgetary practices generally involve developing new budgetary allocations on the basis of prior period expenditures adjusted for increases or decreases projected for the next period. Such an arrangement can easily allow previously approved but currently unnecessary or inefficient activities to continue indefinitely.

The concept of zero-base budgeting was proposed by President Carter in 1977 for various federal agencies as a modification of the more conventional budgeting procedures then followed by those agencies. It is designed to require every segment of the governmental unit to identify each function it performs and to project the personnel and other costs associated with performing those functions at various levels of service. Thus it is supposed to require a clear description of the results that can be expected from every dollar spent. It seems to have the advantages of requiring complete financial planning before the budget is prepared, a more direct accountability on the part of segment managers for all of their activities, and increased involvement of lower-level supervisory personnel in the budgetary process. The one major disadvantage is the increased time and effort required to develop the budget.

General Fund Expenditures Budget

In the preceding section we described the general philosophy underlying source and disposition fund budgeting procedures. In this section we shall list and briefly describe the procedures that should be followed in developing a general fund budget. That budgetary process typically involves the following steps:

1. The annual budgetary process generally is initiated in the finance or accounting department, and the first projection of budgeted expenditures is based on historical data.

2. The finance or accounting department passes the projected data developed in Step 1 along with an explanation of those data on to the various department heads.

3. The department heads review the budgeted data and return the

data with suggested changes. The level of priority assigned to each suggested addition to the budget should be indicated.

4. The finance or accounting department checks the changes proposed in Step 3. The checked figures are then sent to appropriate upper-level supervisory personnel for consideration.

5. Upper-level managers review the budgetary data and return the data with their suggestions to the finance or accounting department.

6. The city manager's office examines the budgetary data to determine the funding levels required to balance the expenditures proposed in the tentative budget.

7. The city manager's office discusses the proposed funding level required, after proposed cuts or additions have been made, with department heads.

8. The finance or accounting department prepares the budget summary for examination by the city council or other legislative body.

9. The city council adopts the final budget after critically reviewing it and making such changes as it judges are desirable.

These budgetary procedures may well span six to nine months between the date on which the budgetary process is initiated and the time the final budget is adopted.

Using the Budget as a Control Device

We have followed the development of a typical object-of-expenditure or line-item budget for a municipality. The budget data developed would then be recorded in the budgetary accounts included in the general fund accounting records. Those records should be organized to provide a continuing comparison between budgeted and actual data as the operations of the period are carried out. We shall now develop the procedures for recording budgetary data and implementing actual to budgetary comparisons by:

1. describing budgetary accounts

2. showing how the budgetary data are recorded

3. explaining how expenditures are controlled within budgetary limits

4. illustrating how closing entries clear the budgetary accounts at the end of each fiscal period.

Budgetary Accounts.   The estimated revenue and planned expenditure data for the general fund developed in the budgetary process are recorded in ledger accounts that appropriately describe them. Budgeted expenditures are recorded in *appropriation accounts,* while budgeted revenues are reflected in *estimated revenue accounts.* Control accounts usually are used to record these data. These control accounts are supported by subsidiary ledgers that show the amounts available to be used for each object of expenditure item and the relationships between estimated and actual amounts for each type of revenue listed in the budget. The subsidiary ledger forms for appropriations generally are designed to reflect, within the same form, appropriations, expenditures, and encumbrances on a line-item basis. Such an arrangement facilitates the comparison of budget and actual data on a continuing basis. The forms shown in Figure 2.3 illustrate how the control and subsidiary ledger data may be accumulated for appropriations, expenditures, and encumbrances.

The estimated revenues control account will also have a subsidiary ledger showing the amounts of revenues expected to be realized from each of the various sources reflected in the budget. Because managers cannot be expected to control actual revenues within the limits of estimates in the same manner as they can expenditures, the subsidiary records for estimated and actual revenues may well be maintained separately. Each subsidiary ledger, however, is expected to balance against its respective control account.

Implementing Controls over Expenditures.   After budgetary data have been given final approval they should be recorded in the respective control accounts of the general fund as follows:

    Dr. Estimated revenues
    Dr. or Cr. Budgetary fund balance for difference
       Cr. Appropriations

As budgetary data are posted to the accounts from the preceding entry, the amounts appropriated for each line item will be entered in the respective line-item subsidiary ledger accounts. They should be reflected in the appropriations column of the subsidiary ledger as is shown in Figure 2.3.

When expenditures are incurred, the control account for expenditures will be debited and the individual expenditure items will be recorded in the expenditures section of the subsidiary ledger. Since a subsidiary ledger account will be maintained for each line item of expenditures, it provides a continuing record of the amount of appropriations and the expenditures against those appropriations for each item appearing in the budget. In that way expenditures can be controlled effectively within the appropriation limits.

The budgetary account *encumbrances* is used to help prevent overspending an appropriation when a significant amount of time is expected to elapse between the commitment to spend resources and the time the actual expenditure occurs. For example, a commitment to buy equipment

FIGURE 2.3 Control Accounts

Expenditures	Encumbrances	Appropriations
(1) 450,000	(1) 40,000	(1) 1,500,000

Subsidiary Ledger
Street Maintenance Services

	Expenditures			Encumbrances			Appropriations		
	Dr.	Cr.	Balance	Dr.	Cr.	Balance	Dr.	Cr.	Balance
Salaries									
Budget entry								200,000	200,000
Expenditure entry	$90,000		$90,000						110,000
Maintenance supplies									
Budget entry								150,000	150,000
Expenditure entry	70,000		70,000						80,000
Maintenance equipment									
Budget entry								50,000	50,000
Expenditure entry	15,000		15,000						35,000
Encumbrance entry				20,000		20,000			15,000

(1) Control accounts include appropriations, expenditures, and encumbrance items for Street Maintenance Services of $400,000, $175,000, and $20,000, respectively.

scheduled for delivery six months later should be recognized in the accounts by recording the following entry:

Dr. Encumbrances
    Cr. Reserve for encumbrances

Encumbrances should also be recorded in a control account as is shown in Figure 2.3. When the individual encumbrance is recorded, it will be reflected in the line-item subsidiary ledger account to show that that part of the appropriation balance has been committed to be spent. By looking at the line-item subsidiary ledger account, the controller can then recognize that the difference between the original appropriation and the sum of expenditures and encumbrances against the appropriation is the remaining amount available to be spent for that item.

End-of-Period Closing Entries. At the end of each fiscal period, after the budgetary (estimated revenues and appropriations) data have served their usefulness as control devices, those account balances should be closed. This is done by reversing the entry originally made to record them, which allows the actual revenues and expenditures to be closed directly to the unreserved fund balance. The amount debited or credited to that account will then reflect the difference between actual revenues and expenditures for the period.

The balance shown in the encumbrances account at the end of the fiscal period should be closed against reserve for encumbrances. The balance in fund balance reserved for encumbrances then should be adjusted to reflect the amount of encumbrances outstanding at the end of the period. The offsetting debit or credit in this entry will be to unreserved fund balance.

Program Budgeting

Earlier in this chapter we discussed briefly the concept of planning-programming-budgeting (PPB) and noted some of the problems involved in implementing such a budgeting system. Conceptually, it is designed to do what the budgetary system for a governmental unit should do, but the practical problems of implementing it have seriously limited its use. We then demonstrated how the object-of-expenditure or line-item budget can be used in planning and controlling the inflows and outflows of resources for the general fund of a governmental unit. Classifications under this system are item-of-expenditure or input oriented. They are designed to reflect the amounts available to be spent for salaries, services, supplies, and so on by each department or subelement of the general fund.

Partially as a result of the conceptual desirability of PPB, program-oriented budgets are often developed as a supplement to the more conventional line-item budget. These budgets include output-oriented classifications based on programs, functions, or activities, and they relate spending to specific activity goals. We see an emphasis on this way of thinking in the requirement that budget requests be based on changes in services and activity levels. To some extent that requires consideration of the programs to be implemented. In this section we shall further develop the concept of program budgeting by:

1. illustrating the relationship between the line-item and program budgets for a general fund

2. explaining how functional unit costs can be developed from program budget data

3. showing how costs can be controlled through the use of program budgetary data.

Program Budgeting Illustrated.   Each department or agency in a governmental entity exists either to produce a service or to assist other departments in providing such services. A review of the budgetary process clearly demonstrates these underlying objectives. We can think of the departments engaged in providing these services as being similar to the productive departments of a manufacturing enterprise. Following that line of thought a bit further, we can then think of the support activities, such as the controller's office, as a service department.

The program budgeting process begins with the identification of the programs or activities provided by the city and the community needs served by those programs or activities. If the programs are to be operated effectively, the next step involves the assignment of priorities to the different activities. That process should include an examination of all programs to determine how well they are achieving their purposes. The final step in the budgetary process is an estimation of the resources required to operate each program over a period of time.

The budgetary procedures described earlier in this chapter clearly include elements of program budgeting. Indeed, a city typically will develop a program budget as well as a line-item budget for its activities. Figures 2.4 and 2.5 show a condensed expenditures budget for the general fund

FIGURE 2.4 Expenditures Budget (Line-Item Basis)

Salaries and wages	$13,675,241
Supplies	1,182,484
Maintenance	1,206,940
Utilities, travel, and contractual services	1,732,174
Pensions and social security	1,677,276
Miscellaneous expense	2,155,977
Contributions	114,910
Capital outlays	1,738,376
Debt service	2,738,474
Total	$26,221,852

FIGURE 2.5   Expenditures Budget (Program Basis)

Administration	$ 4,683,272
Crime and delinquency	3,510,468
Health	1,452,942
Manpower	628,537
Environmental protection and development	8,967,777
Housing	217,783
Transportation	3,832,146
Recreation and culture	2,618,248
Social service	23,816
Unallocated balance	286,863
Total	$26,221,852

on line-item and program bases, respectively. An examination of these two illustrations shows that they represent the same total of projected expenditures classified in two different ways. The process of converting the information from one reporting format to the other is frequently referred to as "cross-walking." By properly coding the items and establishing the allocation processes to be followed, the cross-walk procedure can be implemented by use of a computer.

Development of Functional Unit Costs.   The terms *program, activity,* and *function* are often used synonymously. Therefore, with the development of appropriate nondollar quantitative data relating to the activities being performed, functional unit costs can be developed. For example, the amount of crime and delinquency (police) service cost per unit of population can be developed by dividing the total police service cost by the population being served. Other unit functional costs can be developed in a similar manner.

Controlling Costs Through Use of Functional Cost Data.   Budgetary data and actual expenditure data should be classified in the same manner. If actual and budgetary data are not projected on a program basis, they can be cross-walked from the line-item type classification into functional expenditure categories. We can then calculate actual functional unit costs by relating nondollar quantitative data to the functional classifications of actual expenditures. Those unit costs can then be compared with the budgetary projections of those costs. Differences between budgeted functional unit costs and actual functional unit costs should then be analyzed so that control measures can be introduced to reduce the deviations between those figures in future periods.[3]

[3] *See* Emerson O. Henke, "Performance Evaluation for Not-for-Profit Organizations," *Journal of Accountancy* (June 1972): 51–55.

We have suggested that functional unit costs can be used in projecting budgetary needs. This process places the primary emphasis on the program budget rather than on the line-item budget. Such an approach to the budgeting process requires that cross-walk procedures be employed to reclassify the program-oriented budgetary data to the line-item classifications required for meeting legally imposed operating requirements. This could well be the next step in improving the efficiency of the budgetary process and the resulting controls over expenditures.

Budgetary Process for Project-Oriented Funds

In the preceding portions of this chapter we have dealt with budgetary procedures for self-sustaining funds and the general fund of governmental entities. Generally speaking, other source and disposition funds follow planning procedures that are similar in many respects to those described for the general fund. However, the sources of authority for acquiring and using certain types of resources and the period covered by the authorization are somewhat different. This is particularly true for capital projects funds, special assessment funds, and debt-service funds.

Capital Projects Funds.   Capital projects funds are created to account for resources designated to be used for the acquisition or construction of general capital facilities of the governmental unit. The budget for each capital projects fund is established on a *project basis rather than on a period basis,* as is the case for the general fund and special revenue funds. As a general rule, a separate capital projects fund will be established for each authorized project.

A capital projects fund tentatively comes into existence with the proposal of a capital improvement program and the development of projected costs of completing the program. Having developed the anticipated expenditures associated with the project, the next step normally involves the clearance of legal authorization to secure financing for the project. Although the revenue side of the budget normally will be provided by the sale of bonds, other types of debt instruments may be used. In other instances financing may be realized from grants provided by other governmental agencies. If general obligation bonds are to be used, legal authorization generally must be secured by a referendum to the voters. A favorable vote would authorize the establishment of the capital projects fund with the proposed expenditure and financing arrangement approved by the voters. This action has essentially the same budgetary implications for the capital projects fund as does the approval of the general fund budget by the appropriate legislative body.

The origination of a capital projects fund to be financed through the issuance of bonds can be recorded as follows:

    Dr. Estimated bond issue proceeds
       Cr. Appropriations

These are budgetary accounts and therefore often are completely omitted from the records of capital projects funds. Nevertheless, the use of this type of entry clearly discloses the revenue and expenditure plans of the fund and facilitates later comparison of actual inflows and outflows with them.

Special Assessment Funds.   Special assessment funds are used to account for the inflows and outflows of resources associated with such public improvements as residential streets, sidewalks, or other types of improvements to be paid for by special assessment levies against benefited property owners. This is one of the features distinguishing special assessment fund activities from capital project improvements. Improvements financed through capital projects funds are presumed to benefit all of the citizens of the governmental unit on a more or less equal basis. Projects financed through special assessment funds, on the other hand, are for improvements that primarily benefit the property owners within a limited geographical portion of the governmental unit. Therefore those property owners typically are expected to pay, through special assessment levies, all or a large part of the cost of the improvement.

In many instances the costs of special assessment projects are paid for jointly by property owners and general fund resources, because, it is reasoned, the municipality will also benefit from the special assessment project and should bear part of its cost. That line of reasoning leads to an arrangement whereby the primarily benefited property owners will pay a major portion, say 75 percent, of the cost with the remaining amount being paid from general fund resources.

Special assessment funds are, like capital projects funds, project oriented. Normally a separate special assessment fund will be created for each special assessment type of improvement, and a budget should be established for each project just as with capital projects funds. Generally speaking the authorization to create a special assessment fund rests with the governing body of the governmental unit. In some instances, however, action may be initiated by citizens in the neighborhood expecting to benefit most from the proposed improvements.

The authorization can be recorded as the initial accounting recognition of the project through the following entry:

    Dr. Estimated financing sources
        Cr. Appropriations

Just as with the capital projects fund, we should recognize that the accounts included in the preceding entry are budgetary accounts and frequently may be omitted from the accounting records. If the authorization entry is omitted, the first entry in the fund will generally occur when the first inflow of revenue is realized.

Debt-Service Funds.   Debt-service funds are originated to account for the inflows and outflows of resources designated for the payment of principal and interest on long-term generally obligation debt. This does not include debt incurred in financing special assessment projects or certain types of enterprise fund activities. Debt-service funds require annual contributions from general fund resources. As resources are received by the debt-service fund, some will be used to pay interest on long-term debt and the balance will be invested for the purpose of producing interest and dividend income. Again, just as with the two previous funds discussed, the debt-service fund is a project-oriented fund covering the period over which the general long-term debt is expected to be outstanding.

The bond indenture provision will generally require the establishment of a debt-service fund for the purpose of accumulating resources to be used in the payment of loan interest and principal. That constitutes the authorization to originate a debt-service fund. At the time of the authorization to issue bonds, budgetary action will have to be taken authorizing transfers from the general fund to the debt-service fund for the purpose of paying interest and ultimately retiring the principal of the bonds. *Because this is an annual authorization, the budgetary entry for fund inflows can be recorded annually as follows:*

> Estimated revenues from investments
> Required general fund contributions
>   Budgetary Fund balance

Again, because this is a budgetary entry, it may be completely excluded from the accounting records of the debt-service fund. In that case the first entry in the debt-service fund would occur as funds are transferred from the general fund to the debt-service fund.

Development and Use of Cost Data

We have discussed how unit cost data can be developed and used in accounting for self-sustaining fund activities. These data are derived from records maintained on the accrual basis of accounting that allows the determination of the full costs of providing services, including depreciation and amortization charges. These costs are properly characterized as *full cost* or *expense per unit* of service performed.

We have also dealt with the possibility of accumulating unit functional cost data for general fund activities to help evaluate the efficiency with which the services of the entity were being performed. However, most of those unit cost data are really *expenditures per unit* rather than *expense per unit*. The only way that an expense per functional unit of service performed can be developed for source and disposition fund operations is to divide expenditures between expense and asset categories, adjust expense items for accrued and prepaid amounts, and recognize depreciation as the expense associated with the usage of fixed assets. If such data are developed, budgetary projections can be based on an extension of the functional units of service needed multiplied by the anticipated full functional cost per unit. Such a budgeting arrangement would not only help provide more efficient control over the conversion of resources but, if generally accepted, would also provide an avenue for a meaningful intergovernmental entity comparison of unit functional costs. That type of comparison should help in evaluating the efficiency of operations of different governmental units. We sometimes refer to this type of budgeting process as performance budgeting.

The development of full, accrual-based projected cost data is currently an idealistic expectation. Present-day governmental accounting practices cling tenaciously to the line-item budget because of the legal requirements associated with the uses of source and disposition fund resources. Some jurisdictions are beginning to use program budgeting, through which expenditures are based primarily on service categories and secondarily on objects of expenditure. This type of budget may be thought of as representing a step toward the performance budget described earlier. Future developments in budgetary and accounting procedures for governmental units probably will see greater use of the program budget and, perhaps, ultimately more use of the performance budget.

SUMMARY

We began this chapter by describing the budgetary process for self-sustaining funds and observing that it was similar to that followed by businesses. We saw how anticipated changes in the level of operations, programmed expenditure changes, and a provision for inflation can be incorporated into the operating budget.

We then described the budgetary procedures normally followed in planning the inflow-outflow activities of source and disposition funds with primary emphasis on general fund budgetary procedures. The basic philosophy underlying the establishment of budgetary allocations within these funds calls for planning the uses of available resources in such a way that the services provided by the governmental entity will be the ones desired by a majority of its citizens. In relating that to budgetary procedures, we have shown how the expenditures budget for the general fund is planned to provide the community services that the elected body perceives to be desired and needed by the citizens of the community. This requires a careful analysis of the services performed by various departments of the governmental entity, including some judgments regarding the priorities that should be assigned to the various services.

After the expenditures plan has been developed, the legislative body must turn its attention to establishing a plan for realizing sufficient revenues to cover the planned expenditures. Much of the revenue needed to meet expenditure plans must be acquired through the assessment of taxes. This requires the establishment and approval of tax rates including a rather delicate balancing of the assessment rates acceptable to the citizens against the volume of services to be provided.

After expenditure and revenue plans have been established, the governmental entity is ready to move from the "plan" phase of the plan-operate-evaluate-plan cycle to the "operate" phase. In that phase of the cycle, expenditures must be carefully controlled against budgetary appropriations on an item-by-item basis. The accounting records should be organized to provide the information required for this type of control. The financial managers must continuously review these data in deciding whether specific expenditures can be approved.

We also discussed briefly the procedures that should be followed in developing program and performance budgets, and we showed how functional unit expenditure or unit expense data can be used in controlling the operations of source and disposition funds. We noted the possibility of using a crossover worksheet to convert line-item budgetary data to program-based data. We illustrated how general fund budgetary data might be presented both within the legally required object-of-expenditure format and a program format.

In the last part of the chapter we described the authorization actions preceding the establishment of capital projects, special assessment, and debt-service funds and showed how the authorization data should be recorded in the records of those funds.

SUGGESTED SUPPLEMENTARY REFERENCES

*Barton, Marvin. "The Impact of Inflation—A Major Problem in Budgeting and Planning." *The Federal Accountant* (December 1975).

Brown, Robert C., and C. Lowell Harriss. "The Impact of Inflation on Property Taxation." *Governmental Finance* (November 1977): 16–23.

Brownsher, Charles A. "Improvements to the Congressional Budget and Impoundment Control Act of 1974." *The Government Accountant's Journal* (Spring 1983): 13–22.

Caldwell, Kenneth S. "The Accounting Aspects of Budgetary Reform: Can We Have Meaningful Reform Without Significant Changes in Traditional Accounting Practices?" *Governmental Finance* (August 1978): 10–17.

Draper, Frank D., and Bernard T. Pitsvada. "Limitations in Federal Budget Execution." *The Government Accountant's Journal* (Fall 1981): 15–25.

* Also available in *Accounting in the Public Sector: A Changing Environment—A Book of Readings* by Robert W. Ingram. Salt Lake City: Brighton Publishing Company, 1980.

Enke, Ernest L. "The Accounting Preconditions of PPB." *Management Accounting* 53 (1972): 33–37.

Frengen, James M. "Fixed Budgets in a Flexible World: The Dilemma of Government Management." *The Government Accountant's Journal* (Summer 1978): 62–68.

Hermanson, Roger H. "A New Era of Budget Philosophy on the Federal Scene—ZBB—How to Make it Work." *The Government Accountant's Journal* (Summer 1977).

*Holder, William W., and Robert W. Ingram. "Flexible Budgeting and Standard Costing: Keys to Effective Cost Control." *The Government Accountant's Journal* (Fall 1976).

Letzkus, William C. "Zero-Base Budgeting: Some Implications of Measuring Accomplishments." *The Government Accountant's Journal* (Summer 1978): 34–42

Minmier, George S., and Rober H. Hermanson. "A Look at Zero-Base Budgeting—The Georgia Experience." *Atlanta Economic Review* 26 (1976): 5–12.

*Pyhor, Peter A. "The Zero-Base Approach to Government Budgeting." *Public Administration Review* (January/February 1977).

*Rehfuss, John. "Zero-Base Budgeting: The Experience to Date." *Public Personnel Management* (May/June 1977).

*Said, Kamal E. "A Goal Oriented Budgetary Process." *Management Accounting* (January 1975).

Simpson, C. R. "Municipal Budgeting—A Case of Priorities." *Governmental Finance* 5 (1976): 12–19.

Stallings, Wayne. "Improving Budget Communications in Smaller Local Governments." *Governmental Finance* (August 1978): 18–25.

Steinberg, Harold I., and James D. Carney, "Program Budgeting for Town and Villages." *Management Controls* 20 (1973): 121–124.

*Steinberg, Harold I., and James D. Carney. "Halting a Rise in a Town's Tax Structure Through PPBS." *Management Adviser* (January/February 1974).

Venketaraman, V. K., and Richard G. Stevens. "Capital Budgeting in the Federal Government." *The Government Accountant's Journal* (Winter 1981–1982): 45–50.

White, Michael J. "Budget Policy: Where Does It Begin and End?" *Governmental Finance* (August 1978): 2–9.

QUESTIONS FOR CLASS DISCUSSION

2.1. Why do governmental units place such a strong emphasis on budgeting as an element of their accounting systems?

2.2. Compare and contrast governmental budgeting practices with those of businesses.

2.3. How are revenues generally projected for a self-sustaining fund?

2.4. Describe the procedures followed in budgeting expenses for a self-sustaining fund.

2.5. Explain the difference between surplus and deficit financing by governmental units.

2.6. What implications are associated with a projected deficit for a governmental unit during a particular period?

2.7. Relate deficit financing to the concept of "generational equity."

2.8. Explain the relationships between appropriations and the property tax rate for a source and disposition fund.

2.9. Describe the procedures followed in PPB systems. What is the primary objective of PPB?

2.10. Explain what is meant by zero-base budgeting. What are the primary advantages and disadvantages of this budgetary process?

2.11. What meaning does a balance in an encumbrance account convey? When is such an account used?

2.12. What is a program budget? How does it relate to functional unit cost data?

2.13. What is meant by the term *cross-walking*? How does it relate to the use of program budgets?

2.14. What is the purpose of a capital projects fund? How does its reporting emphasis differ from that of the general fund?

2.15. Describe the distinguishing features of a special assessment fund.

2.16. What is the operating objective of a debt-service fund? How is it related to the general long-term debt account group?

2.17. Compare a program budget with an object-of-expenditure budget. Can we have an object-of-expenditure budget for a particular program? Explain.

EXERCISES

2.1. The assessed value (equal to 70% of current market value) of all property in Denver City is $35,000,000. The city council adopts a budget calling for total expenditures in the amount of $775,000. They estimate that $75,000 of revenue will be realized from sources other than property taxes.

Required:

1. Calculate the tax rate that should be assessed by Denver City.
2. What percentage of current market value is currently being assessed as taxes?

2.2. The general fund of the city of Denby has, among others, the following account balances at the end of the fiscal period:

Estimated revenues	$500,000
Appropriations	485,000
Revenues	508,000
Expenditures	460,000
Encumbrances	20,000
Reserve for encumbrances	20,000

Required:

Journalize the closing entries.

2.3. The subsidiary ledger for police department expenditures shows, among others, the following balances:

Appropriation—supplies	$5,000
Expenditures—supplies	2,500
Encumbrances for supplies	500

Required:

What amount does the department still have available to spend for supplies? Explain.

2.4. The police department's budgeted expenditures for the current year are as follows:

	Fixed Expenditures	Expenditures That Vary with the Level of Population	Total Expenditures
Salaries	$400,000		$400,000
Equipment repairs	21,000	$24,000	45,000
Vehicle services	100,000	10,000	110,000
Other expenditures	14,000	16,000	30,000
Totals	$535,000	$50,000	$585,000

Although salaries of police personnel are listed as a fixed expenditure, the city contemplates adding one new officer at a starting salary of $12,000 per year with each 5 percent growth in population. The city expects population to increase 8 percent next year over the current year. An inflation rate of 6 percent is anticipated. Presently employed personnel are scheduled to receive a salary increase amounting to 9 percent of their current salaries.

Required:

Prepare the police department budget for next year.

2.5. The *budgeted expenditures* for the general fund of the city of Huntsburg for 19XX were:

Police expenditures	$560,000
Recreation expenditures	120,000
Sanitation expenditures	410,000
Fire protection expenditures	595,000
Unallocated expenditures	75,000

Assume that unallocated expenditures are to be allocated to the various service programs on the basis of direct expenditure charges.

Required:

1. Prepare a budget that shows all expenditures allocated to specific service programs.
2. Calculate the percentages of total expenditures expected to be incurred in providing each type of service for the city.

2.6. Refer to Exercise E2-5. Assume that the city being served by these programs has a population of 100,000.

Required:

Calculate the amount of expenditures per capita being used to provide each of the services.

2.7. The general fund subsidiary ledger shows the following account balances for selected expenditures as of December 31, 19XX:

	Budget	Expenditures	Encumbrances
Salaries	$115,000	$107,500	$ 7,400
Misc. equipment	4,000	3,900	200
Supplies	5,000	4,000	800
Vehicles	36,000	18,000	17,500

Required:

Calculate the differences between the budgeted expenditures and those incurred and committed for each line item and in total. Comment on your findings.

2.8. City Motor Pool provides maintenance and repair services for a city's fleet of 100 vehicles. This internal service fund operated with the following budget last year. This budget was based on the assumption that all vehicles would be driven an average of 1,000 miles per vehicle per month.

	Total Expenses	Fixed Expenses	Variable Expenses
Salaries and wages	$125,000	$100,000	$25,000
Auto parts	45,000	18,000	27,000
Supplies	15,000	10,000	5,000
Depreciation	25,000	25,000	

The anticipated rate of inflation for next year is 6 percent. Salaries and wages are expected to increase 8 percent.

Required:

1. Prepare an expense budget for City Motor Pool on the assumption that vehicle mileage can be reduced to 800 miles per month per vehicle.
2. Prepare the budget assuming that vehicle mileage is expected to increase to 1200 per vehicle per month.
3. Calculate the average cost per mile to maintain city vehicles under each assumption.

2.9. The following program budgets have been prepared covering general fund activities for Home City:

Fire services
    1. Salaries $540,000
    2. Equipment   80,000
    3. Misc.   58,000
    4. Supplies   22,000

Police services
    1. Salaries $420,000
    2. Equipment 24,000
    3. Misc. 19,000
    4. Supplies 22,000

Recreational services
    1. Salaries $85,000
    2. Equipment 2,000
    3. Misc. 3,500
    4. Supplies 1,700

Required:

Develop an object-of-expenditure budget for Home City general fund.

PROBLEMS

2.1. (AICPA adapted.) Select the best answer for each of the following items:

1. In preparing the general fund budget of Brockton City for the

forthcoming fiscal year, the city council appropriated a sum greater than expected revenues. This action of the council will result in:

(a) a cash overdraft during that fiscal year
(b) an increase in encumbrances by the end of that fiscal year
(c) a decrease in the fund balance
(d) a necessity for compensatory offsetting action in the debt-service fund

2. The budget that relates input of resources to output of services is the:

(a) line-item budget
(b) object-of-expenditure budget
(c) performance budget
(d) resource budget

3. If a credit was made to the fund balance in the process of recording a budget for a governmental unit, it can be assumed that:

(a) estimated expenses exceed actual revenues
(b) actual expenses exceed estimated expenses
(c) estimated revenues exceed appropriations
(d) appropriations exceed estimated revenues

4. A performance budget relates a governmental unit's expenditures to

(a) objects of expenditure
(b) expenditures of the preceding fiscal year
(c) individual months within the fiscal year
(d) activities and programs

5. A city's general fund budget for the forthcoming fiscal year shows estimated revenues in excess of appropriations. The initial effect of recording this will result in an increase in:

(a) taxes receivable
(b) fund balance
(c) reserve for encumbrances
(d) encumbrances

6. Which of the following accounts is a budgetary account in governmental accounting?

(a) reserve for inventory of supplies
(b) fund balance
(c) appropriations
(d) estimated uncollectible property taxes

7. When the budget of a governmental unit is adopted and the estimated revenues exceed the appropriations, the excess is:

(a) debited to reserve for encumbrances
(b) credited to reserve for encumbrances

(c) debited to fund balance

(d) credited to fund balance

2.2. (AICPA adapted.) The comptroller of the city of Helmaville recently resigned. In his absence, the deputy comptroller attempted to calculate the amount of money required to be raised from property taxes for the general fund for the fiscal year ending June 30, 19AB. The calculation is to be made as of January 1, 19AA, to serve as a basis for setting the property tax rate for the following fiscal year. The mayor has asked you to review the deputy comptroller's calculations and obtain other necessary information to prepare a formal statement for the general fund that will disclose the amount of money needed to be raised from property taxes for the fiscal year ending June 30, 19AB. The following calculations were prepared by the deputy comptroller:

City resources other than proposed tax levy:

Estimated general fund working balance, January 1, 19AA	$ 352,000
Estimated receipts from property taxes (January 1, 19AA–June 30, 19AA)	2,222,000
Estimated revenue from investments (January 1, 19AA–June 30, 19AB)	442,000
Estimated proceeds from sale of general obligation bonds in August 19AA	3,000,000
Total	$6,016,000

General fund requirements:

Estimated expenditures (January 1, 19AA–June 30, 19AA)	$1,900,000
Proposed appropriations (July 1, 19AA–June 30, 19AB)	4,300,000
Total	$6,200,000

Additional Information:

(a) The general fund working balance required by the city council for July 1, 19AB, is $175,000.

(b) Property tax collections are due in March and September of each year. Your review indicates that during the month of February 19AA, estimated expenditures will exceed available funds by $200,000. Pending collection of property taxes in March 19AA, this deficiency will have to be met by the issuance of thirty-day tax-anticipation notes of $200,000 at an estimated interest rate of 9 percent per annum.

(c) The proposed general obligation bonds will be issued by the City Water Fund and will be used for the construction of a new water-pumping station.

Required:

Prepare a statement as of January 1, 19AA, calculating the property tax levy required for the city of Helmaville general fund for the fiscal year ending June 30, 19AB.

2.3. A self-sustaining fund incurred the following expenses during the past year:

Salaries	$ 64,000
Other operating expenses	90,000
Depreciation	6,000
Total expenses	$160,000

Depreciation is a fixed expense. It is estimated that $40,000 of salaries and $50,000 of other operating expenses are also fixed. The remaining amount of each item is considered variable.

In preparing the expense budget for next year, the department anticipates a 10 percent increase in its level of operations. An 8 percent rate of inflation is expected for the year. Salaries are expected to be increased to compensate for inflation plus 3 percent (total, 11%).

Required:
Prepare an expense budget for the self-sustaining fund for next year.

2.4. A city's general fund incurred the following expenditures during the past year:

Salaries	$140,000
Supplies	30,000
Equipment	50,000
Other expenditures	20,000
Total	$240,000

This fund provides services that should vary directly with the level of population within the city. The city manager anticipates a 10 percent growth in population and an inflation rate for next year over the past year of approximately 8 percent. Property taxes are the only source of revenue, and revenue was equal to expenditures last year. City property currently has an assessed value of $9,600,000. The population increase should provide a 6 percent increase in the assessed valuation of property. The city council is concerned about taxpayer reaction to any increase in the tax rate.

Required:
You have been engaged to assist the city manager in preparing a budget for the coming year. Within the constraint of not increasing the tax rate, what observations and suggestions can you make to help her in that task? Be specific and include the development of useful numerical data.

2.5. The following object-of-expenditure budget has been prepared for the general fund of a city:

Salaries and wages	$6,000,000
Supplies	500,000
Maintenance	600,000
Employee benefits	800,000
Capital outlays	900,000
Other expenditures	500,000
Total	$9,300,000

Services provided by these expenditures include administration, police protection, recreation and culture, and sanitation services. The city wants to prepare a program budget as a first step in determining the amounts of different types of service expenditures per person to be provided for its citizens. Analysis of the various object-of-expenditure items discloses that they should be allocated to the various service functions as follows:

	Administration	Police	Recreation and Culture	Sanitation
Salaries and wages	40%	30%	10%	20%
Supplies	20%	20%	40%	20%
Maintenance	10%	30%	20%	40%
Employee benefits	40%	30%	10%	20%
Capital outlays	20%	30%	10%	40%
Other expenditures	On basis of total allocated expenditures			

Required:
1. Prepare a program budget for general fund operations.
2. Assume the city has a population of 100,000. Calculate the budgeted expenditures per person for each service provided.

2.6 Last year's budget for the city of Panola is presented as follows:

Estimated revenues	
General property taxes	$ 7,500,000
City sales taxes	3,500,000
Permits, licenses, and fees	1,500,000
User fees	2,000,000
Miscellaneous	500,000
Total estimated revenues	$15,000,000
Budgeted expenditures	
Salaries and wages (including fringe benefits)	$ 7,000,000
Supplies and services	1,500,000
Maintenance of facilities	1,000,000
Capital expenditures	2,000,000
Debt service	2,000,000
Miscellaneous expenditures	1,300,000
Total budgeted expenditures	$14,800,000

The city expects to have a 5 percent increase in population and in assessed value of property next year. The price level for all expenditures except debt service and salaries and wages is expected to increase 7 percent.

An analysis of expenditures shows that the following amounts from last year's budget are expected to vary directly with changes in population:

Supplies and services	$400,000
Maintenance of facilities	200,000
Miscellaneous expenditures	800,000

Other expenditures are fixed except as noted next. Salaries and wages will be increased by 8 percent. The volume of capital expenditures are to be budgeted at the same volume as last year.

Permits, licenses, and fees are expected to vary with the level of population but will not be adjusted for inflation. Individual user fees are being increased by 6 percent to partially compensate for inflationary changes. These fees are also expected to increase in direct relationship to any increase in population. City sales taxes are based on retail sales within the city. Miscellaneous revenues are expected to increase by 10 percent.

Required:

1. Prepare a budget for the city of Panola for next year. The budget should provide for a $100,000 excess of revenues over expenditures. No new services will be added. The city council has asked that last year's operating plan simply be adjusted for the anticipated changes cited previously. All budget amounts are to be rounded to the nearest thousand dollars. Property tax rates will be established at the level required to meet budgetary goals.
2. Comment on the effect which the budget will have on property tax rates.

ACCOUNTING FOR GENERAL FUND RESOURCES

3

In Chapter 1 we showed how accounting practices followed by nonprofit organizations differ from those used by profit enterprises. We observed that those practices place a strong emphasis on dollar accountability (controlling operations by monitoring spendable resource inflows and outflows), which in turn requires special emphasis on the budgetary controls described in Chapter 2.

In this chapter we develop the specialized accounting procedures followed by governmental units in accounting for general fund resources. The procedures described in this chapter are consistent with the provisions of NCGA Statement 1. The interpretations of that statement included in GAAFR, however, are the ones followed in our illustrated journal entries. With a few minor exceptions, these journal entries are also consistent with the AICPA Industry Audit Guide for governmental units.[1] The differences include useful clarifications and alternative methods.

We will develop the logical framework supporting the recommended practices, as well as the specific procedures to be followed, by:

1. recalling briefly the *unique operational characteristics* of governmental entities

2. describing the *nature of general fund operations*

3. *illustrating the procedures* followed in accounting for general fund transactions

[1] *Audit of State and Local Governmental Units* (New York: American Institute of Certified Public Accountants, 1974), pp. 8–21.

4. showing the *financial statements for a general fund*

5. citing some of the *special problems* associated with general fund accounting procedures

6. illustrating how a *transactions worksheet* can be used to summarize the general fund transactions for a period.

UNIQUE OPERATIONAL CHARACTERISTICS

A governmental entity is created to provide services for its citizens. As observed in Chapter 2, the resources needed to provide these services generally are acquired through a tax levy based on some measure of the taxpayer's ability to pay, rather than on the value of the services rendered to each individual taxpayer. The overall result is to *provide services according to needs and to collect resources to pay for those services on the basis of ability to pay,* rather than requiring service recipients to pay individually for the services they receive.

In this section we begin to develop the unique accounting procedures used to provide information about the acquisitions and disposals of resources within a governmental entity by identifying and describing:

1. the fund entities used by governmental units

2. the account groups typically included within the accounting records of a governmental unit.

Governmental Fund Entities

A governmental unit achieves dollar accountability and control by using separate fund entities and account groups, by using designated claims accounts, and by adhering closely to budgetary appropriation controls. As noted in Chapter 1, legal constraints on the uses of specified groups of resources and the organizational structure of a governmental unit itself require the use of separate fund entities. Each fund is made up of appropriable resources to be used in carrying out specific activities or attaining certain objectives.

Each fund entity also requires a separate set of self-balancing accounting records. These records always include asset and fund balance accounts and generally will also include liability, revenue, and expenditure accounts. Specific fund entities may be established by law, charter, or managerial directive. The number of separate fund entities will depend on the extent of the legal constraints placed on the uses of resources, and on managerial judgment regarding the level of control required to account for resources whose uses are not legally restricted.

The NCGA suggests that governmental funds be classified according

to the kinds of activities carried out through them, as follows (see pages
14–15):

1. source and disposition funds characterized as *governmental* or *expenditure funds* in the governmental area:
   a. general fund   P. 63
   b. special revenue funds   P. 102
   c. capital projects funds   P. 103
   d. special assessment funds   P. 115
   e. debt-service funds   P. 108

2. self-sustaining funds characterized as *proprietary funds* in the governmental area:
   f. enterprise funds   P. 126 - 127
   g. internal service funds

3. hybrid funds, sometimes called *fiduciary funds,* that have some
   operating characteristics of both source and disposition funds and
   self-sustaining funds:
   h. trust and agency funds   P. 123

Every governmental unit will have a general fund as well as any other
funds in the preceding list needed to account for its financial activities.
The range of funds maintained by a particular governmental entity may
extend from the general fund alone to all eight kinds of funds.

Account Groups

In addition to the eight types of funds just listed, the NCGA recommends
the establishment of two self-balancing groups of accounts, the *general fixed-
assets account group* and the *general long-term debt account group* (see page 15).
The first accounting group provides a record of the fixed assets of a governmental unit other than those carried in internal service funds, trust and
agency funds, and enterprise funds. The second account group reflects
the obligations associated with all unmatured long-term debt representing
general obligations of the governmental unit.

GENERAL FUND OPERATIONS

The general fund of a governmental unit is composed of the unrestricted
resources available for carrying on the unit's operating activities. It is a
source and disposition type fund characterized as a governmental fund
in the governmental accounting literature. The records of this fund constitute an independent fiscal and self-balancing accounting entity and accord-
ingly include those accounts necessary to reflect properly the flows of re-

sources as well as the residual assets and obligations outstanding as of the end of each period. In the pages that follow, we describe the procedures used in accounting for general fund transactions. Specifically, we shall:

1. examine the types of accounts appearing in the general fund records

2. consider briefly some of the subclassifications used to provide more detailed data on the major account classifications

3. show the relationship between budgetary control and the accounting procedures

4. describe end-of-the-year closing entries.

General Fund Accounts

The general fund accounting entity contains, as a minimum, asset, liability, fund balance, and revenue and expenditure accounts. It also often contains budgetary accounts for estimated revenues and appropriations, as well as encumbrance, encumbrance reserve, and interfund accounts.

An *asset,* defined primarily from the viewpoint of profit entities, is a probable future economic benefit obtained or controlled by a particular entity as a result of past transactions.[2] General fund assets, however, are limited to *appropriable resources* such as cash and near-cash items. The same source defines a *liability* as a probable future sacrifice of economic benefits arising from the present obligation of an entity to transfer assets or provide services to other entities in the future, as a result of past transactions or events.[3] This definition applies in both profit and nonprofit accounting; however, because profit entities use the accrual basis of accounting, they include long-term obligations, accrued expenses, and prepaid income items as liabilities, all of which are omitted from the general fund accounts because we use the modified accrual basis of accounting for that fund.

The general fund of a governmental unit has a fund balance account that roughly corresponds to the capital balance of a corporation. This account is defined in GAAFR as "the fund equity of governmental and trust funds." The 1980 publication of GAAFR suggests that this equity account should be divided into three separate elements. The first of these, labeled "budgetary fund balance," is used to reflect the difference between estimated revenues and appropriations as the budgetary data are recorded in the accounts. The second, entitled "fund balance reserved for encumbrances," reflects the portion of fund equity reserved to cover expenditure commitments outstanding at the end of a fiscal period. The third, reflecting the portion of the net assets of the fund that is available for meeting future

[2] FASB Statement of Financial Accounting Concepts. No. 3 (Stamford, CT: Financial Accounting Standards Board, 1980), p. 9.

[3] Ibid., p. 14.

expenditures, is characterized as an "unreserved fund balance."[4] We should observe that while this practice is recommended by GAAFR, it is not prescribed by Statement 1 and may not necessarily be followed in actual practice.

Revenue and expenditure accounts, defined in Chapter 1 (page 7), may be thought of as the primary nominal accounts for the general fund. They are closed at the end of each period, as are the income and expense accounts for businesses. Unlike business income and expense accounts, however, these accounts are designed to reflect the inflows (revenues) and the outflows (expenditures) of appropriable resources. Appropriable resources are the liquid assets that, within the concept of the going concern, are anticipated to be available to meet fund expenditures during the reporting period or within 60 days after the end of the period.

As we observed in Chapter 2, budgetary accounts are used to record budget plans within the formal accounting records. Estimated revenues are recorded to show the anticipated flows of appropriable resources into the general fund. Appropriation accounts show the budgeted outflows of such resources. The NCGA defines an *appropriation* as "a legal authorization for government spending activities during the year."[5] In that way, spending limits are established that cannot be exceeded unless subsequently amended by the board authorizing them. Kohler defines an appropriation as

> an expenditure authorization with specific limitations as to amount, purpose, and time; a formal approval of an expenditure or class of expenditures from designated resources available or estimated to be available. An appropriation may vary in binding force from an expression of intent by the management of a business concern to a restrictive limitation by the legislature imposed on a government agency.[6]

Both the estimated revenue and appropriation accounts are closed at the end of each period and are, therefore, classified as nominal accounts.

The strong emphasis on appropriation control makes the use of encumbrance and encumbrance reserve accounts highly desirable in accounting for general fund operations. Kohler defines an *encumbrance* as "an anticipated expenditure, evidenced by a contract or a purchase order, or determined by administrative action."[7] The encumbrance account is another nominal account. It is reversed against reserve for encumbrances either when the related expenditure is recognized or at the end of the reporting period. If encumbered appropriations outstanding at the end of the period do not lapse, another entry should then be made to record

---

[4] *Governmental Accounting, Auditing, and Financial Reporting* (Chicago: Municipal Finance Officers Association, 1980) p. 42.

[5] Ibid., p. 2.

[6] Eric L. Kohler, *A Dictionary for Accountants* (Englewood Cliffs, NJ: Prentice–Hall, Inc., 1975), p. 30.

[7] Ibid., p. 173.

an amount equal to that balance in an account entitled "fund balance reserved for encumbrances." The offsetting debit will be to unreserved fund balance. These entries are illustrated on pages 68 and 78. If performance on an encumbered appropriation is virtually complete, *substance over form treatment* permits it to be recognized as an expenditure and liability at the end of the period.

Interfund accounts represent claims against and obligations to other fund entities. Although they may be thought of, respectively, as assets and liabilities of the fund, they cannot be construed as assets and liabilities of the governmental unit.

General fund nominal accounts are designed to account for the flows of appropriable resources into and out of the operating entity. *Revenue accounts should disclose the sources of inflows, and expenditure accounts should show how resources have been used.* Thus, through the use of these accounts and other related nominal accounts, dollar accountability is maintained for general fund resources. In accordance with this concept of control, capital and revenue items are accounted for in much the same manner. For example, except for the difference in account names, a purchase of equipment from general fund resources is recorded within the general fund exactly as is the payment of payroll. Each is treated as an expenditure, or an outflow of spendable resources.

Each type of nominal account may describe a group of individual accounts found in the general fund ledger or may serve as a control account in that ledger with appropriate supporting subsidiary records. If the nominal accounts are assumed to be control accounts, subsidiary ledgers will be maintained in support of them. A portion of a subsidiary ledger is shown in Figure 3.1.

Account Subclassifications

As we have noted, each major nominal account may be further subdivided to provide more adequate disclosure of the data and to achieve more specific control over the flows of resources. Generally, these subsidiary records are organized to show more specific information about various types of revenues and expenditures.

Revenue Accounts.   Revenue items are subclassified primarily by source. This helps users of financial statements see where resources used by the governmental entity have originated. Typical categories for the revenues of a general fund are:

1. revenues from taxes

2. revenues from fines and forfeits

3. revenues from licenses and permits

4. charges for services

FIGURE 3.1 Subsidiary Appropriations Ledger—Street-Maintenance Services

Salaries

	Encumbrances Dr.	Cr.	Balance	Expenditures Dr.	Cr.	Balance	Appropriations Dr.	Cr.	Balance
(1)								$200,000	$200,000
(5)				$200,000		$200,000	$200,000		0
(C-2)					$200,000	0			0

Maintenance

	Encumbrances Dr.	Cr.	Balance	Expenditures Dr.	Cr.	Balance	Appropriations Dr.	Cr.	Balance
(1)								50,000	50,000
(5)				48,000		48,000	48,000		2,000
(C-2)(C-1)					48,000	0	2,000		0

Equipment

	Encumbrances Dr.	Cr.	Balance	Expenditures Dr.	Cr.	Balance	Appropriations Dr.	Cr.	Balance
(1)								150,000	150,000
(6)	$150,000		$150,000				150,000		0
(7b)		$150,000	0					150,000	150,000
(7a)				145,000		145,000	145,000		5,000
(C-2)(C-1)					145,000	0	5,000		0

5. intergovernmental revenues

6. miscellaneous revenues.

These classifications may be further subdivided to explain more adequately the sources from which the revenues were realized. For example, revenues from taxes may be subdivided to show the amounts realized from sources such as property taxes and sales taxes. Other categories may be similarly subdivided.

Expenditure Accounts.   Expenditures generally are subclassified first by *function.* Typical functional classifications might include:

1. general government

2. public safety

3. highways and streets

4. sanitation services

5. culture and recreation services

6. health services

7. welfare services

8. education services.

The specific functional classifications used within a general fund will, of course, depend on the services provided by the governmental unit. Furthermore, the major functional classifications typically are further subdivided into subfunctions or departments. For example, the general government function may be subdivided into executive, legislative, and judicial subfunctions or departments. Within each of these categories, expenditures are generally subclassified by *object.* The executive function, for example, typically would be subdivided into object categories to establish item-by-item budgetary control.

Budgetary Control and Accounting Procedures

Budgetary control through the appropriation technique is a natural instrument for implementing dollar accountability for general fund resources. For that reason, budgetary data usually are recorded in the general fund accounting records. We shall now explain how these data are used to relate the budget plan formally to actual general fund operations.

Budgetary Accounts.   Estimated revenues and appropriations are budgetary accounts. The manager of a governmental entity is responsible for accounting for the sources and dispositions of dollars and for showing that expenditures were made in accordance with the approved budget. Consequently, accounting practices that allow managers to have a running comparison between actual data and budget data, at levels where budgetary limitations are imposed, are generally used. This aspect of general fund accounting practices is illustrated in the transactions and financial reports shown later in this chapter. As was observed in Chapter 2, the budgetary data, requiring a type (1) entry (see page 19), are formally recorded in the general fund record as follows:

> Dr. Estimated revenues
>> Dr. or Cr. Budgetary fund balance
>> Cr. Appropriations

Encumbrance Accounts.   The high degree of control necessary to prevent expenditures from exceeding appropriations gives rise to the use of encumbrance accounts. When management commits itself to an expenditure of resources in the future, the available appropriation for that category of expenditure should be encumbered. An encumbrance, a type (4) transaction (see page 19), is recorded as follows:

> Dr. Encumbrances
>> Cr. Reserve for encumbrances

When the commitment becomes an expenditure within the accounting period, the encumbrance entry is reversed and the expenditure is recorded in the normal manner.

When a balance remains in the encumbrances account at the end of the fiscal period, it should, as we have observed, be reversed against the reserve for encumbrances account. If the encumbered appropriation does not lapse, the following entry generally should be recorded to show the amount of net assets that are reserved to meet encumbrances outstanding at the end of the period:

> Dr. Unreserved fund balance
>> Cr. Fund balance reserved for encumbrances

Closing Procedures

In business entities, *closing entries* are organized to emphasize the matching of revenues and expenses in an income summary account. General fund revenue and expenditure-related nominal accounts are closed in two steps. First, the entry used to record the budgetary data is reversed. Then revenues and expenditures are matched against each other, and the balance is debited or credited to the unreserved fund balance. These closing entries are recorded as follows:

> Dr. Appropriations
> Dr. or Cr. Budgetary fund balance
>> Cr. Estimated revenues

Dr. Revenues
Dr. or Cr. Unreserved fund balance
    Cr. Expenditures

ACCOUNTING FOR GENERAL FUND TRANSACTIONS

In this chapter and Chapter 4 we will show how a series of assumed transactions for Model City should be recorded in the city's accounting records. We begin the Model City illustration in this chapter by journalizing and posting to T-accounts a series of transactions assumed to have occurred in connection with activities of the city's general fund. All transactions are recorded as they would appear in the separate general fund records.

General Fund Transactions

We begin our illustration by presenting the beginning-of-the-period balance sheet for the general fund of Model City.

Model City—General Fund Balance Sheet

Assets		Liabilities and Fund Balance	
Cash	$20,000	Vouchers payable	$10,000
		Unreserved fund balance	10,000
	$20,000		$20,000

During the year, the following transactions occur:

1. The city council adopts the following budget for the next fiscal year:

Estimated Revenues by Sources

Property taxes	$1,450,000
Sales taxes	300,000
Municipal court fines	50,000
Traffic fines	50,000
Retail store permits	100,000
Taxes for special services	25,000
Other revenues	25,000
Total estimated revenues	$2,000,000

Appropriations by Functional Classifications

General government	$ 350,000
Police services	250,000
Street-maintenance services	400,000
Recreation services	200,000
Sanitation services	165,000
Transfer to debt-service fund	50,000
School services	400,000
Transfer to special assessment fund	25,000
Transfer to municipal garage fund	85,000
Miscellaneous	25,000
Total appropriations	$1,950,000

(With this budget, the city council is planning to receive $50,000 more revenue than it plans to use during the fiscal period.)

2. The property tax rate is determined by dividing the estimated revenue needed from this source by the assessed valuation, which is assumed to be $36,250,000. The tax rate is calculated as follows:

$$\frac{1,450,000}{36,250,000} = .04 \text{ per dollar}$$

This rate is commonly expressed as $4.00 per hundred dollars of assessed valuation.

After certain adjustments are made, tax bills in the amount of $1,460,000 are sent out. At this point, a subsidiary ledger showing taxes receivable from individual taxpayers is prepared to support the debit to the control account for taxes receivable. The revenue control account and the subsidiary ledger account for revenue from property taxes are credited.

3. Other revenues in the amount of $545,000 are received during the year. The entry to record this fact is actually a summary of many entries recorded during the year as the individual revenue receipts were realized.

Revenues by Sources

Sales taxes	$320,000
Municipal court fines	60,000
Traffic fines	35,000
Retail store permits	90,000
Fees for special services	20,000
Other revenues	20,000
	$545,000

4. Property taxes in the amount of $1,445,000 are collected. Individual accounts in the taxes receivable subsidiary ledger are also credited as the entry is made to the control account.

5. During the year, expenditures and transfers in the amount of $1,739,000 are made against the appropriations shown below. These are summations of numerous transactions that occurred as salaries were paid, as equipment was purchased, and so forth.

Expenditures by Functional Classifications

General government	$ 348,000
Police services	249,000
Street-maintenance services	248,000
Recreation services	175,000
Sanitation services	160,000
Payment into debt-service fund	50,000
School services	375,000
Payment toward special assessment project	25,000
Transfer to municipal garage fund	85,000
Miscellaneous expenditures	24,000
Total	$1,739,000

6. Contracts are signed for the purchase of equipment estimated to cost $200,000. The equipment includes street-maintenance units estimated at $150,000, miscellaneous recreational equipment estimated at $25,000, and school equipment estimated at $25,000.

Encumbrances by Functional Category

Street-maintenance services	$150,000
Recreational services	25,000
School services	25,000
Total	$200,000

7. The street-maintenance equipment is received. Its actual cost is $145,000.

8. Vouchers and amounts due to other funds in the amount of $1,800,000 are paid during the year.

9. Old street-maintenance equipment originally costing $60,000 is sold as scrap for $5,000.

Journal Entries To Record Transactions in Control Accounts

We now present the journal entries that are used to record the Model City general fund transactions. Each entry shows the number of the corresponding transaction described in the preceding paragraphs.

Transaction (1)

Estimated revenue	$2,000,000	
Appropriations		$1,950,000
Budgetary fund balance		50,000

Estimated Revenues Subsidiary Ledger (Debits)

Property taxes	$1,450,000
Sales taxes	$ 300,000
Municipal court fines	50,000
Traffic fines	50,000
Retail store permits	100,000
Fees for special services	25,000
Other revenues	25,000
	$2,000,000

Appropriations Subsidiary Ledger Credits (Expenditures Section)

General government	$ 350,000
Police services	250,000
Street-maintenance services	400,000
Recreation services	200,000
Sanitation services	165,000
Transfer to debt-service fund	50,000
School services	400,000
Transfer to special assessment fund	25,000
Transfer to municipal garage fund	85,000
Miscellaneous expenditures	25,000
Total	$1,950,000

This entry records in the formal accounting records the amounts of revenues that Model City expects to realize and the amounts appropriated for the proposed services. The description of transaction (1) on page 69 shows that $400,000 is appropriated for the city's street-maintenance services. The subsidiary ledger (Figure 3.1) shows further limitations placed on the use of these funds. It shows that $200,000 is earmarked for salaries, $50,000 for maintenance, and $150,000 for equipment purchases. In this way, the dollar accountability for the street-maintenance services appropriation is maintained on an item-by-item basis.

Estimated revenues, subclassified by the sources of the revenues, are also recorded in this entry. A subsidiary ledger for revenues normally is used to show the relationship between revenues budgeted by sources and actual revenues realized from each source.

Transaction (2)

Taxes receivable	$1,460,000	
Revenue		$1,460,000

Revenues Subsidiary Ledger Credit

Property taxes	$1,460,000

Transaction (3)

Cash	$ 545,000	
Revenue		$ 545,000

Revenues Subsidiary Ledger Credits

Sales taxes	320,000
Municipal court fines	60,000
Traffic fines	35,000
Retail store permits	90,000
Fees for special services	20,000
Other revenues	20,000
	$ 545,000

Transaction (4)

Cash	$1,445,000	
Taxes receivable		$1,445,000

The journal entry to record transaction (2) shows the result of billing taxpayers for their respective obligations. Credits are entered in the control amount for revenues and in the revenues subsidiary ledger. Other revenues are recorded as they are realized. Journal entry (3) shows the summation of transaction (3) entries. Entry (4) records the collection of taxes entered as receivables in transaction (2).

Transaction (5)

Transfer to debt-service fund	$ 50,000	
Transfer to special assessment fund	25,000	
Transfer to municipal garage fund	85,000	
Expenditures	1,579,000	
Vouchers payable		$1,544,000
Due to debt-service fund		50,000
Due to municipal garage fund		120,000
Due to special assessment fund		25,000

Expenditures Subsidiary Ledger Debits

General government	$ 348,000
Police services	249,000
Street-maintenance services	248,000
Recreation services	175,000
Sanitation services	160,000
School services	375,000
Miscellaneous expenditures	24,000
Total	$1,579,000

The journal entry for transaction (5) records $1,739,000 of expenditures and transfers. Supporting details show that $248,000 of this amount is for street-maintenance services, which includes $200,000 for salaries and $48,000 for maintenance. After entering these amounts in the subsidiary ledger (Figure 3.1), we see that the entire appropriation for salaries has been used and that $2,000 remains for maintenance. Of the total outlays, $195,000 represents a recognition of interfund obligations. This fact is recorded by crediting accounts showing the amounts due to the debt-service fund, municipal garage fund, and special assessment fund. The balance, amounting to $1,544,000, is credited to vouchers payable.

It is interesting to observe that $85,000 of the $120,000 due to the municipal garage fund is shown in the transfer to municipal garage fund account while the difference amounting to $35,000 is recorded as an expenditure. The amount in the transfer account reflects the contribution that the general fund made to establish the municipal garage. The amount included in expenditures is for services rendered to the general fund during the period (see page 86 for a further explanation).

Transaction (6)

Encumbrances	$ 200,000	
Reserve for encumbrances		$ 200,000

Encumbrances Subsidiary Ledger Debits

	Debit
Street-maintenance services	$ 150,000
Recreational services	25,000
School services	25,000
Total	$ 200,000

The entry for transaction (6) records an encumbrance against appropriations for equipment purchases. In the subsidiary ledger (Figure 3.1), the effect on the balance available for street-maintenance equipment is shown by extending the effect of the encumbrance in the appropriation balance column. This column shows that the city has no more resources to spend for street-maintenance equipment during the fiscal period. The reserve for encumbrances is credited to show the extent to which appropriable resources are committed.

Transaction (7a)

Expenditures	$ 145,000	
Vouchers payable		$ 145,000

Expenditures Subsidiary Ledger Debit

Street-maintenance services	$ 145,000

Transaction (7b)

Reserve for encumbrances	$ 150,000	
Encumbrances		$ 150,000

Encumbrances Subsidiary Ledger Credit

Street-maintenance services	$ 150,000

The transaction (7a) entry shows the actual cost of equipment purchases, and the transaction (7b) entry reverses the previously recorded
encumbrance. These amounts are also recorded in the equipment section
of the street-maintenance services subsidiary ledger. The net effect of these
two entries is to leave $5,000 available for equipment purchases (see Figure
3.1). Not all expenditures are encumbered before they are incurred, as
shown in transaction (5). Encumbrance accounts are used only when a
significant period is expected to elapse between the dates of commitment
to spend and expenditure recognition.

Transaction (8)

Due to municipal garage fund	$ 120,000	
Vouchers payable	1,605,000	
Due to special assessment fund	25,000	
Due to debt-service fund	50,000	
Cash		$1,800,000

The entry for transaction (8) records payment of $1,605,000 in vouch-
ers payable plus amounts due to the debt-service fund, special assessment
fund, and municipal garage fund of $50,000, $25,000, and $120,000, re-
spectively.

Transaction (9)

Cash	$ 5,000	
Revenue		$ 5,000

Revenue in the amount of $5,000 from the sale of old street-cleaning
equipment is recorded in the entry for transaction (9). Cash is debited,
and revenue is credited. Because the equipment was charged to expenditures when it was purchased, the only record of its original cost will be
found in the fixed-assets accounting records developed in Chapter 4.

Posting the Transactions

The preceding journal entries are posted to general fund accounts, as
shown in the following T-accounts. Each posting is keyed to the transaction
giving rise to it.

T-Accounts for Model City

(Numbers in parentheses represent transaction numbers used in the text.)

Estimated Revenue			
(1)	$2,000,000	(C-1)	$2,000,000

Appropriations			
(C-1)	$1,950,000	(1)	$1,950,000

Revenues			
(C-2)	$2,010,000	(2)	$1,460,000
		(3)	545,000
		(9)	5,000

Expenditures			
(5)	$1,579,000	(C-2)	$1,724,000
(7a)	145,000		

Transfers to Debt-Service Fund			
(5)	$ 50,000	(C-2)	$ 50,000

Transfers to Special Assessment Fund			
(5)	$ 25,000	(C-2)	$ 25,000

Budgetary Fund Balance			
(C-1)	$ 50,000	(1)	$ 50,000

Tranfers to Municipal Garage Fund			
(5)	$ 85,000	(C-2)	$ 85,000

Unreserved Fund Balance			
(C-4)	$ 50,000	Bal.	$ 10,000
		(C-2)	126,000

Encumbrances			
(6)	$ 200,000	(7b)	$ 150,000
		(C-3)	50,000

Taxes Receivable			
(2)	$1,460,000	(4)	$1,445,000

Reserve for Encumbrances			
(7b)	$ 150,000	(6)	$ 200,000
(C-3)	$ 50,000		

Cash			
Bal.	$ 20,000	(8)	$1,800,000
(3)	545,000		
(4)	1,445,000		
(9)	5,000		

Vouchers Payable			
(8)	$1,605,000	Bal.	$ 10,000
		(5)	1,544,000
		(7a)	145,000

Due to Special Assessment Fund			
(8)	$ 25,000	(5)	$ 25,000

Due to Municipal Garage Fund			
(8)	$ 120,000	(5)	$ 120,000

Fund Balance Reserved for Encumbrances			
		(C-4)	$ 50,000

Due to Debt-Service Fund			
(8)	$ 50,000	(5)	$ 50,000

Closing Entries

At the end of the fiscal period, the following C-entries (posted in the T-accounts illustrated on page 77) are recorded to close the nominal accounts of the general fund:

(C-1)

Dr. Appropriations	$1,950,000	
Dr. Budgetary fund balance	50,000	
Cr. Estimated revenues		$2,000,000

(C-2)

Dr. Revenues	$2,010,000	
Cr. Expenditures		$1,724,000
Cr. Transfers to debt service fund		50,000
Cr. Transfers to special assessment fund		25,000
Cr. Transfers to municipal garage fund		85,000
Cr. Unreserved fund balance		126,000

(C-3)

Dr. Reserve for encumbrances	$ 50,000	
Cr. Encumbrances		$ 50,000

(C-4)

Dr. Unreserved fund balance	$ 50,000	
Cr. Fund balance reserved for encumbrances		$ 50,000

Entry (C-1), recorded at the end of the fiscal period, reverses the original budgetary entry (1). Entry (C-2) is used to close the revenue and expenditure accounts to the unreserved fund balance account. Subsidiary records for all those items are also closed at this time. Entry (C-3) reverses the balances shown in the encumbrance and reserve for encumbrances accounts. Entry (C-4) records the portion of the unreserved fund balance that should be reserved for encumbrances.

As a result of these entries, we can see that the budgetary plan contemplated an unreserved fund balance of $60,000: $10,000 plus a $50,000 budgeted increase. The fund actually ended up with an unreserved fund balance of $86,000: $10,000 beginning balance plus $126,000 from entry (C-2) minus $50,000 from entry (C-4).

During the next year, when the encumbrance-related expenditure is recognized, it will be recorded as an expenditure but will be labeled to show that it relates to the prior fiscal period. At the end of the next year, the balance in the fund balance reserved for encumbrances should again be adjusted to reflect the amount of year-end encumbrances outstanding. To illustrate how that should be done, let's assume that the encumbrances outstanding at the end of the next year amount to $40,000. That would require the fund balance reserved for encumbrances to be adjusted as follows:

Dr. Fund balance reserved for encumbrances	$10,000	
Cr. Unreserved fund balance		$10,000

In the subsidiary ledger (Figure 3.1), credits of $200,000, $48,000, and $145,000 to expenditures for salaries, maintenance, and equipment, respectively, are parts of the credit to expenditures of $1,724,000 shown in entry (C-2). As explained earlier, all debits to the appropriations sections of this subsidiary ledger are part of the $1,950,000 debit to appropriations (see C-1).

Subsidiary Ledgers

Detailed subsidiary ledgers should be maintained for each control account used in the preceding illustrations. This allows management to exercise item-by-item control, which is particularly important in accounting for expenditures. Appropriations are made for the budget period, and authorization to commit resources for them usually expires at the end of that period.

Control of expenditures requires item-by-item coordination of appropriations, expenditures, and encumbrances. This control usually is attained by combining the subsidiary records of these accounts as they relate to each specific type of expenditure. Figure 3.1 (page 66) shows the street-maintenance services section of the subsidiary appropriations, expenditures and encumbrances ledger with the assumed transactions recorded in it.

FINANCIAL STATEMENTS FOR THE GENERAL FUND

Governmental units prepare separate financial statements for each fund and account group. In this section, we consider the financial statements that should be prepared for the general fund of Model City. More specifically, we will:

1. examine the objectives of general fund financial statements

2. illustrate the preparation of a statement of revenues, expenditures, and changes in fund balance

3. cite selected observations that can be made from reading the statement of revenues and expenditures

4. present an illustrated balance sheet.

Objectives of Financial Statements

Adherence to the concept of dollar accountability for reporting financial data for the general fund requires that the statements show:

1. the sources and uses of funds

2. the extent to which the budgetary plan has been achieved

3. the financial position of the fund at the end of the period with respect to appropriable resources.

Statement of Revenues, Expenditures, and Changes in Fund Balance

The first two of these objectives are accomplished by preparing a statement showing both budgeted and actual revenues and expenditures. This information generally should be combined in one statement, with expenditures offset against revenues. Governmental entities, however, may present these data for internal use in two statements—one for revenues and another for expenditures and transfers. The relationships between actual and budgeted amounts are emphasized in each statement. Figure 3.2 is prepared using this plan of reporting to show general fund revenues, expenditures, and changes in fund balance for the illustrated fiscal period. Generally accepted accounting practice (GAAP), as spelled out in NCGA Statement 1, requires that these statement data also be combined with those of other funds, as illustrated in Chapter 4.

In reporting for business enterprises, a statement showing changes in retained earnings is prepared to show a connecting-link history of the business. Similar information showing the changes in the fund balance account should also be included among the general fund financial statements. The lower part of Figure 3.2 shows changes in the general fund balance of Model City during the fiscal period. This is the statement format recommended in NCGA Statement 1.

Interpreting the Operating Statements

Financial statements are prepared to be read and interpreted. In the following paragraphs we discuss some important facts that can be observed from the statement of revenues, expenditures, and changes in fund balances, as well as their implications for the users of these statements.

The statement in Figure 3.2 shows that Model City has realized actual revenues amounting to $10,000 more than was budgeted. The realization of excess amounts from property taxes, sales taxes, and municipal court fines more than offset deficiencies in amounts realized from other budgeted sources of revenue. Also, the unanticipated sale of assets accounted for $5,000 of the excess revenues. Because the amount of taxes collected is

**FIGURE 3.2. Model City General Fund
Statement of Revenues, Expenditures, and
Changes in Fund Balances for Fiscal Period**

	Budget	Actual	Variances Favorable/ (Unfavorable)
Revenues			
Property taxes	$1,450,000	$1,460,000	$ 10,000
Sales taxes	300,000	320,000	20,000
Municipal court fines	50,000	60,000	10,000
Traffic fines	50,000	35,000	(15,000)
Retail store permits	100,000	90,000	(10,000)
Fees for special services	25,000	20,000	(5,000)
Revenue from water department	25,000	20,000	(5,000)
Revenue from sale of assets	0	5,000	5,000
Total	$2,000,000	$2,010,000	$ 10,000
Expenditures			
General government	$ 350,000	$ 348,000	$ 2,000
Police services	250,000	249,000	1,000
Sanitation services	165,000	160,000	$ 5,000
Recreation services	200,000	175,000	25,000
Street-maintenance services	400,000	393,000	7,000
School services	400,000	375,000	25,000
Miscellaneous	25,000	24,000	1,000
Total	$1,790,000	$1,724,000	66,000
Excess (deficiency) of revenues over expenditures	$ 210,000	$ 286,000	$ 76,000
Transfers			
To debt-service fund	50,000	50,000	0
To special assessment fund	25,000	25,000	0
To municipal garage fund	85,000	85,000	0
Total	$ 160,000	$ 160,000	$ 0
Excess (deficiency) of revenues over expenditures and transfers	$ 50,000	$ 126,000	$ 76,000
Fund balances at beginning of period	$ 10,000	$ 10,000	
Fund balances at end of period	60,000	$ 136,000	$ 76,000
Fund balance reserved for encumbrances		$ 50,000	
Unreserved fund balance		86,000	
Total fund balances		$ 136,000	

a function of governmental taxing power, the excess amount realized from these sources cannot be said to be either good or bad; it simply shows the extent to which the budget plan for revenues has been achieved. As an example, the deficiency in revenues from traffic fines could be caused by inadequate traffic control or by a general tendency toward fewer traffic violations.

The expenditures and transfer parts of the statement disclose the extent to which the actual outflows of appropriable resources have coincided with the original plan for the uses of these resources. It is important, however, to understand the significance of the differences between appropriations and actual amounts expended. For example, the failure of sanitation services to spend $5,000 of its appropriation could mean that less service was provided than was planned. Because each appropriation anticipates a certain level of service, a saving can always be achieved by failing to provide the full amount of service planned. On the other hand, actual expenditures can include outflows of resources caused by inefficiencies in rendering the services. The conventional statement of revenues and expenditures does not provide sufficient information to determine exactly what has caused the differences between budgeted and actual expenditures.

The presently accepted practice of emphasizing funds flow, rather than income and expense data, in the operating reports of governmental funds often leads to the use of funds without adequate regard for the benefits realized from them. For example, this practice may occur when management decides to spend resources simply because they have been appropriated rather than because of a real need for providing more or better services.

Revenue and expenditure statements generally are characterized as statements of operations. We must be careful to recognize that such statements of operations disclose information that is significantly different from that contained in the income statements of profit enterprises. Operating statements for businesses show periodic revenues and expenses offset against each other to determine net income for the period, whereas revenue and expenditure statements show inflows and outflows of appropriable resources for the period. Because revenue and expenditure statements include things such as the sales of assets or expenditures for capital items, they are more appropriately described as *statements of sources and uses of appropriable resources*.

The Balance Sheet

The balance sheet shows the financial position of the general fund, and its primary emphasis is on the appropriable resources available to the fund. The general fund balance sheet for Model City shows $230,000 of appropriable resources (Figure 3.3). Commitments against these resources amount to $144,000, leaving an unreserved fund balance of $86,000, which reflects the amount of nonappropriable resources available for use in future periods.

FIGURE 3.3.   Model City General Fund Balance Sheet, End of Fiscal Period

Assets		Liabilities, Reserves, and Fund Balance	
Cash	$215,000	Vouchers payable	$ 94,000
Taxes receivable	15,000	Fund balance reserved for encumbrances	50,000
		Unreserved fund balance	86,000
Total	$230,000	Total	$230,000

SPECIAL PROBLEMS ASSOCIATED WITH GENERAL FUND ACCOUNTING

The preceding examples of general fund accounting procedures and financial statements show how routine, regularly recurring transactions are recorded and reported. Familiarity with this framework is basic to an understanding of accounting procedures for source and disposition (governmental) type funds. A number of problems can arise, however, that demand special attention in the accounting records and reports. These special problems include:

1. practical deviations in accounting practices

2. accounting for capital items

3. disclosure of inventory data

4. transactions involving short-term borrowing

5. accounting for probable losses in the collection of taxes receivable.

Practical Deviations

We have described how to record budgetary data in the formal accounting records in transaction (1) (page 72). As a practical matter, however, these items are not always recorded in the formal records. In many instances only actual revenues, expenditures, and transfer items are reflected as nominal accounts in the general fund records. When this practice is followed, budgetary accountability is shown only by the periodic supplementary comparisons of actual and budgeted amounts for each revenue and expenditure item.

In other instances, accounting records for the general fund may be maintained strictly on a cash basis. Revenues are recognized when received in cash, and expenditures are recorded when paid. Such an arrangement omits the recognition of taxes receivable and vouchers payable.

Capital Items

The lack of distinction between capital and revenue items is one of the unique characteristics of governmental type fund accounting. Because of it, some of the specific record-keeping procedures are significantly different from those found in the profit area.

Governmental type fund accounting practices relating to capital expenditures require that transactions such as retirement of long-term debt and purchase of fixed assets by the general fund, both of which represent outflows of appropriable resources, be recorded as debits to expenditure accounts. For example, the following journal entries are used to record a bond retirement:

> Expenditures
>   Matured bonds payable (or Vouchers payable or Due to debt-service fund)
>
> Matured bonds payable (or Vouchers payable or Due to debt-service fund)
>   Cash

The following journal entry records the purchase of a fixed asset:

> Expenditures
>   Vouchers payable or Cash

Cash realized from the issuance of bonds is recorded with an offsetting credit to an inflow account called "bond issue proceeds" (a revenue type of account). Cash realized from the sale of fixed assets is recorded with an offsetting credit to revenue, similar to the way inflows from taxes or fines are recorded.

Inventories: Expenditure or Consumption Method

Another problem of reporting centers around the disclosure of supplies and other similar nonappropriable resources on hand. The balance sheet for the general fund is designed to show the appropriable resources, along with the claims against them. When the cost of supplies is charged to expenditures at the time of purchase, an inventory of supplies is considered a nonappropriable resource and therefore would be omitted from the assets of the general fund. It may be desirable, however, to disclose the cost of the supplies still on hand at the balance sheet date if it is a significant amount. Such an item can be disclosed by originating the following memo entry:

> Supplies on hand
>   Fund balance reserved for supplies on hand

When the amount of supplies on hand at the end of the next period declines, the balances in these accounts can be reduced by reversing the difference out of them. If the balance becomes larger, the additional amount is recorded by another memo entry similar to the one just shown.

Although the method just cited generally is used in accounting for supplies, the 1980 edition of GAAFR also permits use of the *consumption method.* Under this method we would account for the acquisitions and uses of supplies much as we do for profit entities. In other words, expenditures for supplies would be recognized when supplies are used rather than when they are purchased. This method treats supplies on hand as an appropriable asset and therefore allows the value assigned to them to be shown as such on the balance sheet.

Although most inflows of cash or other appropriable resources are recorded as revenue to the general fund, not every inflow of cash represents revenue. For example, an inflow of cash as a result of borrowing on a short-term note does not increase the net appropriable assets and should not be recorded as revenue. That type of transaction is recorded as follows:

Cash
    Notes payable

Similarly, an obligation must be recognized when cash from taxes is received in advance. In such a case, the liability account offsetting the debit to cash is labeled as "advance payment of taxes" or some similar name.

The general fund may also borrow from other funds within the governmental unit. If the general fund borrows cash from another fund, that fact is recorded as follows:

Cash
    Due to other fund

What determines whether a revenue account, a liability account, or an interfund account is to be credited when cash is received? The determining factor seems to be whether the amount must be repaid from appropriable resources available, or expected to be available, to the general fund during the reporting period. Long-term obligations, for example, will be paid from resources to be realized in subsequent years. Short-term notes payable, on the other hand, generally are paid from noncash resources, such as taxes receivable, already available in the general fund. When tax assessments are collected in advance, "advance payment of taxes" is offset by the asset "taxes receivable." In cases where such short-term obligations are incurred, a liability account rather than a revenue account is credited.

Recent discussions of interfund resource flows suggest that they may be classified into three categories, as follows[8]:

[8] NCGA Statement 1 (Chicago: Municipal Finance Officers Association, 1979), pp. 15–16.

1. Those appropriately designated as expenditures, expenses, or revenues. These are characterized as *quasi-external transactions* that would be treated as expenditures, expenses, or revenues if they involved outside organizations. For example, amounts paid to a municipal garage fund by the general fund for maintenance of vehicles would be recognized as expenditures by the general fund and as revenues by the municipal garage fund.

2. Those that represent loans to be reimbursed and their related reimbursements. Transactions that involve the use of funds that are later to be reimbursed should be treated as loans and reflected as "due from" and "due to" items in the accounts for the respective funds. This type of transaction occurs, for example, when an obligation is paid by the general fund that is properly chargeable to some other fund. A "due from" account should be debited in the general fund accounts, and a "due to" account should be credited in the other fund's accounts. When payments of this type are made without the knowledge that they will later be reimbursed, the related expenditure and revenue entries should be reversed.

3. Those that should be reflected as transfers to and from funds involved in the transaction. All payments between funds that do not fall into either of the first two categories fall into this group and should be reflected as transfers to and transfers from other funds. Such transfers are divided into two categories in NCGA Statement 1: *residual equity transfers* and *operating transfers.* Residual equity transfers are reported as additions to or deductions from beginning fund balances. Operating transfers may be thought of as special types of expenditures and revenues for the respective funds, characterized as "other financing sources (uses)." The uses of these accounts are illustrated in Chapter 4.

Possible Losses in the Collection of Taxes Receivable

The possibility of losses occurring in the collection of taxes receivable is another problem that requires special consideration. To provide for losses in collecting accounts receivable, a business entity charges an expense account for the anticipated losses. Because taxes receivable do not actually become a resource available for meeting expenditures until collected, they should be recorded as revenue at their cash realizable value. Such an arrangement means that the anticipated losses in collecting taxes are *recorded as a reduction of revenue* rather than as an expenditure. This is referred to as the *net revenue* approach. In our illustration of Model City, we assumed that all taxes were collectible. If past experience had shown that $10,000 probably would not be collected during the period, the entry to show the recognition of tax revenue would have been recorded as follows:

Taxes receivable	$1,460,000	
Allowance for uncollectible taxes		$ 10,000
Revenues		1,450,000

The entry for taxes receivable designates the amount receivable from the current tax levy. When taxes become delinquent, the amounts still receivable should be so designated by recording them in a taxes receivable–delinquent taxes account. As penalties are assessed on delinquencies, they are recorded in a penalties receivable account with an offsetting credit to revenues.

When delinquent taxes are not paid within a specified time, they are converted to tax liens receivable in much the same manner as taxes receivable are converted to taxes receivable–delinquent taxes. Eventually, cash will be realized on such claims, or they will cease to be an asset of the general fund. If the latter occurs, the tax liens receivable balance should be written off against the allowance for uncollectible tax liens account.

TRANSACTION WORKSHEET

In actual practice, formal journals and ledgers are used to record financial transactions for the general fund. For problem-solving purposes, however, a transactions worksheet, similar to that shown in Figure 3.4 (pages 88–89) may serve as a better recording device. It can save a significant amount of time without sacrificing any of the technical understanding expected to be realized through problem solving. The worksheet simply combines on one page of columnar paper the essential elements of the transactions and statements for Model City illustrated and discussed in this chapter.

SUMMARY

The organizational characteristics of governmental units require that operations be controlled by a budget that specifies the amounts appropriated for each item of expenditures. The fiduciary nature of these entities requires the use of fund accounting techniques, which divides the accounting records for the resources of the governmental unit into a number of separate, self-balancing accounting entities called funds.

Resources available for general operating purposes flow through the general fund. Therefore, the primary objective in accounting for general fund operations is to show the sources and uses of resources available for general operating purposes. Accounting records designed to accomplish

FIGURE 3.4.   Model City Transactions Worksheet

	Balances, Beginning of Period	
Cash	$20,000	
Taxes receivable		
Vouchers payable		10,000
Due to debt-service fund		
Due to special assessment fund		
Due to municipal garage fund		
Unreserved fund balance		10,000
Budgetary fund balance		
Fund balance reserved for encumbrances		
Reserve for encumbrances		
Estimated revenues		
Appropriations		
Revenues		
Transfers to debt-service fund		
Transfers to special assessment fund		
Transfers to municipal garage fund		
Expenditures		
Encumbrances		
Totals	$20,000	$20,000
Balance to unreserved fund balance		
Totals	$20,000	$20,000

a Transaction numbers keyed to journal entries illustrated in this chapter.

this objective and the financial statements resulting from them were illustrated and interpreted in this chapter.

Another objective of general fund accounting is to show the extent to which the actual acquisitions and disposals of resources coincide with the budget plan. For this reason, budget data generally are recorded in the accounts and are directly related to revenues realized and expenditures incurred.

A number of special problems relating to general fund accounting practices were discussed in the last part of the chapter. These include the special considerations associated with recording expenditures for long-

Transactions[a]		Revenues, Expenditures, and Transfers		End-of-Period Balance Sheet	
(3) $ 545,000	(8) $1,800,000			$215,000	
(4) 1,445,000					
(9) 5,000					
(2) 1,460,000	(4) 1,445,000			15,000	
(8) 1,605,000	(5) 1,544,000				$ 94,000
	(7a) 145,000				
(8) 50,000	(5) 50,000				
(8) 25,000	(5) 25,000				
(8) 120,000	(5) 120,000				
(C-4) 50,000				40,000	
	(1) 50,000				50,000
	(C-4) 50,000				50,000
(7b) 150,000	(6) 200,000				
(C-3) 50,000					
(1) 2,000,000		$2,000,000			
	(1) 1,950,000		$1,950,000		
	(2) 1,460,000		2,010,000		
	(3) 545,000				
	(9) 5,000				
(5) 50,000		50,000			
(5) 25,000		25,000			
(5) 85,000		85,000			
(5) 1,579,000		1,724,000			
(7a) 145,000					
(6) 200,000	(7b) 150,000				
	(C-3) 50,000				
$9,589,000	$9,589,000	$3,884,000	$3,960,000	$270,000	$194,000
		76,000			76,000
$9,589,000	$9,589,000	$3,960,000	$3,960,000	$270,000	$270,000

term assets, revenues from long-term borrowing, interfund transactions, proceeds from the sale of long-term assets, and anticipated losses in the collection of taxes. We also considered the special problems associated with the disclosure of supplies inventories in the general fund balance sheet.

QUESTIONS FOR CLASS DISCUSSION

3.1. Explain the differences in the ways the term *revenues* is used in governmental and in business accounting.

3.2. Contrast the terms *expense* and *expenditure*.

3.3. (a) Why are the terms *revenues* and *expenditures* rather than *revenues* and *expenses* used as nominal accounts for governmental units? (b) How do these terms relate to the disclosure of the flows of resources through the fund entity?

3.4. Compare and contrast a balance sheet for a business with a typical general fund balance sheet.

3.5. (a) What is meant by the term *encumbrance*? (b) Could an encumbrance account be used in accounting for the transactions of a business enterprise? (c) If so, why is it not used there?

3.6. (a) Define the term *appropriation*. (b) Are funds ever appropriated within business entities? (c) If so, why don't their accounting records reflect the appropriated funds?

3.7. (a) How do the budgeting practices of governmental units differ from those followed by businesses? (b) Why are the budget data generally recorded in the accounts of the general fund?

3.8. What is meant by the term *appropriable resources*?

3.9. How may nonappropriable resources, such as unused supplies, be shown in the balance sheet of the general fund?

3.10. (a) How does governmental treatment of anticipated losses in the collection of taxes receivable differ from the treatment of anticipated losses in the collection of trade receivables for a business enterprise? (b) Justify the difference.

3.11. Joe and Jim live in different cities. Joe, seeking to extol the merits of his city, cites the fact that the city tax rate is only $2.35 per $100 of assessed value. Jim states that he cannot understand how Joe's tax rate can be so low, since he pays $4.00 per $100 of assessed value and enjoys fewer municipal benefits than Joe. Is this a valid comparison? Explain.

3.12. It is often difficult for municipal accountants to determine properly the costs of rendering a particular service. Why does this problem exist?

EXERCISES

3.1. Stone City has property with an assessed valuation of $50,000,000. The city council adopts a budget calling for expenditures of $500,000. They estimate that $50,000 of revenue will be realized from sources other than property taxes. Past experience has shown that approximately 2 percent of all taxes assessed become uncollectible. What tax rate should be assessed by Stone City?

3.2. The city of Beebe agrees to buy two pieces of street-maintenance equipment estimated to cost $50,000.

(a) How should this fact be recorded in the accounts?

(b) Explain the significance of the account balances.

3.3. The equipment referred to in Exercise 3.2 is received. The billed price is $48,000. How should this transaction be recorded? Explain.

3.4. Encumbrances for Jamesville at the end of the preceding year were $35,000. During the first month of the current year, items involved in these encumbrances are billed at $34,500. How should the billing be recorded? Explain.

3.5. At the end of the year the city of Alpha finds that its general fund shows supplies on hand valued at $5,000. These supplies were recorded as expenditures when purchased. What entry should be made to provide for disclosure of the inventory of supplies in the general fund balance sheet? Explain.

3.6. The city of Denby has, among others, the following account balances at the end of the fiscal period:

Estimated revenues	$500,000
Budgeted appropriations	485,000
Revenues	508,000
Expenditures	460,000
Encumbrances	20,000
Reserve for encumbrances	20,000

(a) Make the necessary closing entries. (b) Explain the significance of the balances resulting from the closing entries.

3.7. The police department has, among others, the following balances in its subsidiary records:

Appropriation—supplies	$ 5,000
Expenditures—supplies	3,000
Encumbrances for supply orders	500

What amount does the department have available to spend for supplies? Explain.

3.8. The balance sheet for the general fund of Texas City shows the following balances at the beginning of the year:

Cash	$25,000	Vouchers payable	$15,000
		Unreserved fund balance	10,000

The following actions and transactions occur during the year:

(a) The city council estimates general fund revenues to be $1,350,000 and has approved a budget authorizing expenditures of $1,490,000.

(b) Property tax notices in the amount of $1,000,000 are mailed.

(c) Property taxes in the amount of $900,000 are collected.

(d) The city realizes $250,000 in sales taxes and collects fines amounting to $70,000.

(e) Expenditures in the amount of $900,000 are incurred.

(f) Checks in the amount of $500,000 are issued in payment of vouchers payable.

(g) A contract to construct a storage building at an anticipated cost of $100,000 is signed.

(h) Budgeted expenditures include $150,000 to be paid to a special assessment fund, $70,000 to be paid to the debt-service fund, and $100,000 to be used to establish a municipal garage fund. These obligations are recognized.

(i) The amount due to the special assessment fund is paid.

(j) Nominal accounts are closed.

Required:

Record the preceding data on a transactions worksheet. Be sure to code each action and transaction with the letter listed beside it.

PROBLEMS

3.1. The balance sheet for the general fund of Bloomville included the following balances at the beginning of the year:

Cash	$40,000
Vouchers payable	20,000
Unreserved fund balance	20,000

The following actions and transactions relating to general fund operations occurred during the year:

(a) The city council approved the following budget for the year:

Estimated revenues	
Property taxes	$2,900,000②
Other revenues	1,100,000
Total	$4,000,000 ①

Appropriations

General government	$ 700,000
Police services	500,000
Street maintenance	800,000
Recreation services	200,000
Sanitation services	330,000
Payment to debt-service fund	100,000
School services	800,000
Payment to special assessment fund	50,000
Establishment of municipal service center	170,000
Other expenditures	250,000
Total	$3,900,000

(b) The property tax rate is determined by dividing estimated revenue from this source by the assessed valuation, which is assumed to be $145,000,000. After the tax rate has been determined, property with an assessed valuation of $1,000,000 was added to the tax rolls. Tax bills were then sent out based on the total assessed valuation of properties.

(c) Other revenues in the amount of $1,090,000 were received during the year.

(d) Property taxes in the amount of $2,890,000 were collected.

(e) The following expenditures and transfers were incurred during the year:

General government	$ 696,000
Police services	498,000
Street maintenance	496,000
Recreation services	150,000
Sanitation services	320,000
Payment to debt-service fund	100,000
School services	750,000
Payment to special assessment fund	50,000
Payment to establish municipal services center	170,000
Other expenditures	248,000
Total	$3,478,000

(f) Contracts are signed for the purchase of equipment at a cost of $400,000. This includes street-maintenance equipment expected to cost $300,000, recreational equipment estimated at $50,000, and school equipment expected to cost $50,000.

(g) The street-maintenance equipment is received. Its billed price is $290,000.

(h) Old street-maintenance equipment costing $120,000 is sold for $10,000.

(i) All amounts due to other funds and vouchers payable, amounting to $3,110,000, were paid.

Required:

1. Enter the beginning-of-year balance sheet items in the first two columns of a worksheet and record the actions and transactions listed previously in a general fund transactions worksheet similar to the one shown in Figure 3.4.
2. Prepare end-of-year financial statements for the general fund of Bloomville.
3. Determine the amounts of unused appropriations for each of the items listed in the approved budget (see Item (a)) as of the end of the year.

3.2. (AICPA adapted.) Select the best answer for each of the following items:

1. The "fund balance reserved for encumbrances" account represents amounts recorded by a governmental unit for:
   (a) anticipated expenditures in the next year
   (b) expenditures for which purchase orders were made in the prior year but disbursement will be in the current year
   (c) excess expenditures in the prior year that will be offset against the current year budgeted amounts
   (d) unanticipated expenditures of the prior year that become evident in the current year

2. Which of the following types of revenue generally would be recorded directly in the general fund of a governmental unit?
   (a) receipts from a city-owned parking structure
   (b) property taxes
   (c) interest earned on investments held for retirement of employees
   (d) revenues from internal service funds

3. The reserve for encumbrances account is properly considered to be a:
   (a) current liability if payable within a year; otherwise, a long-term debt
   (b) fixed liability
   (c) floating debt
   (d) reservation of the fund's equity

4. The initial transfer of cash from the general fund to establish an internal service fund would require the general fund to credit cash and debit:
   (a) accounts receivable—internal service fund
   (b) a "transfer to" account
   (c) reserve for encumbrances
   (d) appropriations

5. The town of Newbold general fund issued purchase orders to vendors and suppliers of $630,000. Which of the following entries should be made to record this transaction?

	Debit	Credit
(a) Encumbrances	$630,000	
Reserve for encumbrances		$630,000
(b) Expenditures	630,000	
Vouchers payable		630,000
(c) Expenses	630,000	
Accounts payable		630,000
(d) Reserve for encumbrances	630,000	
Encumbrances		630,000

6. The sequence of entries listed next indicates which of the following?

   (a) An adverse event was foreseen, and a reserve of $12,000 was created; later the reserve was canceled, and a liability for the item was acknowledged.

   (b) An order was placed for goods or services estimated to cost $12,000; the actual cost was $12,350, for which a liability was acknowledged on receipt.

   (c) Encumbrances were anticipated but later failed to materialize and were reversed. A liability of $12,350 was incurred.

   (d) The first entry was erroneous and was reversed; a liability of $12,350 was acknowledged.

Encumbrances	$12,000	
Reserve for encumbrances		$12,000
Reserve for encumbrances	12,000	
Encumbrances		12,000
Expenditures	12,350	
Vouchers payable		12,350

7. Assuming appropriate governmental accounting principles were followed, the entries:

   (a) occurred in the same fiscal period
   (b) did *not* occur in the same fiscal period
   (c) could have occurred in the same fiscal period, but it is impossible to be sure of this
   (d) reflect the equivalent of a "prior period adjustment," had the entity concerned been one operated for profit

8. Immediately after the first entry was recorded, the municipality had a balanced general fund budget for all transactions. What would be the effect of recording the second and third entries?

   (a) *No* change in the balanced condition of the budget.
   (b) The municipality would show a surplus.

(c) The municipality would show a deficit.

(d) *No* effect on the current budget, but the budget of the following fiscal period would be affected.

9. Entries similar to those for the general fund may also appear on the books of the municipality's

(a) general fixed-assets group

(b) general long-term debt group

(c) trust fund

(d) special revenue fund

10. Kingsford City incurred $100,000 of salaries and wages for the month ended March 31, 19X2. How should this be recorded at that date?

	Dr.	Cr.
(a) Expenditures—salaries and wages	$100,000	
Vouchers payable		$100,000
(b) Salaries and wages expense	$100,000	
Vouchers payable		$100,000
(c) Encumbrances—salaries and wages	$100,000	
Vouchers payable		$100,000
(d) Fund balance	$100,000	
Vouchers payable		$100,000

3.3. (AICPA adapted.) Information concerning the accounting records for the city of Bruceville on December 31, 19X1, is presented in the following table.

Additional information:

On December 31, 19X1, unfilled purchase orders for the general fund totaled $20,000.

City of Bruceville
General Fund
Partial General Ledger Trial Balance (Before Adjustments)
December 31, 19X1

	Debit	Credit
Supplies inventory (physical inventory, 12/31/X1)	$10,000	
Estimated revenue—miscellaneous	20,000	
Estimated revenue—taxes	95,000	
Appropriatons		$112,000
Revenue—miscellaneous		29,900
Revenue—taxes		85,000
Encumbrances	20,000	
Expenditures	80,000	
Expenditures chargeable against prior year encumbrances	7,100	

	Debit	Credit
Fund balance reserved for encumbrances (balance, 1/1/X1, $7,000)		27,000
Fund balance reserved for supplies inventory (balance, 1/1/X1)		12,000
Unreserved fund balance, 1/1/X1		3,300
Budgetary fund balance		3,000

Required:

1. Prepare an adjusting journal entry or entries for general fund accounts for December 31, 19X1.
2. Prepare a closing journal entry or entries for general fund accounts for December 31, 19X1.
3. Prepare in columnar form an analysis of changes in unreserved fund balance for the year 19X1. Use the following column headings: "Estimated," "Actual," and "Excess or deficiency of actual compared with estimate."

3.4. (AICPA adapted.) The following summary of transactions was taken from the accounts of the Annaville School District general fund *before* the books had been closed for the fiscal year ended June 30, 19X2:

	Postclosing Balances June 30, 19X1	Preclosing Balances June 30, 19X2
Cash	$400,000	$ 700,000
Taxes receivable	150,000	170,000
Estimated uncollectible taxes	(40,000)	(70,000)
Estimated revenues	—	3,000,000
Expenditures	—	2,842,000
Expenditures—prior year	—	—
Encumbrances	—	91,000
	$510,000	$6,733,000
Vouchers payable	$ 80,000	$ 408,000
Due to other funds	210,000	142,000
Fund balance reserved for encumbrances	60,000	91,000
Unreserved fund balance	160,000	182,000
Revenues from taxes	—	2,800,000
Miscellaneous revenues	—	130,000
Appropriations	—	2,980,000
	$510,000	$6,733,000

Additional information:

(a) The estimated taxes receivable for the year ended June 30, 19X2, were $2,870,000, and taxes collected during the year totaled $2,810,000.

(b) An analysis of the transactions in the vouchers payable account for the year ended June 30, 19X2, follows:

	Debit (Credit)
Current expenditures	$(2,600,000)
Expenditures for prior year	(58,000)
Vouchers for payment to other funds	(210,000)
Cash payments during year	2,540,000
Net change	$ (328,000)

(c) During the year the general fund was billed $142,000 for services performed on its behalf by other city funds.

(d) On May 2, 19X2, commitment documents were issued for the purpose of new textbooks at a cost of $91,000.

Required:

Based on the preceding data, reconstruct the *original detailed journal entries* that were required to record all transactions for the fiscal year ended June 30, 19X2, including the recording of the current year's budget. Do *not* prepare closing entries at June 30, 19X2.

3.5. (AICPA Adapted) The general fund trial balance of the city of Solna at December 31, 19X2, was as follows:

	Dr.	Cr.
Cash	$ 62,000	
Taxes receivable—delinquent	46,000	
Estimated uncollectible taxes—delinquent		$ 8,000
Stores inventory—program operations	18,000	
Vouchers payable		28,000
Fund balance reserved for stores inventory		18,000
Fund balance reserved for encumbrances		12,000
Unreserved undesignated fund balance		60,000
	$126,000	$126,000

Collectible delinquent taxes are expected to be collected within 60 days after the end of the year. Solna uses the "purchases" method to account for stores inventory. The following data pertain to 19X3 general fund operations:

(a) Budget adopted:

Revenues and other financing sources	
Taxes	$220,000
Fines, forfeits, and penalties	80,000
Miscellaneous revenues	100,000
Share of bond issue proceeds	200,000
	$600,000

Expenditures and other financing uses

Program operations	$300,000
General administration	120,000
Stores—program operations	60,000
Capital outlay	80,000
Periodic transfer to special assessment fund	20,000
	$580,000

(b) Taxes were assessed at an amount that would result in revenues of $220,800, after deduction of 4 percent of the tax levy as uncollectible.

(c) Orders placed but not received:

Program operations	$176,000
General administration	80,000
Capital outlay	60,000
	$316,000

(d) The city council designated $20,000 of the unreserved undesignated fund balance for possible future appropriation for capital outlay.

(e) Cash collections and transfer:

Delinquent taxes	$ 38,000
Current taxes	226,000
Refund of overpayment of invoice for purchase of equipment	4,000
Fines, forfeits, and penalties	88,000
Miscellaneous revenues	90,000
Share of bond issue proceeds	200,000
Transfer of remaining fund balance of a discontinued fund	18,000
	$664,000

(f) Canceled encumbrances:

	Estimated	Actual
Program operations	$156,000	$166,000
General administration	84,000	80,000
Capital outlay	62,000	62,000
	$302,000	$308,000

(g) Additional vouchers:

Program operations	$188,000
General administration	38,000
Capital outlay	18,000
Transfer to special assessment fund	20,000
	$264,000

(h) Albert, a taxpayer, overpaid his 19X3 taxes by $2,000. He applied for a $2,000 credit against his 19X4 taxes. The city council granted his request.
(i) Vouchers paid amounted to $580,000.
(j) Stores inventory on December 31, 19X3, amounted to $12,000.

Required:

Prepare journal entries to record the effects of the foregoing data. Omit explanations.

ACCOUNTING FOR SPECIAL FUNDS AND ACCOUNT GROUPS

4

Although a governmental unit can conceivably handle only general fund resources and, thus, require records for only one fund entity, this is not the typical situation. Limitations on uses of certain resources and the fiduciary responsibilities of persons managing governmental units make it mandatory or, in some cases, simply desirable to divide the resources and accounting records among a number of fund entities. The need for additional information about general long-term assets and general long-term liabilities makes it desirable to establish other self-balancing accounting entities, generally called *account groups.* As we learned in Chapter 1, the overall financial records of a governmental entity can be divided into four general categories:

1. source and disposition funds called *governmental funds* (pages 102–123)
2. hybrid fiduciary-type trust and agency funds (pages 123–126)
3. self-sustaining funds called *proprietary funds* (pages 126–130)
4. account groups (pages 130–138).

The first portion of this chapter deals with the accounting practices associated with these different types of funds (excluding the general fund) and the account groups frequently used in accounting for the resources of a governmental entity. The last part of the chapter explains and illustrates interfund relationships.

SOURCE AND DISPOSITION OR GOVERNMENTAL FUNDS

The general fund discussed in Chapter 3 is an example of a source and disposition type fund. In addition to the general fund, governmental entities typically use several other funds of this type. For the fund to fall within the category of source and disposition type funds, the operating objective associated with managing the money and/or other resources of the fund must center around receiving and using those resources in accordance with an established plan of action. Special revenue funds, capital projects funds, debt-service funds, and special assessment funds clearly are included in this classification. The primary objective in accounting for the resources of these funds is to *show how the resources were acquired and used.* Some funds, such as trust and agency funds, are primarily source and disposition type funds but may also include some of the characteristics of self-sustaining funds.

In this section, we explain and illustrate the practices followed in accounting for governmental type funds other than the general fund. First we will relate the accounting practices followed for special revenue funds to the ones described in Chapter 3 for the general fund. Then we will describe and illustrate the accounting procedures followed for:

1. capital projects funds

2. debt-service funds

3. special assessment funds.

Special Revenue Funds

A governmental unit may have many, one, or no special revenue funds. Such a fund is established when a statute, charter provision, or local ordinance requires that a specific segment of the tax levy be used exclusively for financing a particular function or activity. Special revenue funds may be established to account for revenues earmarked for such things as schools, museums, and parks. The school fund is, perhaps, the most common special revenue fund of municipal governmental units. From the point of view of the school system, the school fund is operated in the same manner as the general fund of the city. The financial statements and accounting practices followed in recording the transactions of any special revenue fund closely parallel those illustrated for the general fund in Chapter 3. Accounts are organized to show the sources and dispositions of resources designated for use by the fund entity.

Capital Projects Funds

A capital projects fund is established to account for resources designated to be used to acquire capital facilities, except for acquisitions financed from general fund or special revenue resources, special assessment resources, or enterprise or internal service funds. Capital projects funds are used to account for the inflows and outflows of resources designated to be used for the acquisition of major capital assets for "general government" use. This type of fund originates, for example, when a governmental unit authorizes the sale of general bonds to finance the acquisition of capital facilities. Although funds to acquire such capital facilities may also come from federal or state government grants or loans or from other sources, most come from the sale of general bonds—bonds issued and backed by the total governmental unit rather than by a specified segment of it.

The primary objective of accounting for a capital projects fund is to *show the acquisitions and dispositions of resources realized from the sale of general bonds and/or other sources.* It is important to recognize that this fund is designed to handle only resources designated to acquire specified assets. The liability for bonds sold for this purpose, for example, is recorded in the accounts of the long-term debt account group described later in this chapter, and the assets acquired through fund expenditures are recorded in the general fixed-assets account group.

As you can observe from the preceding description, capital projects funds are *project oriented rather than period oriented.* A particular capital projects fund will continue to exist until the project using its resources has been finished. Nevertheless, we develop periodic financial reports for capital projects funds at the end of each period during which the fund operates.

Illustrative Transactions. We now illustrate and explain the record-keeping practices followed in accounting for the activities of a capital projects fund. The entries for this fund show how a group of assumed transactions for a Model City capital projects fund are recorded. These transactions continue the overall illustration begun in Chapter 3 and are assumed to occur within the same fiscal period as the transactions illustrated for the general fund.

Let us assume that the capital projects fund for Model City has the following transactions during the fiscal period:

(CP-1) A general bond issue of $500,000 is authorized for financing street improvements.

(CP-2) The bonds are sold for $502,000.

(CP-3) Expenditures of $350,000 are made for part of the street improvement program. Of this amount, $5,000 is used for services performed by the municipal garage.

(CP-4) Contracts amounting to $140,000 are signed for the balance of the improvements.

(CP-5) A contract (see transaction (CP-4)) amounting to $50,000 is completed, and a voucher is prepared to cover it. Because of changes in certain specifications, the amount to be paid is agreed on as $52,000. The contract stipulates that, pending satisfactory performance of the improvements, the city may retain 10 percent of the original contract price.

Journal Entries To Record Transactions.   The following journal entries record the transactions in the accounting records of the capital projects fund:

Transaction (CP-1)

Estimated bond issue proceeds	$500,000	
Appropriations		$500,000

The authorization of a bond issue is to the capital projects fund what the approval of the budget is to the general fund. Entry (CP-1) records this authorization in the accounts. This entry, a type (1) transaction as discussed in Types of Transactions (see page 19), reflects the plan for the operation of the capital projects fund. Because resources are not actually being received or disbursed, these data are sometimes omitted from the formal accounting records, in which case transaction (CP-2) would be the first one recorded. The authorization of a bond issue, however, is normally the signal for formally establishing a capital projects fund accounting entity.

Transaction (CP-2)

Cash	$502,000	
Premium on bonds		$ 2,000
Proceeds from sale of bonds P. 136		500,000

This entry, a type (2) transaction (see page 19), records the sale of the bonds at a premium of $2,000. The fact that the amount appropriated for this project is equal to the face value of the bonds raises a question as to how the premium may be used. Legal provisions can govern the use of the premium. It may be made available as additional financing for the project. In this case, the appropriations account should be credited for an amount equal to the premium. When there are no legal provisions, *any premium received from the sale of bonds should logically be paid to the debt-service fund* so that it may be used in liquidating the bond issue. When this procedure is followed, an interfund obligation account entitled "due to debt-service fund" is credited for the amount of the premium. Because the bonds carry a contractual rate of interest that is higher than market, causing them to be sold at a premium, it is theoretically sound to require that any premium be paid to the debt-service fund.

If the bonds are sold at a discount, the disposition of the discount also depends on legal requirements. Thus, the appropriation balance might be reduced, or the amount of the discount might be transferred from the debt-service fund or general fund to the capital projects fund. In our illustration, the transfer of the premium is recorded as follows:

Transaction (CP-2a)

Premium on bonds	$ 2,000	
Due to debt-service fund		$ 2,000

See reciprocal entry on page 112.

Transaction (CP-2b)

Due to debt-service fund	$ 2,000	
Cash		$ 2,000

See reciprocal entry on page 112.

Transaction (CP-3)

Expenditures	$350,000	
Vouchers payable		$345,000 (CP-6)
Due to municipal garage fund		5,000 (CP-6)

Transaction (CP-4)

Encumbrances	$140,000	
Reserve for encumbrances		$140,000

Transaction (CP-5a)

Reserve for encumbrances	$ 50,000	
Encumbrances		$ 50,000

Transaction (CP-5b)

Expenditures	$ 52,000	
Vouchers payable		$ 47,000 (CP-6)
Contract payable—retained percentage		5,000

Encumbrance and expenditure entries, reflecting type (3), (4), and (5) transactions (see page 19), involve little that is different from similar entries illustrated for the general fund except for use of the account "contract payable—retained percentage" in entry (CP-5b). This account represents the amount designated for delayed payment pending satisfactory performance of the streets improved by the contractor. When the city has had an opportunity to check this performance, the obligation will be paid in the normal manner. If the street improvement does not function satisfactorily, the contractor will be required to make the necessary corrections before this amount will be paid.

Transaction (CP-6)

Due to municipal garage fund	$ 5,000	
Vouchers payable	387,000	
Cash		$392,000

This entry records the payment of an interfund payable and a voucher.

Closing Entries.   Either at the end of the fiscal period or when the project is completed, the nominal accounts will be closed. When all proceeds from the sale of bonds have been properly used, the capital projects fund accounts will be closed and eliminated from the city's accounting records. If the books of the capital projects fund are closed after the illustrated transactions have been completed, the following closing entries should be recorded. Behind these entries is the assumption that outstanding encumbrances can be met at their recorded value and that resources unused and uncommitted will be held in a fund balance account pending their ultimate disposal.

(C-1)

Dr. Appropriations	$500,000	
Cr. Estimated bond issue proceeds		$500,000

(C-2)

Dr. Proceeds from the sale of bonds	$500,000	
Cr. Unreserved fund balance		$ 98,000
Cr. Expenditures		402,000

(C-3)

Dr. Reserve for encumbrances	$ 90,000	
Cr. Encumbrances		$ 90,000

(C-4)

Dr. Unreserved fund balance	$ 90,000	
Cr. Fund balance reserved for		
encumbrances		$ 90,000

In the preceding illustration, we assume that no action has been taken regarding disposition of unused resources—that is, resources equal to the balance reflected in the account entitled "unreserved fund balance." If this amount is to be transferred to the debt-service fund, an entry should be recorded debiting transfer to debt-service fund and crediting an account entitled "due to debt-service fund."

In our illustration, we assume that this capital project is financed entirely from proceeds of a bond issue. If revenues are realized from other sources, they should be recorded with an entry similar to that shown for transaction (CP-2), except that the credit will specify the source of the revenues.

Posting the Transactions. The preceding entries are posted to the capital projects fund ledger accounts as illustrated in the following T-accounts. Each amount is keyed to its respective transaction by the transaction number listed in parentheses beside it.

Estimated Bond Issue Proceeds				Appropriations		
(CP-1)	$500,000	(C-1)	$500,000	(C-1)	$500,000	(CP-1)	$500,000

Proceeds from Sale of Bonds				Expenditures		
(C-2)	$500,000	(CP-2)	$500,000	(CP-3)	$350,000	(C-2)	$402,000
				(CP-5b)	52,000		

Cash				Encumbrances		
(CP-2)	$502,000	(CP-6)	$392,000	(CP-4)	$140,000	(CP-5a)	$ 50,000
		(CP-2b)	2,000			(C-3)	90,000

Vouchers Payable				Reserve for Encumbrances		
(CP-6)	$387,000	(CP-3)	$345,000	(CP-5a)	$ 50,000	(CP-4)	$140,000
		(CP-5b)	47,000	(C-3)	90,000		

Contract Payable— Retained Percentage				Due to Debt-Service Fund		
		(CP-5b)	$ 5,000	(CP-2b)	$ 2,000	(CP-2a)	$ 2,000

Premium on Bonds				Due to Municipal Garage Fund			
(CP-2a)	$ 2,000	(CP-2)	$ 2,000	(CP-6)	$ 5,000	(CP-3)	$ 5,000

Unreserved Fund Balance				Fund Balance Reserved for Encumbrances			
(C-4)	$ 90,000	(C-2)	$ 98,000			(C-4)	$ 90,000

Financial Statements.   Financial statements for the capital projects fund are prepared to show financial position and revenues, expenditures, and other changes in the fund balance of the fund. Figures 4.1 and 4.2 show statements for the capital projects fund of Model City after recording the assumed transactions.

Debt-Service Funds

A debt-service fund is used to account for resources designated to be used for the retirement of general long-term debt. Interest payments on such debt may also be paid through this fund. The primary objectives of its accounting records are to show the sources of the funds and their uses in paying interest on and in retiring general long-term debt.

In many respects, the debt-service fund is similar to a sinking fund used by businesses to accumulate resources to retire bonded debt. It is different, however, in that it provides a higher degree of resource segregation than is normally found in sinking funds of profit enterprises. The debt-service fund goes beyond a simple earmarking of assets to the creation

FIGURE 4.1   Model City Capital Projects Fund Balance Sheet

End of Period			
Assets		*Liabilities*	
Cash	$108,000	Vouchers payable	$ 5,000
		Contract payable— retained percentage	5,000
		Total liabilities	$ 10,000
		Fund balance	
		Fund balance reserved for encumbrances	$ 90,000
		Unreserved fund balance	8,000
			$ 98,000
		Total liabilities, reserves, and fund	
Total assets	$108,000	balance	$108,000

**FIGURE 4.2   Model City Capital Projects Fund
Statement of Revenues, Other Financing Sources,
Expenditures, and Changes in Fund Balance**

For Period

	Budget	Actual	Variances Favorable (Unfavorable)
Revenues			
Proceeds from sale of bonds	$500,000	$500,000	$ –0–
Expenditures	500,000	402,000	98,000
Excess of revenues over expenditures	$ –0–	$ 98,000	$98,000
Fund balance at beginning of period	–0–	–0–	$ –0–
Fund balance at end of period	–0–	$ 98,000	$98,000
Fund balance reserved for encumbrances		90,000	
Unreserved fund balance		8,000	
Total		$ 98,000	

of a separate, self-balancing accounting entity. This section illustrates and explains accounting procedures associated with typical transactions for debt-service funds.

Establishment of Debt-Service Fund. A general bond issue may have a specified term, or it may mature in series over a number of years. Regardless of which kind of issue is involved, resources realized from taxes must be set aside each year toward payment of interest and retirement of the bonds. Therefore, when general bonds are sold, a debt-service fund should be established to *accumulate and temporarily invest* the earmarked resources. Those resources not used for the payment of interest are held in the debt-service fund until the bonds mature. When serial bonds are issued, resources will flow through the debt-service fund more rapidly, because of the periodic payments made in retiring these bonds. This significantly reduces the investing responsibilities associated with the operations of the debt-service fund.

The establishment of a debt-service fund is often required by provisions of the bond indenture originated when term bonds are issued. The first evidence of the need for a debt-service fund as a separate accounting entity occurs when the amount of required contributions from the general fund or other sources is determined. At this time, the budget or authorization entry may be recorded to establish the fund.

Investment of Debt-Service Fund Assets. As resources are accumulated in the fund, they are invested to produce revenue until they are needed for the payment of interest or to retire the bonds, or both. Operationally, this practice creates a need for recording interest or dividend revenue in the fund in much the same manner as such revenues are recorded in the sinking fund of a profit enterprise. If interest is measurable and available, it should be recorded as accrued interest receivable and revenue.

Illustrative Transactions. Let us assume that Model City establishes a debt-service fund to retire the bonds whose proceeds were accounted for in the preceding illustration. Furthermore, assume that the bonds have a ten-year life and that the required contribution for this year from the general fund (see general fund transaction (1), page 72) is $50,000. The following typical transactions illustrate the record-keeping practices followed in accounting for the acquisitions and uses of debt-service fund resources:

(DS-1) The bond indenture (see capital projects funds, pages 102–123) includes a provision that requires the general fund to pay $50,000 per year into a debt-service fund (see appropriation in general fund transaction (1), page 72). It is estimated that investment earnings will amount to $2,000 for the first year.

(DS-2) The obligation of the general fund to contribute the appropriate amount to the debt-service fund is recognized (see general fund transaction (5), page 74).

(DS-3) Payment is received from the general fund (see general fund transaction (8), page 76).

(DS-4) Debt-service fund resources of $49,000 are invested.

(DS-5) Interest income of $1,950 is received by the debt-service fund.

(DS-6) Premium in the amount of $2,000 realized from the sale of bonds (see capital projects fund, page 105) is acquired by the debt-service fund.

Journal Entries To Record Transactions. The following entries record the assumed transactions of the debt-service fund:

Transaction (DS-1)		
Estimated revenues from investment	$ 2,000	
Required general fund contributions	50,000	
Budgetary fund balance		$52,000

The bond indenture provision, requiring the establishment of a debt-service fund to which the general fund will contribute $50,000 per year, is to the debt-service fund what the approval of the budget is to the general fund. Entry (DS-1), a type (1) transaction (see page 19), records this requirement in the debt-service fund records. When the budget for the general fund was approved, the required amount was appropriated and recorded in the general fund accounts.

Although it is generally desirable to show the items included in entry (DS-1) in the debt-service fund records, because of the nature of budgetary accounts, they may be left unrecorded.

Transaction (DS-2)

Due from general fund	$50,000	
Transfers from general fund		$50,000

See reciprocal entry on page 74.

Transaction (DS-3)

Cash	$50,000	
Due from general fund		$50,000

See reciprocal entry on page 76.

Entry (DS-2), a type (2) transaction (see page 19), records the amount receivable from the general fund. It is the first transaction that involves actual financial data. "Transfers from general fund" shows the resources acquired from the general fund. The debit to "due from general fund" is an interfund account that constitutes an asset to the debt-service fund. The collection of this claim against the general fund is shown in entry (DS-3).

Transaction (DS-4)

Investments	$49,000	
Cash		$49,000

This entry records the investment of debt-service fund cash.

Transaction (DS-5)

Cash	$ 1,950	
Revenue from investments		$ 1,950

The fact that interest amounting to $1,950 has been earned from debt-service fund investments is recorded in entry (DS-5).

Transaction (DS-6a)		
Due from capital projects fund	$ 2,000	
Bond issue premium		$ 2,000

See reciprocal entry on page 105.

Transaction (DS-6b)		
Cash	$ 2,000	
Due from capital projects fund		$ 2,000

See reciprocal entry on page 105.

This entry records the receipt of $2,000 from the capital projects fund.

Closing Entries. The T-accounts illustrated on page 113 show that sources of actual revenues and other financing sources are as follows:

Transfers from general fund	$50,000
Interest earned on investments	1,950
Bond issue premium	2,000

The budgetary accounts show that these figures are in line with the estimates, except for a difference of $50 in income from investments and $2,000 realized from the capital projects fund. The following closing entries facilitate this disclosure:

(C-1)		
Dr. Budgetary fund balance	$52,000	
Cr. Estimated revenues from investment		$ 2,000
Cr. Required general fund contributions		50,000

(C-2)		
Dr. Transfers from general fund	$50,000	
Dr. Revenue from investments	1,950	
Dr. Bond issue premium	2,000	
Cr. Fund balance		$53,950

Posting the Transactions. The preceding entries are posted to the debt-service fund ledger accounts as illustrated in the following T-accounts. Each amount is keyed to its respective transaction by the transaction number listed in parentheses beside it.

Required General Fund Contributions				Bond Issue Premium			
(DS-1)	$50,000	(C-1)	$50,000	(C-2)	$ 2,000	(DS-6a)	$ 2,000

Estimated Revenue from Investments				Transfers from General Fund			
(DS-1)	$ 2,000	(C-1)	$ 2,000	(C-2)	$50,000	(DS-2)	$50,000

Due from Capital Projects Fund				Budgetary Fund Balance			
(DS-6a)	$ 2,000	(DS-6b)	$ 2,000	(C-1)	$52,000	(DS-1)	$52,000

Due from General Fund				Cash			
(DS-2)	$50,000	(DS-3)	$50,000	(DS-3)	$50,000	(DS-4)	$49,000
				(DS-5)	1,950		
				(DS-6b)	2,000		

Investments		Revenue from Investments			
(DS-4)	$49,000	(C-2)	$ 1,950	(DS-5)	$ 1,950

Fund Balance		
	(C-2)	$53,950

Statements. Statements are prepared for the debt-service fund at the end of each fiscal period. They should disclose essentially the same information about the debt-service fund that previously illustrated statements for the general fund and capital projects fund show for those accounting entities. Statements prepared from the debt-service fund T-accounts are shown in Figures 4.3 and 4.4.

Figure 4.3 Model City Debt-Service Fund Balance Sheet, End of Period

Assets		Fund Balance	
Cash	$ 4,950		
Investments	49,000	Fund balance	$53,950
Total assets	$53,950	Total fund balance	$53,950

FIGURE 4.4   Model City Debt-Service Fund Statement of Revenues, Other Financial Sources, Expenditures, and Changes in Fund Balance, End of Period

	Requirements and Estimates	Actual Revenues and Expenditures	Variances Favorable (Unfavorable)
Transfer from general fund	$50,000	$50,000	$ 0
Revenues from investments	2,000	1,950	(50)
Transfer from capital projects funds	0	2,000	2,000
Total	$52,000	$53,950	$1,950
Fund balance at beginning of period	0	0	0
Fund balance at end of period	$52,000	$53,950	$1,950

Disposal of Debt-Service Fund Resources.   No expenditures are included among the transactions for the debt-service fund illustrated in the preceding paragraphs. If interest had been paid from debt-service fund resources, the entry to record the obligation for interest would be reflected as follows:

Expenditures	XXXXXX	
Interest payable		XXXXXX

The payment of the interest obligation would be recorded as follows:

Interest payable	XXXXXX	
Cash		XXXXXX

Expenditures to reflect the retirement of bond obligations would be recorded in a similar manner. In the illustration for Model City, the fund probably will show only resource acquisitions and interest payments during the first years of its existence. By the bond maturity date, assets amounting to approximately $500,000 should have accumulated in the debt-service fund for the purpose of retiring the bonds, and they will be so used. If a balance remains in the debt-service fund after all requirements of the bond issue have been met, it is generally turned back to the general fund to be used as needed for operations of the city, or possibly to another debt-service fund.

Special Assessment Funds

Special assessment funds are established to account for resources used to construct certain public improvements that are financed fully or partially from special assessments levied against the primarily benefited property owners. The primary objectives of accounting records for this fund are to *show the sources and uses of financial resources associated with the specified improvement.* This includes the responsibility of accounting for all liabilities of the fund and for the assessments levied against individual property owners that are frequently paid in installments over a period of several years.

Aspects Peculiar to Special Assessment Funds.   The accounting records for special assessment funds closely resemble those of the other funds discussed in this chapter, but they are also distinctive in some respects. For example, a secondary objective of the records is disclosure of subordinate intrafund restrictions placed on uses of fund resources and of long-term obligations of the fund. Thus, figuratively speaking, you may find elements of typical general fund, capital projects fund, and debt-service fund transactions as well as items normally thought of as part of the long-term debt account group among the accounting data for such funds. These relationships are discussed further in explanations of the entries for the special assessment fund of Model City.

Illustrative Transactions.   A typical set of transactions for a special assessment fund for Model City follows. Some of these entries can be related to some of the general fund entries illustrated in Chapter 3, whereas others are more directly related to accounting entities discussed in this chapter. Therefore, let us assume that the special assessment fund has the following transactions:

(SA-1) A special assessment fund is authorized for the construction of streets in a new residential area. The general fund portion of these expenditures has been approved within the general fund appropriations (see transaction (1), page 72) for $25,000. This approval depended on the assessment of a special tax levy of $225,000 against property owners in the area. The total authorized improvement is $250,000. The special tax levy is to be paid over a period of ten years. *deferred*

(SA-2) The general fund contribution is received (see general fund transactions (5) and (8), pages 74 and 76).

(SA-3) Special assessment fund bonds with a free value of $225,000 are issued at face value to provide funds for construction.

(SA-4) Construction expenditures amounting to $200,000 are incurred. Of this amount, $10,000 is for services performed by the municipal garage.

(SA-5) Contracts amounting to $45,000 for completion of the street improvements are signed.

(SA-6) The contracts in transaction (SA-5) are completed, and obligations relating to them are recognized. It is agreed that 10 percent of the contract price will be retained pending satisfactory use of the streets for three months.

(SA-7) The first installment of the special tax levy ($22,500) is received.

(SA-8) Interest amounting to $6,075 is received on deferred assessments receivable.

(SA-9) Vouchers amounting to $230,000 are paid.

(SA-10) Interest amounting to $4,050 is paid to bond holders.

(SA-11) Interest amounting to $2,000 is due to be paid on bonds payable.

(SA-12) Interest amounting to $900 is due to be received on deferred assessments receivable.

Journal Entries To Record Transactions.   The following journal entries record, in the manner recommended by the 1980 edition of GAAFR, the transactions we have listed.

Budgetary Computation

Transaction (SA-1a)		
Estimated financing sources	$250,000	
Appropriations		$250,000

Inter-fund receivable

Transaction (SA-1b)		
Due from general fund	$ 25,000	
Other financing sources		$ 25,000

See reciprocal entry on page 74.

Transaction (SA-1c)		
Dr. Special assessment receivable—current	$ 22,500	
Dr. Special assessments receivable—deferred *Bond*	202,500	
Cr. Revenues		$ 22,500
Cr. Deferred revenues *liability (balance sheet acct.)*		202,500

On authorization of the street improvement project, entry (SA-1a) is made to establish the special assessment fund. Because this is a type

(1) transaction (see page 19), comparable to the budget entry for the general fund, it is often omitted from the special assessment fund records.

Entry (SA-1b), a type (2) transaction (see page 19), is recorded as the general fund recognizes its obligation to the special assessment fund. Entry (SA-1c), also a type (2) transaction, is recorded to reflect the special tax levy originated to cover the portion of the cost assessed against the primarily benefited property owners. Because $202,500 of the special assessments will not be available for use until after the end of the current period, however, that amount has been credited to deferred revenues—a liability account.

Transaction (SA-2)

Cash	$ 25,000	
Due from general fund		$ 25,000

See reciprocal entry on page 76.

Transaction (SA-3)

Cash *(selling of bonds)*	$225,000	
Other financing sources *(Bond payable)*		$225,000

Entry (SA-2) shows the receipt of cash from the general fund. Entry (SA-3) shows the realization of cash from the sale of special assessment bonds. Because these resources will be used for construction purposes, they could be separated from other resources by debiting them to a "cash for construction" account. As a practical matter, however, they will often be debited to a general cash account for the fund.

In entry (SA-3), the receipt of cash from the sale of special assessment bonds is recorded as other financing sources. As you will see, this account is later closed to bonds payable in entry (C-2). After that entry has been made, the liability for bonds payable will be included in the special assessment fund accounts. This treatment is reasonable because these bonds are obligations against the special assessment project rather than against the general resources of Model City. As a result of these entries we include elements paralleling both capital projects fund and long-term debt account group transactions in the special assessment fund.

Transaction (SA-4)

Expenditures	$200,000	
Vouchers payable		$190,000
Due to municipal garage fund		10,000

Transaction (SA-5)

Encumbrances	$ 45,000	
Reserve for encumbrances		$ 45,000

Transaction (SA-6a)

Reserve for encumbrances	$ 45,000	
Encumbrances		$ 45,000

Transaction (SA-6b)

Expenditures	$ 45,000	
Vouchers payable		$ 40,500
Contracts payable—retained percentage		4,500

Transaction (SA-7)

Cash	$ 22,500	
Special assessments receivable—current		$ 22,500

Entries (SA-4), (SA-5), and (SA-6) are similar to those used to record the transactions illustrated for other funds of Model City. They are type (3), (4), and (5) transactions (see page 19), respectively. Entry (SA-7) reflects the collection of the first installment of the special tax levy. The cash so received is to be used for the retirement of the special assessment bonds. Such a restriction suggests that the cash would be placed in a debt-service fund for the retirement of special assessment bonds. In accounting for special assessment bonds, however, a lower level of separation of resources is considered adequate; therefore, we earmark those resources through the medium of a reserved fund balance account (see balance sheet).

Transaction (SA-8)

Cash	$ 6,075	
Revenues from interest		$ 6,075

The collection of interest on deferred tax assessments receivable is recorded in entry (SA-8). Here again, proceeds are designed to be used in meeting interest payments on bonds payable. That restriction is reflected through the medium of a fund balance reserved for debt-service account (see balance sheet).

Transaction (SA-9)

Vouchers payable	$230,000	
Cash		$230,000

Transaction (SA-10)

Expenditures for interest	$ 4,050	
Cash		$ 4,050

Transaction (SA-11)

Expenditures for interest	$ 2,000	
Interest payable		$ 2,000

Transaction (SA-12)

Interest receivable	$ 900	
Revenues from interest		$ 900

Entry (SA-9) requires no explanation. Entry SA-10), however, involves the payment of interest on bonds payable. Observe that under the modified accrual basis the amount of the payment is debited to expenditures rather than to interest expense. Observe also that the difference between these expenditures and the revenues realized in the form of interest on deferred tax assessments receivable is accounted for through the medium of a fund balance reserved for debt service (see balance sheet).

Closing Entries.   We assume that the special assessment project was completed during the period. When that occurred, the nominal accounts of this fund would be closed with the following entries:

Reversal of budget entry (C-1)

Appropriations	$250,000	
Estimated financing sources		$250,000

(C-2)

Other financing sources	$250,000	
Bonds payable		$225,000
Transfers from general fund		25,000

(C-3)

Revenues from interest	$ 6,975	
Revenues	22,500	
Transfers from general fund	25,000	
Fund balance reserved for debt service	196,575	
Expenditures		$245,000
Expenditures for interest		6,050

Posting the Transactions. The preceding journal entries are posted to the special assessment fund accounts as illustrated in the following T-accounts. Each amount is keyed to its respective transaction by the number listed in parentheses beside it.

Estimated Financing Sources				Cash			
(SA-1a)	$250,000	(C-1)	$250,000	(SA-2)	$ 25,000	(SA-9)	$230,000
				(SA-3)	$225,000	(SA-10)	4,050
				(SA-7)	$ 22,500		
				(SA-8)	$ 6,075		

Appropriations				Bonds Payable			
(C-1)	$250,000	(SA-1a)	$250,000			(C-2)	$225,000

Due from General Fund				Expenditures			
(SA-1b)	$ 25,000	(SA-2)	$ 25,000	(SA-4)	$200,000	(C-3)	$245,000
				(SA-6b)	45,000		

Other Financing Sources				Vouchers Payable			
(C-2)	$250,000	(SA-1b)	$ 25,000	(SA-9)	$230,000	(SA-4)	$190,000
		(SA-3)	225,000			(SA-6b)	40,500

Special Assessments Receivable—Current				Due to Municipal Garage Fund			
(SA-1a)	$ 22,500	(SA-7)	$22,500			(SA-4)	$ 10,000

Special Assessments Receivable—Deferred				Encumbrances			
(SA-1a)	$202,500			(SA-5)	$ 45,000	(SA-6a)	$ 45,000

Revenues		
(C-3)	$ 22,500	(SA-1c) $ 22,500

Reserve for Encumbrances		
(SA-6a) $ 45,000	(SA-5) $ 45,000	

Deferred Revenues	
	(SA-1c) $202,500

Contracts Payable—Retained Pct.	
	(SA-6b) $ 4,500

Transfer from General Fund		
(C-3) $ 25,000	(C-2) $ 25,000	

Interest Payable	
	(SA-11) $ 2,000

Fund Balance Reserved for Debt Service	
(C-3) $196,575	

Interest Receivable	
(SA-12) $ 900	

Revenues from Interest		
(C-3) $ 6,975	(SA-8) $ 6,075	
	(SA-12) 900	

Expenditures for Interest		
(SA-11) $ 2,000	(C-3) $ 6,050	
(SA-10) 4,050		

Financial Statements. Special assessment fund financial data are disclosed in financial statements similar to those illustrated for other funds. As you can see in Figure 4.5, however, the balance sheet for the special assessment fund includes a number of items, such as interest receivable, interest payable, deferred revenues, and bonds payable, not found in previously illustrated source and disposition fund statements. Also, the fund balance reserved for debt service reflects a debit balance of $196,575. This occurs primarily because the special assessments receivable—deferred are not treated as revenues until the periods during which they will be paid.

The statement of revenues, expenditures, and changes in fund balance reflects revenues and transfers from the general fund for the period, offset by expenditures, to arrive at the debit balance in the fund balance reserved for debt service at the end of the period (Figure 4.6).

As you can see, the procedures recommended by the 1980 edition of GAAFR produce some unusual balances in the financial statements of the special assessment fund. Many governmental accountants believe that all revenues from special assessments (both current and deferred as recorded in our illustration) should be recognized as revenue in the period the assessment is levied. Such treatment will produce a credit rather than a debit balance in the fund balance account. That treatment seems to be a reasonable alternative when we have interim financing through bonds, as is assumed in our illustration.

FIGURE 4.5   Model City Special Assessment Fund Balance Sheet

End of Period

Assets		Liabilities and Fund Balances	
Cash	$ 44,525	Vouchers payable	$ 500
Special assessments		Due to municipal garage	
receivable—deferred	202,500	fund	10,000
Interest receivable	900	Contract payable—	
		retained percentage	4,500
		Interest payable	2,000
		Deferred revenues	202,500
		Bonds payable	225,000
		Total liabilities	$ 444,500
		Fund balance reserved	
		for debt service	(196,575)
		Total liabilities and	
Total assets	$247,925	fund balances	$247,925

FIGURE 4.6   Model City Special Assessment Fund Statement of Revenues and Expenditures and Changes in Fund Balance

Revenues		
Special assessments		$ 22,500
Interest		6,975
Total revenues		$ 29,475
Expenditures		
Construction	$245,000	
Interest	6,050	$251,050
Excess (deficiency of revenues over expenditures)		($221,575)
Transfers from general fund		25,000
Excess (deficiency) of revenues over expenditures and other sources		($196,575)
Fund balance at beginning of period		0
Fund balance at end of period		($196,575)

Termination of a Special Assessment Fund.   Once established, a special assessment fund continues to exist as a separate accounting entity until all special assessments have been collected and the bonds associated with the project have been retired. If resources remain in the fund after all obligations have been met, they may be transferred to the general fund unless other provisions (such as a pro rata return to the persons against whom the special assessments were levied) were made for their disposition when the fund was established. General fund assets may be used to meet a small shortage of resources, which can occur if interest expenditures exceed interest revenues or construction expenditures exceed the amount anticipated for them. The use of general fund resources for such purposes usually requires approval by the governing body.

Implications of Judgments Regarding Fund Entities. A more complete analysis of entry (C-2) shows how judgment can be used in the establishment of separate fund entities. By the introduction of separate, self-balancing accounting entities, the facts shown in the entries (SA-3), (SA-1c), and (C-2) could be recorded in two funds and an account group. *This practice is not followed in accounting for special assessment fund transactions.* We illustrate that procedure in the following example, however, to show how the supervising accountant may in some instances make judgments regarding the specific accounting entities that should be used.

Special Assessment "Capital Projects" Fund

Cash	$225,000	
Proceeds from sale of bonds		$225,000

Special Assessment "Debt-Service" Fund

Special assessment receivable	$225,000	
Revenues		$ 22,500
Deferred revenues		202,500

Special Assessment "Long-Term Debt Account Group"

Account to be provided for retirement of bonds	$225,000	
Bonds payable		$225,000

The general practice in accounting for special assessment fund resources is to rely on restrictions within the fund entity for the appropriate segregation of resources.

TRUST AND AGENCY FUNDS

Trust and agency funds are used to account for resources received and held by the government in the capacity of trustee, custodian, or agent. As the name implies, this group of funds includes both resources to be held over a long period (trust funds) and others that can be used currently (agency funds). We include the two types of resources in one fund because in both cases the governmental unit has a fiduciary responsibility for all such resources that it holds under a trust or agency agreement. The governmental entity cannot use these resources at its discretion; it must invest, spend, or remit them in accordance with the trust or agency agreement.

Trust and agency fund resources may be expendable, nonexpendable, or a combination of partially expendable and partially nonexpendable. Perhaps the most frequently encountered type of expendable trust fund is the one used to account for the resources of pension and retirement systems. A fund used to account for resources made available to the city to provide loans that must be repaid to maintain the original fund balance is an example of a nonexpendable trust fund. An expendable/nonexpendable trust and agency fund can be created when the city receives resources to be invested to produce income to be used for specified purposes. Within this arrangement, the principal of the fund must be kept intact and only the resources associated with the income it produces are available to be spent for designated purposes.

The accounting procedures for this type of fund require a careful distinction between expendable and nonexpendable resources and, therefore, involve some elements of accounting procedures normally found in accounting for self-sustaining funds. With some exceptions, the criteria for distinguishing between principal and income items are the same as those followed in distinguishing between capital and revenue items in the profit area. For example, the question of whether depreciation should be recognized will depend on the donor stipulations or laws governing the operations of these entities. In the absence of specific contractual provisions to the contrary, however, gains and losses on the sales of securities are credited or charged to the principal fund balance rather than to income and expense.

When a governmental unit receives resources under an arrangement like the one just described, a separate accounting entity is established to reflect accountability in accordance with the agreement under which the assets were received. The accounting records for these funds ordinarily are maintained on an accrual basis, which requires revenues to be recognized as they are earned. The governmental entity must account for the acquisitions and uses of resources to show that fund operations and investments comply with the trust or agency agreement.

Illustrative Transactions

To illustrate the accounting procedures for trust and agency funds, we assume that Model City receives a contribution of $100,000 with the stipulation that income from its investment be used to provide free band concerts in the parks during the summer season. The following transactions occur:

(TA-1) The city receives $100,000, under the stipulated terms, from a wealthy citizen.

(TA-2) The cash is invested.

(**TA-3**) Interest income amounting to $2,500 is received.

(**TA-4**) Expenditures of $2,000 are made.

Journal Entries To Record Transactions

Transaction (TA-1)

Principal cash	$100,000	
Fund balance—principal		$100,000

Transaction (TA-2)

Investments—principal	$100,000	
Principal cash		$100,000

Transaction (TA-3)

Income cash	$ 2,500	
Interest income		$ 2,500

Transaction (TA-4)

Expenditures against income	$ 2,000	
Income cash		$ 2,000

The following entry is used at the end of the period to close the nominal accounts:

(C-1)

Interest income	$ 2,500	
Expenditures against income		$ 2,000
Fund balance—income		500

These entries involve only one significant departure from other entries illustrated in this chapter. This difference is *the distinction made between principal and income resources, which is required by the trust indenture.* We could make this distinction by using separate fund entities for income assets and principal assets. Generally, however, we use a lower level of restriction that involves a designation of assets according to their sources complemented by separate fund balance accounts.

Posting the Transactions

The preceding journal entries are posted to the trust and agency fund accounts as illustrated in the following T-accounts. Postings are keyed to their transactions by the numbers in parentheses beside them.

Principal Cash				Fund Balance—Principal		
(TA-1)	$100,000	(TA-2)	$100,000		(TA-1)	$100,000

Investments—Principal				Fund Balance—Income		
(TA-2)	$100,000				(C-1)	$ 500

Income Cash				Interest Income		
(TA-3)	$ 2,500	(TA-4)	$ 2,000	(C-1)	$ 2,500	(TA-3)	$ 2,500

Expenditures Against Income			
(TA-4)	$ 2,000	(C-1)	$ 2,000

Financial Statements

Trust and agency funds generally require three statements: a balance sheet, a statement of changes in fund balances, and a statement of revenues and expenditures, or expenses. Because these statements are relatively simple to prepare from the ledger accounts and the format is the same as that used for other funds, we omit them here.

SELF-SUSTAINING OR PROPRIETARY FUNDS

Self-sustaining funds (called *proprietary funds* in the governmental area) are reservoirs of resources established to carry on specified activities on a self-sustaining basis. They fall into two principal categories, frequently referred to as *enterprise funds* and *internal service funds. Enterprise funds* are used to account for resources committed to self-supporting activities of governmental units that render services to the general public on a user charge basis, or where the governing body has decided that periodic determinations of revenues earned, expenses incurred, and/or net income are appropriate for capital maintenance, public policy, management control accountability or other purposes.[1] *Internal service funds* are used to account for resources committed to self-supporting activities of governmental units that provide goods or render services to other departments on a cost reimbursement basis.[2] Accounting procedures for an internal service fund are demonstrated in the following pages.

The accounting procedures for all fund entities discussed up to this point, with the exception of the trust fund, have been designed primarily to disclose accountability for the acquisitions and disposals of appropriable resources. Revenue realized by these funds is not primarily dependent on the earning power of assets held by the fund. It is determined either directly or indirectly by the right to tax. In developing records for these funds, the accountant's primary responsibility is to *show dollar accountability by reflecting the flows of dollars through the fund.*

Fund entities established within a plan that requires them to be self-sustaining function in much the same manner as do profit enterprises. Therefore, their accounting records should be organized in a manner similar to that used for profit entities; that is, they must distinguish between capital and revenue items, recognize accrued and prepaid items, and account for the depreciation of fixed assets.

Illustrative Transactions

The governmental activities most frequently carried on through internal service funds are maintenance and supply functions. Illustrations follow of the procedures involved in accounting for such funds. Let us assume that Model City has established a municipal garage to maintain city vehicles. The following transactions relating to the operations of this municipal garage fund occur during the fiscal period. The code letters *SS* are used to designate the fund as a self-sustaining fund.

(SS-1) A contribution of $85,000 is received from the general fund to establish a vehicles maintenance center (see general fund transactions (1), (5), and (8), pages 72, 74, and 76). This becomes the residual equity balance of the new fund.

(SS-2) Equipment costing $35,000 and supplies costing $10,000 are purchased.

(SS-3) Expenses of $40,000 are incurred during the period, and $4,000 worth of supplies are used.

---

[1] *Governmental Accounting, Auditing, and Financial Reporting* (Chicago: Municipal Finance Officers Association, 1980), p. 59.

[2] Ibid., p. 6.

(SS-4) Services and parts are billed to other funds as follows:

General fund	$35,000
Special assessment fund	10,000
Capital projects fund	5,000

(SS-5) Cash is received from billings to the general fund and capital projects fund.

(SS-6) Vouchers amounting to $75,000 are paid.

(SS-7) Equipment is depreciated over a ten-year life.

Journal Entries To Record Transactions

The following journal entries record these transactions:

Transaction (SS-1)

Cash	$85,000	
Capital contribution from general fund (Paid incpital)		$85,000

Transaction (SS-2)

Equipment	$35,000	
Supplies	10,000	
Vouchers payable		$45,000

Transaction (SS-3)

Expenses	$44,000	
Supplies		$ 4,000
Vouchers payable		40,000

Transaction (SS-4)

Due from general fund	$35,000	
Due from special assessment fund	10,000	
Due from capital projects fund	5,000	
Revenue from services		$50,000

Transaction (SS-5)

Cash	$40,000	
Due from general fund		$35,000
Due from capital project fund		5,000

Transaction (SS-6)		
Vouchers payable	$75,000	
Cash		$75,000

Transaction (SS-7)		
Expenses	$ 3,500	
Allowance for depreciation _(Depreciation expense)_		$ 3,500

Closing Entries

The accounts of the municipal garage fund are closed with the following entry:

(C-1)		
Revenue from services	$50,000	
Expenses		$47,500
Retained earnings		2,500

Posting the Transactions

The preceding journal entries are posted to the self-sustaining fund accounts as illustrated in the following T-accounts. Items are keyed to their transactions by the numbers in parentheses beside them.

Cash				Capital Contribution from General Fund			
(SS-1)	$85,000	(SS-6)	$75,000			(SS-1)	$85,000
(SS-5)	40,000						

Equipment				Vouchers Payable			
(SS-2)	$35,000			(SS-6)	$75,000	(SS-2)	$45,000
						(SS-3)	40,000

Supplies				Expenses			
(SS-2)	$10,000	(SS-3)	$ 4,000	(SS-3)	$44,000	(C-1)	$47,500
				(SS-7)	3,500		

Due from General Fund				Revenue from Services			
(SS-4)	$35,000	(SS-5)	$35,000	(C-1)	$50,000	(SS-4)	$50,000

Due from Special Assessment Fund		Allowance for Depreciation	
(SS-4) $10,000			(SS-7) $ 3,500

Due from Capital Projects Fund		Retained Earnings	
(SS-4) $ 5,000	(SS-5) $ 5,000		(C-1) $ 2,500

Financial Statements

The financial statements for a self-sustaining fund are similar to those for a profit enterprise. A statement of revenues, expenses, and changes in retained earnings shows the operations for the period, and a balance sheet reflects residual balances. A statement of changes in financial position should also be prepared to show the sources and uses of working capital or cash during the period.

Related Considerations

Governmental units often own and operate their own utilities, airports, and other service enterprises. Generally, these enterprises are expected to operate on much the same basis as profit entities furnishing similar services. Therefore, business accounting practices are followed in maintaining the accounting records for these activities. They are, in effect, treated as individual business enterprises. Financial statements are also prepared to show the results of operations, the financial position, and the changes in financial position for each of these activities.

The residual equity capital for these entities, which serves much the same purpose as owners' equity for a business, generally comes from the resources of the governmental unit. Capital accounts labeled to show the sources of the capital contributions then become the equity accounts. Capital can also be realized from issuance of bonds secured by assets or anticipated income. Such bonds are generally obligations of the particular fund rather than of the governmental unit; consequently, they are retired from revenues earned by fund activities rather than from tax revenues. A retained earnings account should be used to account for accumulated earnings.

ACCOUNT GROUPS

Governmental units also use accounting entities whose primary objective is to *provide data relating to the acquisition values of fixed assets and relating to the status of general long-term debt.* No expendable resources are associated with these accounting entities. The *general fixed-assets* and *general long-term debt account groups* are examples of accounting entities in this category.

An account group is different from a fund in that it is not a reservoir for appropriable resources. It is designed to disclose financial facts not normally provided by source and disposition (governmental type fund) records because these make no ultimate distinction between capital and revenue items. Because of their position in the overall framework of fund accounting, account groups are sometimes referred to as "memo" account groups. Because they are expected to meet a disclosure weakness of source and disposition fund accounting, there are typically two of these account groups—one for general fixed assets and another for general long-term debt.

General Fixed Assets Account Group

The general fixed assets account group discloses the acquisition values of a governmental unit's fixed assets that are not accounted for in self-sustaining or proprietary funds and the sources of the resources that were used to acquire them. The account group is established as general fixed assets are acquired through use of resources from various source and disposition, or governmental type funds. Entries for asset acquisitions in this accounting entity are directly related to expenditure entries of the general, special revenue, capital project, and special assessment fund records. Assets associated with self-sustaining funds and trust funds are reflected in the accounts of those funds.

The accounting equation for the general fixed assets account group can be stated as follows:

Assets = investments in fixed assets

Assets are debited to reflect increases and credited to reflect decreases. Investments in fixed assets are credited to show increases and debited to show decreases.

We now illustrate how the records of the general fixed-asset account group are maintained. To clarify the need for this accounting entity, we first compare entries used by a governmental unit with those used by a business to record the acquisition of a fixed asset.

Entries for a City
General Fund Entry

Expenditures	XXXXXX	
Vouchers payable or cash		XXXXXX

General Fixed-Assets Account Group Entry

Asset	XXXXXX	
Investment in fixed assets—from general fund		XXXXXX

Entry for Business Entity

Asset	XXXXXX	
Vouchers payable or cash		XXXXXX

If we eliminate the debit to "expenditures" from the general fund entry and the credit to "investment in fixed assets" from the general fixed-asset account group, we leave the same account balances open for the city as are shown in the records of the business entity. In that way we can see that the fragmentation of accounting data into separate fund entities, with no distinction between capital and revenue items within source and disposition fund records, necessitates the use of this account group to provide records of fixed assets. We can therefore think of the journal entries in this account group as entries that *complement* fixed-asset acquisition and disposal entries in the various source and disposition funds.

Illustrative Transactions. Because each transaction recorded in the general fixed assets account group complements an entry in some fund, each entry listed for this accounting entity is keyed to the fund entry giving rise to it. Assume that the following balances existed in the accounts before the current fiscal period began:

	Dr.	Cr.
Equipment	$450,000	
Structures and improvements	900,000	
Investment in general fixed assets—from general fund		$750,000
Investment in general fixed assets—from capital projects fund		400,000
Investment in general fixed assets—from special assessment fund		200,000

Transactions from the various fund entities that affect the fixed assets account group are as follows:

(FA-1) New street-maintenance equipment costing $145,000 is acquired (from general fund entry (7), page 75).

(FA-2) Old street-maintenance equipment originally costing $60,000 is sold for $5,000 (from general fund entry (9), page 76).

(FA-3) Street improvements amounting to $350,000 are completed (from capital projects fund entry (CP-3), page 105).

(FA-4) Another unit of street improvements costing $52,000 is completed (from capital projects fund entry (CP-5b), page 105).

(FA-5) Street improvements costing $245,000 are completed (from special assessment fund entries (SA-4) and (SA6-b), pages 177 and 178.

Journal Entries To Record Transactions. The following journal entries record the preceding transactions in the records of the general fixed assets account group.

Transaction (FA-1)

Equipment	$145,000	
Investment in general fund assets—from general fund		$145,000

Transaction (FA-2)

Investment in general fixed assets—from general fund	$ 60,000	
Equipment		$ 60,000

Transaction (FA-3)

Structures and improvements	$350,000	
Investment in general fixed assets—from capital projects fund		$350,000

Transaction (FA-4)

Structures and improvements	$ 52,000	
Investment in general fixed assets—from capital projects fund		$ 52,000

Transaction (FA-5)

Structures and improvements	$245,000	
Investment in general fixed assets—from special assessment fund		$245,000

The accounts for this accounting entity are designed to show the original costs of general fixed assets owned by the city and the sources of funds used to acquire them. Acquisitions are recorded as shown in entries (FA-1), (FA-3), (FA-4), and (FA-5).

When assets are retired, the entry originally made to reflect the acquisition is reversed. Entry (FA-2) illustrates this removal procedure. Revenue from the disposal of this asset is recorded in the general fund. The fund authorized to receive cash realized from the disposal of a fixed asset is determined by laws or operating policies. In the absence of any legal or established policy requirements, these proceeds are credited either to the fund that originally financed the asset or to the general fund.

Posting the Transactions.   The preceding journal entries are posted to the accounts of the general fixed-asset account group as illustrated in the following T-accounts:

Equipment				Investment in General Fixed Assets—from General Fund		
Balance $450,000	(FA-2)	$ 60,000	(FA-2)	$ 60,000	Balance	$750,000
(FA-1) 145,000					(FA-1)	145,000

Structures and Improvements		Investment in General Fixed Assets—from Capital Projects Fund	
Balance $900,000		Balance	$400,000
(FA-3) 350,000		(FA-3)	350,000
(FA-4) 52,000		(FA-4)	52,000
(FA-5) 245,000			

Investment in General Fixed Assets—from Special Assessment Fund	
Balance	$200,000
(FA-5)	245,000

Statements.   Because the general fixed assets account group is a memo record and is not involved with the flow of appropriable resources, it does not require a statement showing the sources and uses of resources. Figure 4.7 illustrates the kind of statement that is generally appropriate for this account group. NCGA Statement 1 also requires that the changes in general fixed assets be disclosed in the notes to this financial statement or in a separate statement entitled "Statement of Changes in General Fixed Assets."

General Long-Term Debt Account Group

We now illustrate the accounting procedures relating to the general long-term debt account group for Model City.

Origin and Objective.   This account group shows the *status of general long-term debt* that is to be liquidated by use of resources provided by general revenues and that constitutes obligations of the governmental unit as a

FIGURE 4.7   Model City Statement of General Fixed Assets, End of Period

Assets Held		Sources of Funds Used To Acquire Assets *OWNERSHIP*	
Equipment	$ 535,000	Investment in general fixed assets	
Structures and improvements	1,547,000	From general fund	$ 835,000
		From capital projects fund	802,000
		From special assessment fund	445,000
Total *How much we have*	$2,082,000	*Who owns it*	$2,082,000

Note: The balances in the equipment and the structures and improvements accounts increased by $85,000 and $647,000, respectively, during the reporting period.

whole. These obligations are most frequently represented by term or serial bonds payable. Obligations arising from long-term leases treated as capital leases, however, will also be included in this account group. The amounts of the long-term liabilities are shown as credits, and the requirements and accumulations toward meeting them are reflected as offsetting debits. This account group includes general indebtedness incurred to acquire fixed assets or to finance operations, and general obligation bonds issued for the benefit of, but not to be paid by, governmental enterprise funds. Enterprise and special assessment fund bonds, on which the city assumes secondary liability, should be footnoted in the statement of general long-term debt.

To illustrate how this accounting entity is used, we compare the entries for the sale of a general bond issue by a city with the entry for the sale of a bond issue on the books of a business entity.

Entries for City

Capital Projects Fund Entry

Cash	XXXXXX	
Proceeds from sale of bonds		XXXXXX

General Long-Term Debt Account Group Entry

Amount to be provided for retirement of bonds	XXXXXX	
Bonds payable		XXXXXX

Entry for Business Entity

Cash	XXXXXX	
Bonds payable		XXXXXX

If we eliminate the credit to "proceeds from sale of bonds" in the capital projects fund and the debit to "amount to be provided for retirement of bonds" in the general long-term debt account group, we have the same account balances for the city as are shown on the books of the business entity. Therefore, we again see that fragmentation of the accounting data into separate fund entities with no distinction between capital and revenue items within source and disposition fund records makes this account group necessary to provide a record of general long-term liabilities.

The accounting equation for this account group can be stated as follows:

Amount to be provided for the retirement of debt + amount provided for retirement of debt = general long-term debt

The accounts on the left side of the equation are debited to show increases and credited to show decreases in them. Increases in long-term debt are reflected as credits, and decreases are shown as debits.

Illustrative Transactions.   Because each transaction in the general long-term debt account group complements some fund entry, each entry listed for this accounting entity is keyed to the fund entry that gave rise to it. Transactions from the various fund entities affecting the general long-term account group are as follows:

(LTD-1)   Proceeds from sale of $500,000 of 8 percent bonds are received (from capital project fund entry (CP-2), page 104).

(LTD-2)   General fund contribution of $50,000 is paid to debt-service fund for retirement of bonds (from debt-service fund entry (DS-3), page 111).

(LTD-3)   Revenue on debt-service fund investments in the amount of $1,950 is earned (from debt-service fund entry (DS-5), page 111).

(LTD-4)   Premium realized in sale of bonds is transferred from the capital projects fund to the debt-service fund (from debt-service fund entry (DS-6), page 112).

Journal Entries To Record Transactions.   The following journal entries record the preceding transactions:

Transaction (LTD-1)

Amount to be provided for retirement of bonds P. 104	$500,000	
Bonds payable		$500,000

Transaction (LTD-2)

Amount available for retirement of bonds	$ 50,000	
Amount to be provided for retirement of bonds		$ 50,000

(handwritten note in left margin: "...ceivable")

Transaction (LTD-3)

Amount available for retirement of bonds	$ 1,950	
Amount to be provided for retirement of bonds		$ 1,950

Transaction (LTD-4)

Amount available for retirement of bonds	$ 2,000	
Amount to be provided for retirement of bonds		$ 2,000

The originating entries for this accounting entity show the general long-term obligations assumed by the city. Subsequent entries show the extent to which resources have been accumulated for the retirement of these obligations. Entries (LTD-1), (LTD-2), (LTD-3), and (LTD-4) illustrate the recording of these data. When the bonds are eventually paid, the related account balances will be reversed and all accounts in the account group will be closed.

Posting the Transactions.   The posting of the preceding entries is illustrated in the following T-accounts for the general long-term debt account group:

Amount to be Provided for Retirement of Bonds			Bonds Payable	
(LTD-1) $500,000	(LTD-2)	$50,000		(LTD-1) $500,000
	(LTD-3)	1,950		
	(LTD-4)	2,000		

Amount Available for Retirement of Bonds	
(LTD-2)	$50,000
(LTD-3)	1,950
(LTD-4)	2,000

FIGURE 4.8   Statement of General Long-Term Debt, End of Period

Amount Available and To Be Provided for Payment of General Long-Term Debt		Obligations	
Amount to be provided for retirement of bonds	$446,050	Bonds payable	$500,000
Amount provided for retirement of bonds	53,950		
Total	$500,000		$500,000

Note: The balance in the bonds payable account increased by $500,000 during the reporting period.

Statements.   Because the general long-term debt account group is a memo record and is not involved with the flows of appropriable resources, it does not require a statement showing the flows of resources. Figure 4.8 illustrates the kind of statement that is generally appropriate for this account group. NCGA Statement 1 requires that changes in general long-term debt be disclosed either in the notes to this financial statement or in a separate statement of changes in general long-term debt.

INTERFUND RELATIONSHIPS

The various funds and account groups are related to one another in much the same way as are business entities that trade with one another. These relationships are of two types: *reciprocal* and *complementing*. Reciprocal relationships occur as resources or obligations are *shifted from one fund entity to another.* Complementing relationships, on the other hand, occur when elements of a transaction must be *recorded in another accounting entity to complete the record of that transaction.* For example, if the general fund loans cash to the capital projects fund or if an internal service fund provides services for the general fund, we have a reciprocal transaction that must be recognized in the records of both the funds involved. On the other hand, source and disposition fund transactions that involve general fixed assets or general long-term debt require complementing entries in the account groups for general fixed assets and general long-term debt, respectively. These relationships evidence themselves both in the recording of the transactions and in the content of combined financial statements.

In this section, we analyze the transactions included in our illustration to identify transactions that require reciprocal or complementing entries and examine the content of two combined financial statements for Model City.

Reciprocal and Complementing Entries

When journal entries were made in Chapter 3 and this chapter to record the transactions occurring within the funds and account groups of Model City, some of the relationships among these accounting entities were noted. To facilitate a more complete understanding of these relationships, code numbers for entries that require related entries in the records of other funds or account groups are shown in Figure 4.9. Fund names and account groups are listed across the top of the figure. Under these headings, you will find the code numbers of entries that reflect the various transactions of these accounting entities that are also recorded in other funds or account groups. These entries reflect either reciprocal or complementing relationships with those accounting entities.

Combined Financial Statements

NCGA Statement 1 requires that the comprehensive annual financial report (CAFR) for a governmental unit include, in the financial section of the report, the following general purpose financial statements (GPFS) and the notes to those statements[3]:

1. Combined Balance Sheet—All Fund Types and Account Groups

2. Combined Statement of Revenues, Expenditures, and Changes in Fund Balances—All Governmental Fund Types

3. Combined Statement of Revenues, Expenditures, and Changes in Fund Balances—Budget and Actual—General and Special Revenue Fund Types (and similar governmental fund types for which annual budgets have been legally adopted)

4. Combined Statement of Revenues, Expenses, and Changes in Retained Earnings (or Equity)—All Proprietary Fund Types.

5. Combined Statement of Changes in Financial Position—All Proprietary Fund Types

6. Notes to the financial statements

(Trust fund operations may be reported in (2), (4), and (5) above, as appropriate, or separately.)

---

[3] NCGA Statement 1 (Chicago: Municipal Finance Officers Association, 1979), p. 19.

FIGURE 4.9 Reciprocal and Complementing Entries

General Fund	Capital Projects Fund	Debt-Service Fund	Special Assessment Fund	Municipal Garage Fund	General Fixed Asset	General Long-Term Debt
(1)		(DS-1)				
(5)		(DS-2)				
(7a)			(SA-1b)	(SS-1)(SS-4)	(FA-1)	(LTD-1)
	(CP-2)					(LTD-4)
	(CP-2a & b)	(DS-6a & b)				(LTD-2)
		(DS-3)	(SA-2)	(SS-1)	(FA-2)	
(8)	(CP-3)				(FA-3)	
(9)	(CP-5b)	(DS-5)		(SS-4)	(FA-4)	
			(SA-4)	(SS-4)	(FA-5)	(LTD-3)
			(SA-6b)		(FA-5)	
	(CP-6)			(SS-5)		

The relationships between these statements and the supporting data developed in Chapter 3 and in this chapter are presented in NCGA Statement 1 in the form of the reporting pyramid shown in Exhibit 4.1.[4]

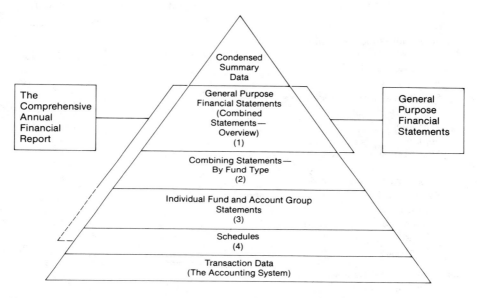

— Required
-- May be necessary
() Refers to "The Financial Section 'Pyramid'" discussion of Statement 1

EXHIBIT 4.1   The Financial Reporting "Pyramid"

Reproduced with permission from National Council on Governmental Accounting, Statement 1, *Governmental Accounting and Financial Reporting Principles* (Chicago: Municipal Finance Officers Association of the United States and Canada, 1979). © Copyright 1979 by the Municipal Finance Officers Association of the United States and Canada.

Because Model City has only one proprietary fund, we present only the combined balance sheet for all fund types and account groups in Figure 4.10 (pages 142–143), and the combined statement of revenues, expenditures, and changes in fund balances for all governmental type funds, in Figure 4.11 (page 144).

[4] Ibid., p. 20.

FIGURE 4.10   Model City Combined Balance Sheet for All Funds and Account Groups—End of Fiscal Period

	General Fund[a]	Capital Project Fund[b]	Debt-Service Fund[c]
Assets and interfund receivables			
Cash	$215,000	$108,000	$ 4,950
Taxes receivable	15,000		
Investments			49,000
Special assessments receivable			
Interest receivable			
Equipment			
Supplies			
Due from special assessment fund			
Allowance for depreciation			
Structures and improvements			
Amount to be provided for retirement of bonds			
Amount provided for retirement of bonds			
Totals	$230,000	$108,000	$53,950
Liabilities and interfund payables			
Vouchers payable	94,000	5,000	
Contract payable—retained pct.		5,000	
Bonds payable			
Interest payable			
Due to municipal garage fund			
Deferred revenues			
Reserves, fund balances, and appropriations			
Reserve for encumbrances	50,000	90,000	
Fund balances	86,000	8,000	53,950
Trust fund—principal balance			
Trust fund—income balance			
Fund balance earnings			
Investment in fixed assets			
Totals	$230,000	$108,000	$53,950

[a] See page 82.
[b] See page 108.
[c] See page 113.
[d] See page 122.

[e] See page 126.
[f] See page 130.
[g] See page 135.
[h] See page 138.

Special Assessment Fund[d]	Trust Fund[e]	Municipal Garage Fund[f]	General Fixed-Asset Account Group[g]	General Long-Term Debt Account Group[h]	Memo Only Total
$ 44,525	$ 500	$50,000			$ 422,975
					15,000
	100,000				149,000
202,500					202,500
900					900
		35,000	$ 535,000		570,000
		6,000			6,000
		10,000			10,000
		(3,500)			(3,500)
			1,547,000		1,547,000
				$446,050	446,050
				53,950	53,950
$247,925	$100,500	$97,500	$2,082,000	$500,000	$3,419,875
500		10,000			109,500
4,500					9,500
225,000				500,000	725,000
2,000					2,000
10,000					10,000
202,500					202,500
					140,000
(196,575)		85,000			36,375
	100,000				100,000
	500				500
		2,500			2,500
			2,082,000		2,082,000
$ 247,925	$100,500	$97,500	$2,082,000	$500,000	$3,419,875

FIGURE 4.11 Model City Combined Statement of Revenues, Expenditures, and Other Changes in Fund Balances for All Governmental Funds for Period

Items	General Fund[a]	Capital Projects Fund[b]	Debt-Service Fund[c]	Special Assessment Fund[d]	Trust Fund[e]	Memo Only Total
Revenues	$2,010,000					$2,010,000
Proceeds from sale of bonds		$500,000				500,000
Transfers from general fund			$50,000			50,000
Bond premium from capital projects fund			2,000			2,000
Interest earned on investments			1,950	$ 6,975		8,925
Transfers from general fund				25,000		25,000
Revenues from special assessments				22,500		22,500
Income					$2,500	2,500
Total	$2,010,000	$500,000	$53,950	$ 54,475	$2,500	$2,620,925
Expenditures	1,724,000	402,000		245,000	2,000	2,373,000
Transfers to municipal garage fund	85,000					85,000
Transfers to debt-service fund	50,000					50,000
Transfers to special assessment fund	25,000					25,000
Interest expenditures				6,050		6,050
Total	$1,884,000	$402,000	$ 0	$251,050	$2,000	$2,539,050
Excess (deficiency) of revenues and other inflows over expenditures and other outflows	$ 126,000	$ 98,000	$53,950	($196,575)	$ 500	$ 81,875
Beginning fund balances	10,000	0	0	0	0	10,000
End-of-period fund balances	$ 136,000	$ 98,000	$53,950	($196,575)	$ 500	$ 91,875

[a] See page 81.
[b] See page 109.
[c] See page 114.
[d] See page 122.
[e] See page 126.

SUMMARY

The special accounting entities for a governmental unit are divided into two main categories: funds and account groups. Funds are subdivided into source and disposition (governmental) type funds and self-sustaining (proprietary) funds.

The primary objective in accounting for the transactions of a source and disposition type fund is to show the flows of resources through the fund entity. As a result, most of the accounting procedures for these funds are similar to those covered in Chapter 3 for the general fund. Another objective of accounting for a special assessment fund is to show the intra-fund restrictions on resources available for the retirement of bonds and payment of interest. The accounts of this fund entity also show the long-term obligations of the special assessment project. Trust and agency funds, classified as source and disposition type funds, also may require a distinction between expendable and nonexpendable resources.

Accounting practices for self-sustaining funds closely resemble those followed by businesses. Expenditures for assets are capitalized, and depreciation is recorded. Revenues and expenses are measured on the accrual basis, which allows an operating statement that matches costs and revenues for the period to be prepared in order to determine the extent of operating profit or loss for the period.

Self-balancing account groups are used to show financial facts relating to general fixed assets and general long-term liabilities. They are different from funds in that they contain no appropriable resources. There are two self-balancing account groups, one for general fixed assets and another for general long-term debt. The general fixed-asset account group shows the acquisition values of fixed assets as debit items and the sources of financing for the assets as credits. The general long-term debt account group shows the amounts of long-term obligations as credits; balancing debits show the extent to which resources have been accumulated for the purpose of retiring the obligations.

QUESTIONS FOR CLASS DISCUSSION

4.1. Does a governmental unit always have (a) a general fund accounting entity? (b) At least one special fund entity? (c) An account group accounting entity? Explain.

4.2. (a) What operational characteristic makes it necessary to divide the accounting records of a governmental unit into separate, self-balancing fund entities? (b) Could a business organize its records along similar lines? Explain.

4.3. Is judgment ever involved in determining whether to create a separate fund entity to account for specified resources? Explain.

4.4. What is the common objective in accounting for the transactions of all source and disposition fund entities?

4.5. Explain the fundamental difference between source and disposition funds and self-sustaining funds.

4.6. Explain the difference between a fund and an account group.

4.7. Budgetary activities are primarily associated with general fund accounts. What actions relating to each of the special source and disposition funds closely parallel the budgetary action for the general fund?

4.8. Is a bonds payable account ever found among the capital project fund accounts? Explain.

4.9. What is the primary objective in accounting for debt-service fund resources?

4.10. Why does a governmental unit have account groups included in its accounting records?

4.11. The only financial statement generally prepared for either of the illustrated account groups is a statement of account balances. Why?

4.12. What information is disclosed by the statement of general long-term debt prepared from the account balances of the long-term debt account group?

4.13. A disbursement by the general fund to another fund may be recorded properly as a receivable, a transfer, or an expenditure. Under what circumstances is each practice appropriate?

4.14. (a) What is the distinguishing characteristic most generally associated with accounting for an agency fund? (b) Why?

EXERCISES

4.1. The citizens of Home City have voted to issue bonds in the amount of $1,000,000 for the construction of a new municipal building. Record the following actions and transactions in the capital projects fund originated to account for proceeds from the sale of the bond issue.

   (a) A bond issue in the amount of $1,000,000 is authorized to finance the construction of the new municipal building.
   (b) The bonds are sold for $1,010,000.

(c) The contract for constructing the new building is negotiated at a cost of $950,000.
(d) Construction of the building is completed at a cost of $965,000, and the building is accepted by the city.
(e) The obligation associated with the construction of the building is paid.
(f) The accounts in the capital projects fund are closed, and unused resources are transferred to the debt-service fund.

Required:
Journalize the preceding actions and transactions in the capital projects fund.

4.2. A city establishes a debt-service fund to account for resources ear-marked for the retirement of a general bond issue in the amount of $700,000. The following actions and transactions are carried out relating to that fund.

(a) The debt-service fund is established in accordance with require-ments of the bond indenture. That indenture requires the general fund to transfer $70,000 to the debt-service fund each year. It is anticipated that $5,000 can be earned from investing these funds during the next year.
(b) The general fund recognizes its obligation to transfer $70,000 to the debt-service fund.
(c) Payment is received by the debt-service fund from the general fund.
(d) Debt-service fund resources are invested in interest-bearing secu-rities.
(e) Interest amounting to $4,500 is received.

Required:
Journalize the preceding transactions in the records of the debt-service fund.

4.3. A city creates a special assessment fund to account for resources contributed jointly by the city and property owners for the purpose of improving the streets and sidewalks in a residential section of the city. The operating arrangement calls for property owners to pay 75 percent of the improvement cost, with the balance being paid from general fund resources. The following transactions relating to this fund occur during the period:

(a) The special assessment fund is authorized under an arrangement calling for property owner assessments of $75,000 and general fund contributions of $25,000 for the project.
(b) The general fund contribution to the project is received.
(c) Assessment notices are sent out to property owners calling for payment of the $75,000 over a period of five years.

(d) The first annual payment of property owner assessments is received.

(e) The city negotiates a loan in the amount of $60,000 to be paid from property owner assessments as they are collected.

(f) The contract for the improvement project is signed. The total cost reflected on the contract is $95,000.

(g) The contract is completed, and the work is accepted by the city at the originally agreed-on price.

Required:

1. Record the preceding transactions in the records of the special assessment fund.
2. Identify the transactions requiring entries in the records of other fund(s) and/or account group(s). Journalize the entries in those fund(s) and/or account group(s).

4.4. Prepare all journal entries required to record the following transactions for the city of Preston:

(a) Bonds valued at $50,000 are authorized and sold at par to finance a general fund deficit.

(b) Special assessment improvements costing $150,000 are authorized.

(c) Special assessments are made in the amount of $120,000.

(d) The city pays $30,000 as its share of the special assessment costs (see Item b).

(e) Special assessment bonds valued at $120,000 are sold to finance construction.

(f) Special assessment construction amounting to $140,000 is completed, and payment is made from special assessment resources.

4.5. Piney Ridge, a city with approximately 100,000 population, creates an internal service center charged with the responsibility of providing printing services for the various operating departments of the city. During the current month the service center completed the following transactions:

(a) Received a contribution from the general fund in the amount of $50,000 to be used in the initial financing of its operations.

(b) Equipment costing $30,000 and supplies costing $5,000 were purchased for cash.

(c) A building was rented from a real estate company at a cost of $3,600 per year. The full amount was paid at the time the lease was negotiated.

(d) Other expenses amounting to $6,000 were incurred during the month.

(e) Services were billed to the general fund in the amount of $9,000.

(f) Equipment is estimated to have a five-year life with no salvage value at the end of that time.

(g) An inventory discloses supplies on hand valued at $3,000 at the end of the month.

Required:

Journalize the preceding transactions in service center accounting records including any adjusting entries implied by them.

4.6. The city of Bend operates an electric power plant that provides electric service for its citizens. The utility is expected to charge fees for electric services that will produce a net income from operations equal to approximately 5 percent of its service revenue. The utility has the following transactions during the period:

(a) Customers are billed for services in the amount of $100,000. The accounts receivable balance at the beginning of the period amounted to $20,000.

(b) Collections on account during the period were $95,000.

(c) Meter deposits of $500 were received from new customers.

(d) General operating expenses amounting to $50,000 were incurred during the period.

(e) Materials and supplies costing $10,000 were purchased on account.

Required:

Journalize the preceding transactions on the books of the utility fund.

4.7. Refer to Exercise 4–6. Assume the following information relating to end-of-the-period adjustments:

(a) Supplies on hand are inventoried at $2,000.

(b) Depreciation on plant and equipment amounts to $10,000.

(c) Operating expenses of $3,000 have accrued.

(d) Accrued interest expense amounting to $5,000 on bonds payable is recognized.

(e) It is estimated that approximately 1 percent of customer accounts receivable will be uncollectible.

Required:

Journalize the adjusting entries required by the preceding information.

4.8. A city receives a contribution of $200,000 from a wealthy citizen with the stipulation that it is to be invested and the earnings from the investment must be used to provide college scholarships to worthy high school graduates living within the city. The city accepts the contribution and creates an agency fund to account for transactions relating to the contributed resources. During its first year of operation, the agency fund had the following transactions:

(a) Cash is received from the contributor.
(b) The cash is invested in securities.
(c) Investment income amounting to $12,000 is received.
(d) Scholarships amounting to $2,000 each are awarded to five worthy high school seniors.

Required:

1. Record the preceding transactions in the agency fund records.
2. Prepare a balance sheet for the fund at the end of the period.

4.9. A municipality completes the following transactions during the current accounting period:

(a) General fund transactions:
    1. Purchased automobiles for police use at a cost of $30,000.
    2. Sold an obsolete piece of equipment originally purchased with general fund resources at a cost of $25,000 for $3,000.
(b) Capital projects fund transaction:
    1. Accepted completed municipal building costing $750,000, which was constructed from the proceeds of a bond issue.
(c) Special assessment fund transaction:
    1. Completed a street improvement program financed jointly by the city and citizens with property adjacent to the street at a cost of $240,000.

Required:

Prepare the journal entries that should be reflected in the fixed-asset account group records as a result of the preceding transactions.

4.10. A city has the following transactions relating to long-term debt during the current period:

(a) Capital projects fund transactions:
    1. Issued bonds in the amount of $1,000,000 in exchange for cash in the amount of $1,010,000.
    2. $1,000,000 of the proceeds from the sale of bonds was spent in constructing a sewage processing plant.
(b) Debt-service fund transactions:
    1. $100,000 received by the debt-service fund from the general fund to be invested and ultimately used in the retirement of general long-term debt.
    2. Interest earned from investing available funds amounts to $8,000.
(c) Special assessment fund transaction:
    1. Special assessment bonds amounting to $250,000 are issued for the purpose of financing a special assessment project.

Required:

Journalize the entries that should be recorded in the general long-term debt account group as a result of the preceding transactions.

PROBLEMS

4.1. This is a comprehensive problem requiring application of accounting procedures discussed and illustrated in Chapters 3 and 4.

New City begins its current year's operations with the following account balances:

Cash	$ 20,000
Vouchers payable	10,000
Unreserved fund balance	10,000
Equipment	900,000
Structure and improvements	1,800,000
Investment in general fixed assets from general fund	1,500,000
Investment in general fixed assets from special assessment fund	400,000
Investment in general fixed assets from capital project fund	800,000

During the year the following transactions and other financial activities occur:

1. The city council approved a budget calling for total estimated revenues of $4,000,000 and appropriations of $3,900,000.

2. Tax notices in the amount of $2,920,000 were sent out.

3. Other revenues in the amount of $1,090,000 were received during the year.

4. Property taxes amounting to $2,890,000 were collected.

5. During the year expenditures and transfers in the amount of $3,478,000 were made against appropriations. These included $200,000 for the acquisition of a water utility company, $100,000 payment into a debt-service fund, $50,000 payment toward a special assessment project, and $170,000 payment into a municipal garage fund for the purpose of establishing a vehicle maintenance center.

6. Contracts were signed for the purchase of equipment estimated to cost $400,000.

7. Part of the equipment ordered in Item 6 estimated to cost $300,000 was received. Its actual cost was $290,000.

8. Vouchers including all amounts due to other funds in the amount of $3,600,000 were paid during the year.

9. Obsolete equipment originally costing $120,000 was sold as scrap for $10,000.

10. A capital projects fund was originated; a general bond issue in the amount of $1,000,000 was authorized to finance the project.

11. The general bond issue (see Item 10) was sold for $1,004,000.

12. Expenditures in the amount of $700,000 were made on the capital project. Of this amount, $10,000 was for services performed by the municipal garage fund.

13. Contracts amounting to $280,000 were signed covering the remainder of the capital project.

14. A contract (see Item 13) amounting to $100,000 was completed and a voucher is prepared to cover it. Because of changes in certain specifications, the amount to be paid is agreed on as $104,000. The contract also stipulates that, pending satisfactory performance of the improvements, the city may retain 10 percent of the original contract price.

15. Vouchers amounting to $774,000 plus the $10,000 due to the municipal garage fund were paid by the capital projects fund.

16. The general bond indenture (see capital projects fund) includes a provision requiring the general fund to pay $100,000 per year into a debt-service fund (see appropriation transaction in general fund). It is estimated that the investment earnings will amount to $4,000 during the first year.

17. The obligation of the general fund to contribute the appropriate amount to the debt-service fund is recognized (see transaction 5).

18. The general fund pays its obligation to the debt-service fund (see transaction 8).

19. Interest income amounting to $3,900 was received by the debt-service fund.

20. The premium on the sale of general bonds in the amount of $4,000 (see capital projects fund transaction) is transferred to the debt-service fund.

21. A special assessment fund was authorized for the construction of streets and sidewalks in a new residential area. The general fund portion of these expenditures was approved as part of the general fund appropriations in the amount of $50,000. This approval was contingent on the assessment of a special tax levy in the amount of $450,000 against property owners in the benefited area. The total authorized improvement is $500,000. A special tax levy scheduled to be paid over a period of ten years was authorized.

22. Special assessment fund bonds amounting to $450,000 were issued at par to provide funds for the project.

23. Construction expenditures amounting to $400,000 were incurred by the special assessment fund. Of this amount, $20,000 was for services performed by the municipal garage.

24. A contract amounting to $90,000, covering the completion of the special assessment improvement project, was signed.

25. The contract (see Item 24) was completed, and the obligation relating to it was recognized. It was agreed that 10 percent of the contract price would be retained pending satisfactory use of the streets for six months.

26. The first installment of the special tax levy amounting to $45,000 was received.

27. Interest amounting to $12,150 was received on the deferred assessments receivable.

28. Special assessment fund vouchers amounting to $460,000 were paid.

29. Interest amounting to $8,100 was paid to special assessment fund bond holders.

30. Interest amounting to $4,000 was payable on special assessment fund bonds payable.

31. Interest amounting to $1,800 was receivable on deferred assessments receivable.

32. The municipal garage fund, after receiving its contribution from the general fund, purchased equipment costing $70,000 and supplies costing $20,000 on account.

33. Expenses in the amount of $80,000 were incurred by the municipal garage during the period.

34. Supplies valued at $8,000 were used in garage operations during the period.

35. Services of the municipal garage were billed to other funds as follows:

> General fund, $70,000
> Special assessment fund, $20,000 (see transaction 23)
> Capital projects fund, $10,000 (see transaction 12)

36. Vouchers amounting to $150,000 were paid by the municipal garage fund.

37. Equipment in the municipal garage fund was depreciated over a ten-year life.

Required:

1. Prepare a transactions worksheet for each of the funds and account groups that should be used by New City in accounting for the year's actions and transactions. The worksheets should be organized to reflect beginning balances, actions and transactions, operating statement (where appropriate), and end-of-period balance sheet.
2. Prepare the combined financial statements required by the GAAFR Statement of Principles (see Chapter 4).

4.2. (AICPA adapted.) The city of Bergen enters into the following transactions during 19XX:

Budgetary accounts

(a) A bond issue is authorized by vote to provide funds for the construction of a new municipal building, estimated to cost $600,000. The bonds are to be paid in ten equal installments from a debt-service fund: payments are due on March 1 of each year. Any balance left in the fund used to account for the bond proceeds is to be transferred directly to the debt-service fund.
(b) An advance of $40,000 is received from the general fund to underwrite a contract to purchase land at a cost of $60,000. The deposit is made.
(c) Bonds valued at $550,000 are sold for cash at 102. A decision is made to sell only a portion of the bonds, because the cost of the land is less than expected.
(d) Contracts amounting to $490,000 are let to Michela and Company, the lowest bidder, for construction of the municipal building.
(e) The temporary advance from the general fund is repaid, and the balance on the land contract is paid.

Warrants Payable

(f) Based on the architect's certificate, warrants are issued for $320,000 for the work completed to date.
(g) Warrants paid in cash by the treasurer amount to $410,000.
(h) Because of changes in the plans, the amount of the contract with Michela and Company is revised to $540,000. The remaining bonds are sold at 101.
(i) The building is finished before the end of the year, and additional warrants amounting to $115,000 are issued to the contractor in final payment for the work. All warrants are paid by the treasurer.

Required:

1. Record the preceding transactions and closing entries in a capital projects fund transaction worksheet. Key the entries in the worksheet by letter to the preceding data.
2. Prepare the applicable fund balance sheet, considering only the

proceeds and expenditures from capital projects fund transactions, as of December 31, 19XX.

4.3. (AICPA adapted.) You were engaged to examine the financial statements of the Mayfair School District for the year ended June 30, 19AA, and were furnished the general fund trial balance. Your examination disclosed the following information:

    (a) The recorded estimate of losses for the current year taxes receivable was considered to be sufficient.

    (b) The local government unit gave the school district twenty acres of land to be used for a new grade school and a community playground. The unrecorded estimated value of the land donated was $50,000. In addition, a state grant of $300,000 was received and the full amount was used in payment of contracts pertaining to the construction of the grade school. Purchases of classroom and playground equipment costing $22,000 were paid from general funds.

    (c) Five years ago a 4 percent, ten-year sinking fund bond issue in the amount of $1,000,000 for constructing school buildings was made and is outstanding. Interest on the issue is payable at maturity. Budgetary requirements of an annual contribution of $90,000 and accumulated earnings to date aggregating $15,000 were accounted for in separate debt-service fund accounts.

    (d) Outstanding purchase orders for operating expenses not recorded in the accounts at year-end were as follows:

Administration	$1,000
Instruction	1,200
Other	600
Total	$2,800

    (e) The school district operated a central machine shop. Billings amounting to $950 were properly recorded in the accounts of the general fund but not in the internal service fund.

Mayfair School District General Fund Trial Balance, June 30, 19AA

	Debit	Credit
Cash	$ 47,250	
Taxes receivable—current year	31,800	
Estimated losses—current year taxes		$ 1,800
Temporary investments	11,300	
Inventory of supplies	11,450	
Buildings	1,300,000	
Estimated revenues	1,007,000	

	Debit	Credit
Appropriations—operating expenses		850,000
Appropriations—other expenditures		150,000
State grant revenue		300,000
Bonds payable		1,000,000
Vouchers payable		10,200
Due to internal service fund		950
Operating expenses:		
Administration	24,950	
Instruction	601,800	
Other	221,450	
Debt service from current funds (principal and interest)	130,000	
Capital outlays (equipment)	22,000	
Revenues from tax levy, licenses, and fines		1,008,200
Unreserved fund balance		87,850
Total	$3,409,000	$3,409,000

Required:

1. Prepare the formal adjusting and closing entries for the general fund.
2. Prepare general fund financial statements as of June 30, 19AA.

4.4. (AICPA adapted.) The town of Sargentville uses budgetary accounts and maintains accounts for each of the following kinds of funds:

Symbol	Fund
A	General fund
B	General long-term debt
C	Capital projects funds
D	General fixed-asset account group
E	Utility funds
F	Special assessment funds
H	Special revenue funds
S	Debt-service funds
T	Internal service funds
U	Trust and agency funds

The chart of accounts for the general fund follows:

Symbol	Account
1	Appropriations
2	Cash
3	Due from other funds
4	Due to other funds
5	Encumbrances
6	Expenditures
7	Reserve for encumbrances

Symbol	Account
8	Revenues
9	Revenues (estimated)
10	Unreserved fund balance
11	19X4 taxes receivable
12	Vouchers payable
13	Transfers to and from other funds

The following transactions are among those that occur during 19X4:

(a) The 19X4 budget, providing for $520,000 of general fund revenue and $205,000 of school fund revenue, is approved.

(b) The budgeted appropriations for the general fund amount to $516,000.

(c) An advance of $10,000 from the general fund is made to a fund for the operation of a central printing service used by all departments of the municipal government. (This has not been budgeted and is not expected to be repaid.)

(d) Taxes totaling $490,000 for general fund revenues are levied.

(e) Contractors are paid $200,000 for constructing an office building. This payment comes from proceeds of a general bond issue of 19X3.

(f) Bonds of a general issue, previously authorized, are sold at par for $60,000 cash.

(g) Orders are placed for supplies, estimated at $7,500, to be used by the Health Department.

(h) Vouchers are approved for payment of salaries amounting to $11,200 for town officers. (No encumbrances are recorded for wages and salaries.)

(i) The supplies ordered in Item g are received, and vouchers are approved for the invoice price of $7,480.

(j) Fire equipment is purchased for $12,500, and the voucher is approved.

(k) A payment of $5,000 is made by the general fund to a fund for eventual redemption of general obligation bonds.

(l) Of the taxes levied in Item d, $210,000 is collected.

(m) Taxes amounting to $1,240, written off as uncollectible in 19X1, are collected. (These collections have not been budgeted.)

(n) One thousand dollars of the advance made in Item (c) is returned because it is not needed.

(o) Supplies for general administrative use are requisitioned from the stores fund. A charge of $1,220 is made for the supplies.

(p) The general fund advances $30,000 to provide temporary working capital for a fund out of which payment will be made for a new sewage installation. Eventual financing will be accomplished by assessments on property holders based on benefits received.

(q) Equipment from the Highway Department is sold for $7,000 cash. (This sale is not included in the budget, and depreciation is not funded.)

(r) The town receives a cash bequest of $75,000 for the establishment of a scholarship fund.

(s) Previously approved and entered vouchers for payments of $6,200 for Police Department salaries and for the transfer of $500 to the police pension fund are paid.

(t) Receipts from licenses and fees amount to $16,000.

Required:

Using an answer sheet like the one shown below, show the account debited and the account credited in the general fund for each transaction. If a transaction requires an entry in any fund(s) other than the general fund, indicate the fund(s) affected by printing the appropriate letter symbol(s) in the column headed "other funds affected." If there is nothing to be entered for a transaction, leave the space blank.

The following transaction is entered on your answer sheet as an example: "Collections of taxes belonging to the county amount to $17,400."

Answer Sheet

| Transaction | General Fund | | Other Funds Affected |
	Debit	Credit	
Ex.	2	4	U
a. through t.			

4.5. Prepare journal entries to record the following unrelated series of events and indicate in which fund or account group each entry would be made:

(a) The city sold $1,000,000 of ten-year, 6 percent bonds at par on an interest payment date to finance the construction of an addition to the city hall. At the beginning of each year, the city will contribute a sufficient amount to cover a $100,000 addition to the debt-service fund and $60,000 interest, minus the amount the sinking fund is able to earn. For the first year, net earnings of the fund are estimated to be $7,000.

(b) A contribution of $120,000 is made by the general fund to the debt-service fund at the beginning of the year. The debt-service fund records the investment of $90,000 of the contribution received. Interest received in the amount of $10,000 is also recorded.

4.6. A capital projects fund has the following transactions:

(a) A $100,000 bond issue was sold at 99 on an interest payment date to finance a capital project. The discount will reduce the amount available for the project.

(b) A contract for the project amounting to $94,000 was signed.

(c) Invoices for half of the project were received, totaling $50,000.

(d) The accounts were closed at year-end.

Required:

1. Journalize the preceding events in a capital projects fund records.
2. Prepare a year-end balance sheet for the capital projects fund.

4.7. The citizens of Pineville authorized the issuance of bonds in the amount of $2,000,000 for the construction of a sewer system. As a result of that action the accounting department originated a capital projects fund to account for the proceeds from the sale of the bonds issued. The following transactions have occurred during the year:

(a) A bond issue in the amount of $2,000,000 was authorized to finance the construction.

(b) The bonds were sold for $2,020,000.

(c) A contract for constructing the sewer system was negotiated at a cost of $1,900,000.

(d) The construction of the sewer system was completed at a cost of $1,930,000 and was accepted by the city.

(e) The obligation associated with the construction of the sewer system was paid.

(f) The capital projects fund was closed.

Required:

1. Journalize the preceding actions and transactions.
2. Journalize any reciprocal or complementing entries required in other funds and account groups. Indicate the fund or account group in which each entry is recorded.

4.8. Gemville has established a debt-service fund to account for resources earmarked for the retirement of a general bond issue in the amount of $1,400,000. The following actions and transactions are carried out by the fund during the year:

(a) The debt-service fund is established in accordance with the stipulation in bond indenture, which requires the general fund to transfer $140,000 to the debt-service fund each year. It is anticipated that the fund will earn $10,000 from investing funds during the year.

(b) The general fund recognizes its obligation to transfer $140,000 to the debt-service fund.

(c) The debt-service fund receives the payment from the general fund.
(d) The payment received from the general fund is invested in interest-bearing securities.
(e) Interest in the amount of $9,000 is received.

Required:

1. Journalize the preceding transactions in the records of the debt-service fund.
2. Journalize the entries required in other funds and account groups and indicate the fund or account group in which each entry is recorded.

4.9. The city of Winslow has worked out an arrangement with a group of its property owners calling for special assessments for the purpose of improving the streets and sidewalks in their section of the city. The agreement calls for property owners to pay 80 percent of the improvement costs with the balance being paid from general fund resources. The following transactions relating to this fund occurred during the period:

(a) The special assessment fund was authorized under an arrangement calling for property owner assessments of $160,000 and general fund contributions of $40,000 for the project.
(b) The general fund contribution to the special assessment fund was received.
(c) Assessment notices are sent out to property owners calling for the payment of the $160,000 over a period of five years.
(d) The first annual payment of property owner assessments was received.
(e) The city negotiated a loan in the amount of $128,000, the proceeds of which will be used to carry out the construction of streets and sidewalks. This amount is expected to be paid from property owner assessments as those assessments are collected.
(f) A contract for the improvement project was signed, calling for total payments in the amount of $190,000.
(g) The project was completed, and the work was accepted by the city at the originally agreed-on price.

Required:

1. Record the preceding transactions in the records of the special assessments fund.
2. Identify any transactions requiring entries in the records of other funds and account groups. Journalize the entries in those funds and account groups. Show the name of the fund or account group in each instance.

4.10. A city carried out the following unrelated transactions during its fiscal year:

(a) General fund cash was used to purchase equipment costing $60,000.

(b) A general fixed asset originally costing $40,000 was sold for $4,000.

(c) General obligation bonds with a par value of $500,000 were sold by the capital projects fund for $505,000.

(d) A municipal building was constructed using capital projects fund resources at a cost of $300,000.

(e) A capital projects fund with a cash balance of $3,000 and no liabilities was closed out.

(f) A special assessment fund sold bonds associated with the special assessment project that had a par value of $200,000 for $202,000.

(g) A special assessment project was completed at a cost of $195,000.

(h) A debt-service fund received $50,000 from the city's general fund.

(i) A debt-service fund earned interest revenue in the amount of $10,000.

(j) A city water utility fund sold revenue bonds with a par value of $100,000 for $103,000.

(k) An enterprise fund transferred $20,000 to a bond redemption fund.

(l) A city collected taxes for the county in which it is located in the amount of $50,000. The city charged $500 for the collection service.

Required:

1. Journalize each of the preceding transactions in the records of the fund originating the transaction. Show the fund name with the transaction.

2. Prepare the reciprocal and complementing entries required for each transaction. Be sure to show the fund or account group name with each entry.

4.11. (AICPA adapted.) Select the best answer for each of the following items:

1. Long-term liabilities of an enterprise fund should be accounted for in the:

	Enterprise fund	Long-term debt account group
(a)	no	no
(b)	no	yes
(c)	yes	yes
(d)	yes	no

2. Which of the following funds of a governmental unit would account for general long-term debt in the accounts of the fund?

   (a) special revenue
   (b) capital projects
   (c) internal service
   (d) general

3. The amount to be provided for retirement of general long-term debt is an account of a governmental unit that would be included in the:

   (a) asset section of the general long-term debt account group
   (b) asset section of the debt-service fund
   (c) liability section of the general long-term debt account group
   (d) liability section of the debt-service fund

4. Which of the following would be included in the Combined Statement of Revenues, Expenditures, and Changes in Fund Balances—Budget and Actual in the comprehensive annual financial report (CAFR) of a governmental unit?

	Enterprise fund	General fixed-asset account group
(a)	yes	yes
(b)	yes	no
(c)	no	yes
(d)	no	no

5. A capital projects fund of a municipality is an example of what type of fund?

   (a) internal service
   (b) governmental
   (c) proprietary
   (d) fiduciary

6. Encumbrances would *not* appear in which fund?

   (a) general
   (b) enterprise
   (c) capital projects
   (d) special revenue

7. Within a governmental unit, two funds that are accounted for in a manner similar to a profit entity are

   (a) general, debt service
   (b) special assessment, enterprise
   (c) internal service, enterprise
   (d) enterprise, general

8. When Harmon City realized $1,020,000 from the sale of a $1,000,000 bond issue, the entry in its capital projects fund was:

Cash	1,020,000	
Proceeds from sale of bonds		1,000,000
Premium on bonds issued		20,000

Recording the transaction in this manner indicates that:

(a) The $20,000 may not be used for the designated purpose of the fund but must be transferred to another fund.

(b) The full $1,020,000 may be used by the capital projects fund to accomplish its purpose.

(c) The nominal rate of interest on the bonds is below the market rate for bonds of such term and risk.

(d) A safety factor is being set aside to cover possible contract defaults on the construction.

9. The activities of a central motor pool that provides and services vehicles for the use of municipal employees on official business should be accounted for in:

(a) an agency fund

(b) the general fund

(c) the internal service fund

(d) a special revenue fund

10. A transaction in which a municipal electric utility issues bonds to be repaid from its own operations requires accounting recognition in:

(a) the general fund only

(b) a debt-service fund only

(c) an enterprise fund only

(d) an enterprise fund, a debt-service fund, and the general long-term debt account group

11. A transaction in which a municipal electric utility paid $250,000 out of its earnings for new equipment requires accounting recognition in:

(a) an enterprise fund only

(b) the general fund only

(c) the general fund and the general fixed-asset account group

(d) an enterprise fund and the general fixed-asset account group

12. The operation of a public library, which receives the majority of its support from property taxes levied for that purpose, should be accounted for in:

(a) the general fund

(b) a special revenue fund

(c) an enterprise fund

(d) an internal service fund

13. Taxes collected and held by a municipality for a school district would be accounted for in a (an)

(a) enterprise fund

(b) intragovernmental service fund

(c) agency fund

(d) special revenue fund

14. Which of the following funds should use the modified accrual basis of accounting?

(a) capital projects

(b) internal service

(c) enterprise

(d) trust

15. Which of the following requires the use of the encumbrance system?

(a) special assessment fund

(b) debt-service fund

(c) general fixed-asset account group

(d) enterprise fund

4.12. (AICPA adapted) Select the best answer for each of the following items.

1. The following items were among Kew Township's expenditures from the general fund during the year ended July 31, 19X1:

Minicomputer for tax collector's office	$22,000
Furniture for Township Hall	40,000

How much should be classified as fixed assets in Kew's general fund balance sheet at July 31, 19X1?

(a) $0

(b) $22,000

(c) $40,000

(d) $62,000

2. The following balances are included in the subsidiary records of Burwood Village's Parks and Recreation Department at March 31, 19X2:

Appropriations—supplies	$7,500
Expenditures—supplies	4,500
Encumbrances—supply orders	750

How much does the department have available for additional purchases of supplies?

(a) $0
(b) $2,250
(c) $3,000
(d) 6,750

3. Kingsford City incurred $100,000 of salaries and wages for the month ended March 31, 19X2. How should this be recorded at that date?

	Dr.	Cr.
(a) Expenditures—salaries and wages	$100,000	
Vouchers payable		$100,000
(b) Salaries and wages expense	$100,000	
Vouchers payable		$100,000
(c) Encumbrances—salaries and wages	$100,000	
Vouchers payable		$100,000
(d) Fund balance	$100,000	
Vouchers payable		$100,000

4. The Board of Commissioners of the city of Rockton adopted its budget for the year ending July 31, 19X2, which indicated revenues of $1,000,000 and appropriations of $900,000. If the budget is formally integrated into the accounting records, what is the required journal entry?

	Dr.	Cr.
(a) Memorandum entry only		
(b) Appropriations	$ 900,000	
General fund	100,000	
Estimated revenues		$1,000,000
(c) Estimated revenues	$1,000,000	
Appropriations		$ 900,000
Fund balance		100,000
(d) Revenues receivable	$1,000,000	
Expenditures payable		$ 900,000
General fund balance		100,000

Item 5 is based on the following information:

The following balances appeared in the City of Reedsbury's general fund at June 30, 19X1:

Account	Balance Dr. (Cr.)
Encumbrances—current year	$ 200,000
Expenditures:	
Current year	3,000,000
Prior year	100,000
Fund balance reserved for encumbrances:	
Current year	(200,000)
Prior year	None

Reedsbury maintains its general fund books on a legal budgetary basis, requiring revenues and expenditures to be accounted for on a modified accrual basis. In addition, the sum of current year expenditures and encumbrances cannot exceed current year appropriations.

5. What total amount of expenditures (and encumbrances, if appropriate) should Reedsbury report in the general fund column of its combined statement of revenues, expenditures, and changes in fund balance for the year ended June 30, 19X1?

   (a) $3,000,000
   (b) $3,100,000
   (c) $3,200,000
   (d) $3,300,000

6. The debt-service fund of Harmon City shows the following journal entry:

Required additions	158,000	
Required earnings	2,000	
Fund balance		160,000

   The journal entry indicates that Harmon City:

   (a) has closed its books for the fiscal period
   (b) has not earned as much as it had anticipated to cover debt service
   (c) has not yet received cash for the $2,000 of earnings
   (d) has received $158,000 from the general fund

Items 7 and 9 are based on the following data relating to Lely Township:

Printing and binding equipment used for servicing all of Lely's departments and agencies, on a cost-reimbursement basis	$100,000
Equipment used for supplying water to Lely's residents	900,000
Receivables for completed sidewalks to be paid for in installments by affected property owners	950,000
Cash received from federal government, dedicated to highway maintenance, which must be accounted for in a separate fund	995,000

7. How much should be accounted for in a special revenue fund or funds?

   (a) $ 995,000
   (b) $1,050,000
   (c) $1,095,000
   (d) $2,045,000

8. How much should be accounted for in an internal service fund?

    (a) $100,000
    (b) $900,000
    (c) $950,000
    (d) $995,000

9. How much should be accounted for in an enterprise fund?

    (a) $100,000
    (b) $900,000
    (c) $950,000
    (d) $995,000

10. Ariel Village issued the following bonds during the year ended June 30, 19X3:

For installation of street lights, to be assessed against properties benefited	$300,000
For construction of public swimming pool; bonds to be paid from pledged fees collected from pool users	400,000

    How much should be accounted for through debt-service funds for payments of principal over the life of the bonds?

    (a) $0
    (b) $300,000
    (c) $400,000
    (d) $700,000

11. The general fixed-asset group of accounts would be used for the fixed assets of the

    (a) special assessment fund
    (b) enterprise fund
    (c) trust fund
    (d) internal service fund

12. Which of the following accounts could be included in the balance sheet of a general long-term debt account group?

	Reserve for encumbrances	Revenue bonds payable	Retained earnings
(a)	no	no	yes
(b)	no	yes	yes
(c)	yes	yes	no
(d)	no	no	no

Items 13 and 14 are based on this information:

The following events relating to the city of Albury's debt-service funds occurred during the year ended December 31, 19X1:

Debt principal matured	$2,000,000
Unmatured (accrued) interest on outstanding debt at January 1, 19X1	50,000
Interest on matured debt	900,000
Unmatured (accrued) interest on outstanding debt at December 31, 19X1	100,000
Interest revenue from investments	600,000
Cash transferred from general fund for retirement of debt principal	1,000,000
Cash transferred from general fund for payment of matured interest	900,000

All principal and interest due in 19X1 were paid on time.

13. What is the total amount of expenditures that Albury's debt-service funds should record for the year ended December 31, 19X1?

    (a) $ 900,000
    (b) $ 950,000
    (c) $2,900,000
    (d) $2,950,000

14. How much revenue should Albury's debt-service funds record for the year ended December 31, 19X1?

    (a) $ 600,000
    (b) $1,600,000
    (c) $1,900,000
    (d) $2,500,000

Items 15 and 16 are based on the following information:

During the year ended December 31, 19X1, Leyland City received a state grant of $500,000 to finance the purchase of buses and an additional grant of $100,000 to aid in the financing of bus operations in 19X1. Only $300,000 of the capital grant was used in 19X1 for the purchase of buses, but the entire operating grant of $100,000 was spent in 19X1.

15. If Leyland's bus transportation system is accounted for as part of the city's general fund, how much should Leyland report as grant revenues for the year ended December 31, 19X1?

    (a) $100,000
    (b) $300,000
    (c) $400,000
    (d) $500,000

16. If Leyland's bus transportation system is accounted for as an enterprise fund, how much should Leyland report as grant revenues for the year ended December 31, 19X1?

(a) $100,000
(b) $300,000
(c) $400,000
(d) $500,000

ACCOUNTING FOR COLLEGES AND UNIVERSITIES

5

Nonprofit organizations such as colleges and universities, hospitals, health and welfare agencies, churches, and public school systems follow accounting practices that are similar in many respects to those followed by governmental entities. In all cases, the managements of these organizations operate under a fiduciary relationship with their constituencies. Many of the operational characteristics of these organizations are similar to those of governmental units; consequently, many of their accounting practices are also similar.

In this chapter we examine the accounting and reporting practices followed by colleges and universities. As we examine these procedures, we shall:

1. compare the statement of fundamental concepts for colleges and universities with the statement of principles for governmental entities

2. summarize the significant changes in accounting practices suggested by the AICPA Audit Guide

3. compare the fund entities suggested for colleges and universities with those recommended for governmental units

4. illustrate the journal entries used to record a series of typical transactions for colleges and universities

5. briefly describe and illustrate the financial statements normally presented in college and university annual reports.

Although we will devote much of our time to defining the specific accounting practices followed by colleges and universities, our initial attention will be focused on how the accounting practices followed by these organizations differ from those previously described for governmental units.

COLLEGE AND UNIVERSITY STATEMENT OF PRINCIPLES COMPARED TO GOVERNMENTAL STATEMENT

The most generally recognized publication covering accounting practices for colleges and universities is *College and University Business Administration,* published by the National Association of College and University Business Officers.[1] (The principal elements of the accounting practices part of that book are reproduced in Appendix A of this book.) An AICPA Industry Audit Guide entitled *Audits of Colleges and Universities*[2] originally called for some reporting practices that differed from those included in an earlier edition of *College and University Business Administration;* however, almost all these differences were eliminated in the 1982 edition.

The statement of principles for colleges and universities is similar in many respects to the one accepted as the guideline in accounting for operations of governmental units. Both cite the *need for following fund accounting practices,* and both specifically indicate the funds or fund groups to be used. *Both reject the practice of recognizing depreciation in the accounts,* except where it is funded or where the assets are associated with a self-sustaining activity. The statements do, however, display some differences that are significant and others that are more apparent than real. In this section we examine some of the differences and explore some of the similarities found within these statements, with particular attention being given to:

1. legal provisions

2. budgetary practices

3. basis of accounting

4. accounting for depreciation

5. accounting for auxiliary enterprises.

---

[1] *College and University Business Administration,* 4th ed. (Washington, DC: National Association of College and University Business Officers, 1982).

[2] *Audits of Colleges and Universities* (New York: American Institute of Certified Public Accountants, 1973).

Legal Provisions

A comparison of the two statements of principles reveals an apparent difference regarding the emphasis on showing compliance with legal provisions. The statement for colleges and universities makes no mention of a need for organizing the system "to show that legal provisions have been complied with." The explanation of fund accounting (see Appendix A, page 312), however, suggests that "in some instances legal provisions and government regulations pertaining to certain funds may require accounting and reporting practices that differ from generally accepted accounting principles. It is recognized that in these instances such legal and regulatory provisions must take precedence." State-supported institutions no doubt experience legal limitations, whereas limitations on the uses of resources by private schools are primarily imposed by their constituencies. In either case, the fiduciary responsibilities must be recognized and met; consequently, this difference in the statements of accounting principles is more apparent than real and, therefore, has only a limited effect on the differences in accounting practices followed. Both types of enterprises must provide accounting data to show compliance with the regulations within which they operate.

Budgetary Practices

Municipal accounting principles require that the accounting system provide budgetary control of both revenues and expenditures. Although the college and university statement does not require such control, a rather complete system of operational budgeting is almost universally followed by these institutions.

While a large number of the individual items included in the budget of a college or university are appropriation controlled, many are also formula controlled, with budget allowances being adjusted to changes in the level of operations achieved. In this respect, the operations of colleges and universities resemble those of profit enterprises. This is because a significant amount of revenue, particularly among private schools, is earned by the provision of services rather than from an assessment based on a predetermined amount of proposed services. For example, if the enrollment is larger than expected, appropriate formula-related increases often are added to the originally budgeted expenditures to enable the institution to meet the requirements of an expanded program. Such adjustments require a careful analysis of costs after dividing them into fixed and variable elements.

Under these circumstances, the college or university budget is a much more flexible instrument than the one typically used by source and disposition type funds of governmental entities. As a result, budgetary data may be given less formal recognition in the accounts of colleges and universities. If budgetary data are formally recorded in the financial records, they may be entered as credits in separate appropriation accounts or they may be entered as credits in the expenditure accounts. Budgeted revenue generally is omitted from the formal accounting records.

Basis of Accounting

Accounting principles for governmental units recommend use of the accrual basis to the extent that it is practicable. This is interpreted to require the full accrual basis for proprietary funds and the modified accrual basis for governmental type funds. Revenues for governmental funds are recognized when they become available and are objectively measurable. Expenditures, with limited exceptions, are recognized when they are incurred and are objectively measurable. Furthermore, no distinction is made between capital and revenue items, and depreciation is not recognized in accounting for the activities of these funds.

The college and university statement also recommends use of the accrual basis in accounting for its operations. This is interpreted to require the recognition of revenues when earned. Expenditures are recognized when "materials or services are received." However, the accrual basis, as defined in the college and university statement of principles, does not distinguish between capital and revenue items or recognize depreciation. In summary, we can conclude that except for proprietary (self-sustaining) funds, *the accrual basis recommended for these institutions falls short of the pure accrual basis used by profit entities.*

Accounting for Depreciation

Among governmental units, depreciation is recognized only on the assets of self-sustaining funds. Principle 7 for governmental entities (see page 15) states that "depreciation on general fixed assets should not be recorded in the accounts of governmental funds." Depreciation is, however, recognized in accounting for the assets of enterprise funds, internal service funds, and other self-sustaining funds.

The college and university statement indicates that, except for real properties that are the investments of endowment funds, "depreciation expense related to assets comprising the physical plant is reported neither in the statement of current funds, revenues, expenditures, and other changes nor in the current funds statement of fund balances" (see Appendix A, page 316). This is not interpreted to preclude provisions for renewals and replacements as a substitute for depreciation in the accounting records of auxiliary enterprises. As we shall see in our analyses of the *AICPA Audit Guide for Colleges and Universities,* the position taken by the accounting profession regarding depreciation is one that would permit the reporting of depreciation in the plant fund section of the statement of changes in fund balances.[3] The statements of principles of both governmental units and

[3] Ibid., p. 2.

colleges and universities suggest, however, that *depreciation may be included in supplementary schedules* for the purpose of computing unit costs when such costs are desired.

Therefore, insofar as depreciation accounting relating to general fixed assets is concerned, there is little fundamental difference between the practices followed by these two kinds of nonprofit organizations.

Auxiliary Enterprises

Auxiliary activities of colleges and universities—for example, intercollegiate athletics, residence halls, and cafeterias—are generally expected to be self-sustaining or to produce an excess of income over expenditures. Although one would logically expect these accounting records to be maintained in a manner similar to those of proprietary funds in the governmental area, they are significantly different in two respects.

The first difference is the *practice of not recording depreciation on the facilities being used in the auxiliary activity.* The college and university statement is permissive in saying that *provisions may be made for renewals and replacements,* with these provisions being reported in the schedules of current expenditures. Where this is done, however, cash or liquid assets are expected to be transferred from current funds to a plant fund subsection maintained for accumulating resources for renewals and replacements. As a result, the statement showing the operations of an auxiliary activity is in reality a statement of income and expenditures rather than an income statement.

The second difference is that, as a general rule, *no separate balance sheet is prepared for the individual auxiliary activity.* Assets used in auxiliary activities are shown as part of the plant fund accounting entity. Short-term assets and liabilities associated with these activities generally are included in the current funds balance sheet. This accounting practice is consistent with the exclusion of auxiliary activities from the fund groups listed in the Statement of Principles (see Appendix A).

SUMMARY OF CHANGES SUGGESTED BY AICPA AUDIT GUIDE

The *AICPA Audit Guide for Colleges and Universities* in many respects clarified and expanded the accounting practices recommended by the statement of principles in the 1968 edition of *College and University Business Administration.* Although the 1974 edition of that publication was revised, for the most part, to comply with the AICPA recommendation, it is worthwhile to point out some of the changes in college and university accounting practices brought about by publication of the AICPA Audit Guide. These changes may be summarized as follows[4] :

[4] Ibid., pp. 2–3.

1. The audit guide *permits* the reporting of depreciation expense in the plant funds section of the statement of changes in fund balances.

2. It allows funds held in trust by others to be included in the financial statements under certain circumstances.

3. Endowment income stabilization reserves permitted by the 1968 college and university publication are indicated to be at variance with generally accepted accounting principles and should, therefore, be eliminated from the financial statements.

4. The audit guide requires that mandatory debt-service provisions relating to auxiliary enterprises be treated as transfers among the funds rather than as expenditures. This treatment is consistent with the requirement of the college and university publication regarding mandatory debt-service provisions relating to educational facilities.

5. *Mandatory transfers* from current funds should be *reported separately* from *nonmandatory transfers*. At the same time, the audit guide requires that the statement of current fund revenues, expenditures, and other changes include all current fund transfers, both mandatory and nonmandatory.

6. The audit guide requires that the accounting procedures followed for encumbrances should be in accordance with the accrual basis of accounting. This means that *expenditures will include only outlays and liabilities incurred* in connection with goods and services received.

7. The audit guide states that agency funds *should not* be included in the statement of changes in fund balances.

8. The audit guide *allows* current market or fair value to be used as an alternative to cost in reporting the carrying value of investments.

9. In addition to the changes in accounting practices described to this point, the audit guide requires certain disclosures that were not specifically mentioned in the college and university publication. These include the disclosure of the total performance of the investment portfolio and a disclosure of pledges in the notes to the financial statements.

10. The audit guide requires that a clear distinction be maintained between the balances of funds that are externally restricted and those that are internally restricted.

11. The audit guide also permits recording the monetary value of services contributed by members of a religious group to an institution operated by that group.

These modifications, with the exception of footnote disclosures, have been incorporated into the financial statements shown in Figures 5.3, 5.4, and 5.5 on pages 192–201.

COMPARISON OF FUND ENTITIES

Both the governmental and college and university principles statements require the use of fund accounting. The fund entities recommended for colleges and universities, however, are significantly different from those suggested for governmental units. One difference is that the college and university statement refers to the entities as fund groups rather than as funds. This practice clearly suggests that each group may have two or more subdivisions, each of which is roughly equivalent to an individual fund.

The college and university statement recommends the following fund groups, each of which is discussed in this section (see Appendix A, page 313):

1. current funds

2. loan funds

3. endowment and similar funds

4. annuity and life income funds

5. plant funds

6. agency funds.

Current Funds

Current funds are used to account for resources available for general operating purposes, auxiliary activities, and current restricted purposes. One element of the total fund balance for all these funds is roughly equivalent to the fund balance of the general fund for a governmental unit. In the college and university balance sheet, however, the total current fund balance will be subdivided into unrestricted and restricted fund balance categories. The unrestricted fund balance indicates the net amount of current fund resources available for *discretional* use by management of the institution within the limits of budgetary restrictions. The restricted fund balance reflects the net amount of current fund resources available to be used for specified purposes only. It is somewhat similar to the special revenue fund for a governmental entity.

Generally, current fund-accounting practices are similar to those followed in accounting for the general fund and special revenue fund activities of a municipal entity. However, the current fund-accounting entity includes separate self-balancing subdivisions for current unrestricted funds and current restricted funds rather than one fund balance account. In addition, the account names must be changed to ones that are appropriate for college and university operations. Some of these accounts are illustrated in the balance sheet (see Figure 5.3) and in the statement of current funds revenues, expenditures, and other changes (see Figure 5.4).

Loan Funds

Loan funds are used to account for resources that may be lent to students, faculty, and staff. Assets of this fund include cash, investments, and accounts receivable from loans. Although there is no governmental fund exactly like it, the loan fund does have many of the characteristics of a self-sustaining fund that is maintained as a revolving loan fund. Thus, accounting practices for this fund entity are similar to those for governmental self-sustaining funds. The accrual basis is employed in determining interest earned by the fund unless the amount so earned is immaterial. Provisions are made for probable losses to be incurred in the collection of the loans. Loan fund assets are shown as part of the combined balance sheet (see Figure 5.3).

Endowment Funds

Endowment funds are used to account for resources that donors or other outside agencies have stipulated shall be *maintained in perpetuity* and invested to produce income, which may be expended or added to the principal. In addition to the pure endowment funds just described, this *funds group* includes *term endowment* and *quasi-endowment* funds. Term endowment funds differ from pure endowment funds in that all or part of the principal may be used after a stated period. Quasi-endowment funds include resources that the governing board of an institution, rather than an outside donor, has designated to be retained and invested. Because these resources are internally designated, the governing board also has the right to use the principal if it so desires. In many respects, endowment funds are similar to the principal segment of the trust fund discussed in Chapter 4.

Resources represented by earnings from the investment of these funds generally flow into current unrestricted or current restricted funds for general or designated uses. As its name suggests, earnings from a *general endowment fund* may be used for general operations; consequently, resources realized from the investment of these funds flow into the current unrestricted fund. On the other hand, revenue earned by a *scholarship endowment fund* flows into a current restricted fund or a segment of the current fund whose resources are restricted to providing scholarships.

Due to the differences in the designated uses of resources realized from revenues, each endowment fund should be accounted for separately.

This could be accomplished by setting up a separate fund for each endowment, but such a fragmentation of the investments and accounting records is often impractical. Instead, most institutions "pool" the assets of the various endowment funds, in which case each fund will simply hold a share of the "pool." Such an arrangement not only is more practical for record keeping, but also allows the financial manager to follow more effective investment practices. Nevertheless, if the terms of the endowment agreement require it, the funds from that endowment must be invested and accounted for separately.

In recent years, a controversy has developed regarding the interpretation of income from endowment funds. These differences of opinion have centered around whether resources resulting from gains realized from the sale of endowment investments or from an increase in market values of these investments can be expended. Historically, these gains have been treated as additions to the principal of the endowment fund. This treatment adheres to the *trust fund theory* held to be legally binding in some states. More recently, however, the Ford Foundation has expressed a sharply contrasting view, saying that there is no authoritative support for treating gains as additions to the principal. People who advocate this point of view, commonly called the *corporate law concept,* hold that the resources resulting from gains can be spent in much the same manner as those earned from interest and dividends on endowment investments. As a result, some colleges and universities have adopted what is referred to as a total approach to endowment fund management. Under this approach resources equal to the total investment return, including the traditional revenues plus or minus gains and losses, have been made available for expenditures permitted under the endowment agreement. This approach generally calls for protection of the endowment principal from its loss of purchasing power before appropriating gains. It appears, however, that conservative, prudent management of endowment resources would still call for the retention of resources equal to the gains on endowment fund resources as additions to endowment fund principal.

Transfers from endowment funds to current funds are properly recorded in the records of the endowment fund by entering a debit to the endowment fund balance account and a credit to endowment fund cash. In the current fund, cash is debited and endowment fund income is credited. Because the endowment fund entry would be a reversal of an earlier entry to record the receipt of cash, however, both that entry and the one to record the transfer of cash out of the endowment fund are often omitted. That arrangement would call for an entry only in a current fund debiting cash and crediting endowment income.

Annuity and Life Income Funds

Annuity and life income funds are used to account for resources held by a college or university that are subject to *annuity or living trust agreements.*

These funds generally provide for payment of specified amounts per period (month, year) to the donor or his or her designee for life or for a specified period. At the end of this period, resources left in the fund generally become the property of the institution and are then available for general use, additions to endowment funds, or other specified uses.

In some respects, annuity funds are similar to endowment funds. When they are relatively small in amount, they may be grouped in this category. Accounting practices for these funds are also similar to those followed in accounting for governmental agency funds. The present values of annuities payable, however, should be recorded as a liability of these funds (see Figure 5.3).

Plant Funds

The plant funds of a college or university are similar to a combination of the governmental account groups for general fixed assets and long-term debt. They are also different from these account groups in one important respect—*they include resources designated for the acquisition of plant assets and retirement of long-term debt.* As a result, transactions recorded in plant funds typically include a mixture of memo account group and source and disposition fund entries. Interestingly enough, a college or university generally will have a number of separate plant funds.

The asset side of the balance sheet for the plant fund group (see Figure 5.3) typically includes subdivisions for unexpended plant funds, funds for renewal and replacement, funds for retirement of indebtedness, and investment in plant. The credit side of the balance sheet includes various fund balances plus notes and mortgages payable.

Agency Funds

Agency funds are *funds in the custody of the institution but not belonging to it.* The institution never expects to own the assets of such funds. The college or university serves only as a depository or fiscal agent to handle resources belonging to student organizations, faculty committees, or other groups connected with the institution.

TYPICAL TRANSACTIONS DESCRIBED AND RECORDED

The operating cycle for colleges and universities typically includes the following types of transactions:

1. realization of current fund revenues

2. recognition of current fund expenditures

3. realization of other resource inflows

4. recognition of nonoperating expenditures

5. transfers between funds

6. auxiliary activity transactions.

In this section we shall describe a series of assumed transactions for Illustration University. We shall then record those transactions in a transactions worksheet to show how they relate to the various funds and the financial statements.

Realization of Current Fund Revenues

Cash and other resource inflows realized by a college or university fall into two general categories:

1. receipts available for operating purposes

2. nonoperating receipts.

Cash and other resources realized by a college or university for direct use in operations are subdivided into *unrestricted* and *restricted* revenues. Resources available for general operating purposes at the discretion of management are characterized as unrestricted revenues. Resources available for operating purposes within *externally imposed* restrictions are classified as current fund restricted revenues. As current fund resources are received, the asset account is debited and the appropriate revenue account is credited. Typical educational and general revenue classifications include amounts received from[5]:

1. student tuition and fees

2. governmental appropriations

3. governmental grants and contracts

4. gifts and private grants

5. endowment income

6. sales and services of educational departments

7. organized activities related to educational departments

8. other sources.

To illustrate the realization of current fund revenues, we shall assume that Illustration University (see transactions worksheet) realizes revenue from the following sources:

[5] Ibid., pp. 20–23.

1. unrestricted revenues received from:
   tuition and fees, $8,000,000
   governmental appropriations, $3,000,000
   gifts, $1,000,000
   other sources, $200,000

2. endowment income, $1,500,000, including $200,000 for specifically designated instruction and research

3. auxiliary enterprises, $2,000,000.

You will find the realization of these revenues reflected in journal entry numbers 1, 2, and 3 in the transactions worksheet for Illustration University (see Figure 5.1).

Recognition of Current Fund Expenditures

As expenditures are made from general operating resources, the appropriate expenditure accounts are debited and the offsetting credits are recorded in the appropriate asset or liability accounts. Educational and general expenditures are normally subdivided into the following functional classifications[6]:

1. instruction and departmental research

2. organized activities related to educational departments

3. sponsored research

4. other separately budgeted research

5. other sponsored programs

6. extension and public service

7. libraries

8. student services

9. operation and maintenance of plant

10. general administration

11. general institutional expense

12. student aid.

In addition to the revenue and expenditure categories listed here, the unrestricted current fund normally includes revenues and expenditures for auxiliary enterprises, as well as transfers to and from other funds. The preceding classifications, including those for transfers among the funds, are included in Figure 5.4.

[6] Ibid., pp. 27–29.

FIGURE 5.1   Illustration University Transactions Worksheet for Fiscal Period Current Funds

	Beginning Balances	
Unrestricted current funds		
Cash	100,000	
Investments	300,000	
Accounts receivable	50,000	
Vouchers payable		40,000
Due to other funds		10,000
Fund balance		400,000
Total—unrestricted current funds	450,000	450,000
Restricted current funds		
Cash	60,000	
Investments	80,000	
Vouchers payable		10,000
Fund balance		130,000
Total—restricted current funds	140,000	140,000
Total for current funds	590,000	590,000

Loan Funds

Cash	20,000	
Investments	100,000	
Loans to students	300,000	
Fund balance		420,000
Total for loan funds	420,000	420,000

Endowment Funds

Cash	50,000	
Investments	15,000,000	
Fund balances		
Endowment		12,050,000
Quasi endowment		3,000,000
Available for distribution		
Total—endowment funds	15,050,000	15,050,000

Annuity Funds

Cash	40,000	
Investments	4,000,000	
Annuities payable		2,500,000
Fund balance		1,540,000
Total—annuity fund	4,040,000	4,040,000

Transactions				Statement of Revenues and Expenditures	Balance Sheet	
(1)	12,200,000	(4)	12,850,000		380,000	
(2)	1,300,000	(9)	70,000			
(3)	2,000,000	(14)	700,000			
		(15)	1,600,000			
					300,000	
					50,000	
						40,000
						10,000
		(21)	280,000			680,000
					730,000	730,000
(16)	107,000	(17)	307,000		60,000	
(2)	200,000					
					80,000	
						10,000
					0	130,000
					140,000	140,000
					870,000	870,000

Loan Funds

Transactions				Statement of Revenues and Expenditures	Balance Sheet	
(5)	400,000	(18)	390,000		30,000	
(18)	60,000				160,000	
(18)	330,000	(5)	275,000		355,000	
		(5)	125,000			545,000
					545,000	545,000

Endowment Funds

Transactions				Statement of Revenues and Expenditures	Balance Sheet	
(2)	1,500,000	(2)	1,500,000		100,000	
(14)	500,000	(19)	450,000			
(6)	2,000,000				17,450,000	
(19)	450,000					
		(6)	2,000,000			14,050,000
		(14)	500,000			3,500,000
(2)	1,500,000	(2)	1,500,000			
					17,550,000	17,550,000

Annuity Funds

Transactions				Statement of Revenues and Expenditures	Balance Sheet	
(7)	320,000	(11)	250,000		110,000	
					4,000,000	
(11)	250,000	(7)	200,000			2,450,000
		(7)	120,000			1,660,000
					4,110,000	4,110,000

continued on next page

FIGURE 5.1 (*continued*)

	Beginning Balances	

Plant Funds

Unexpended plant funds		
Cash	150,000	
Investments	2,000,000	
Notes payable		100,000
Bonds payable		500,000
Fund balance		1,550,000
Total—unexpended plant funds	2,150,000	2,150,000
For retirement of indebtedness		
Cash	50,000	
Deposits with trustees	300,000	
Fund balance		350,000
Total for retirement of indebtedness	350,000	350,000
Investment in plant		
Land	500,000	
Buildings	20,000,000	
Equipment	12,000,000	
Library books	400,000	
Bonds payable		2,000,000
Net investment in plant		30,900,000
Total—investment in plant	32,900,000	32,900,000
Total for plant funds	35,400,000	35,400,000

Agency Funds

Cash	40,000	
Investments	80,000	
Deposits held for others		120,000
Total—agency funds	120,000	120,000

Unrestricted Current Funds—Nominal Accounts

Educational and general revenues
  Tuition and fees
  Governmental appropriations
  Gifts
  Endowment income
  Other sources
Auxiliary activities

Transactions				Statement of Revenues and Expenditures	Balance Sheet	

Plant Funds

(8)	1,000,000	(12)	1,100,000		350,000	
(9)	100,000					
(14)	200,000					
					2,000,000	
						100,000
						500,000
(12)	1,100,000	(8)	1,000,000			1,750,000
		(9)	100,000			
		(14)	200,000			
					2,350,000	2,350,000
(9)	70,000	(20)	100,000		20,000	
(20)	100,000	(13)	150,000		250,000	
(13)	150,000	(9)	70,000			270,000
					270,000	270,000
					500,000	
(12)	800,000				20,800,000	
(12)	300,000				12,300,000	
(4)	300,000				700,000	
(13)	100,000					1,900,000
		(12)	1,100,000			32,400,000
		(13)	100,000			
		(4)	300,000			
					34,300,000	34,300,000
					36,920,000	36,920,000

Agency Funds

(10)	7,000				47,000	
					80,000	
		(10)	7,000			127,000
					127,000	127,000

Unrestricted Current Funds—Nominal Accounts

(1)	8,000,000		8,000,000		
(1)	3,000,000		3,000,000		
(1)	1,000,000		1,000,000		
(2)	1,300,000		1,300,000		
(1)	200,000		200,000		
(3)	2,000,000		2,000,000		

continued on next page

FIGURE 5.1 (*continued*)

Beginning Balances

Educational and general expenditures
    Instruction and research
    Libraries
    Student services
    Plant operations
    General administration
    Other expenditures
Mandatory transfers
    Principal and interest
Auxiliary activities
Other transfers
    To plant fund
    To endowment fund
    To fund balance
Total—revenues and expenditures
Excess of revenues over expenditures
Total

Restricted Current Funds—Nominal Accounts

Educational and general revenue
    Endowment income
    Gifts and grants
    Other revenues
Educational and general expenditures
    Instruction and research
    Student aid

Total

For the purpose of illustrating the accounting procedures followed in recording expenditures, we shall assume that Illustration University incurs expenditures as follows:

1. instruction and research, $11,000,000
2. libraries (for books), $300,000
3. student services, $200,000
4. plant operations, $1,000,000
5. general administration, $300,000
6. other expenditures, $50,000.

You will find these expenditures recorded as journal entry number 4 in the transactions worksheet for Illustration University (see Figure 5.1). Al-

	Transactions		Statement of Revenues and Expenditures	Balance Sheet
(4)	11,000,000		11,000,000	
(4)	300,000		300,000	
(4)	200,000		200,000	
(4)	1,000,000		1,000,000	
(4)	300,000		300,000	
(4)	50,000		50,000	
(9)	70,000		70,000	
(15)	1,600,000		1,600,000	
(14)	200,000		200,000	
(14)	500,000		500,000	
(21)	280,000			
			15,220,000 15,500,000	
			280,000	
			15,500,000 15,500,000	

Restricted Current Funds—Nominal Accounts

		Transactions	Statement of Revenues and Expenditures	Balance Sheet
(2)		200,000		200,000
(16)		100,000		100,000
(16)		7,000		7,000
(17)	200,000		200,000	
(17)	107,000		107,000	
			307,000 307,000	

though the expenditure transaction is recorded as a credit to cash in our illustration, in actual practice it would often go through a vouchers payable account.

Observe that the expenditures for long-term assets (libraries) are recorded as expenditures in the current fund and as additions to plant assets in the plant fund.

Realization of Other Resource Inflows

Nonoperating receipts include cash and other property *externally designated* to be added to the fund balance accounts of nonoperating funds. The receipt of such resources, restricted by the donor or granting agency, is added to the fund balance of the designated fund. *Receipts of this type are recorded directly in plant funds, endowment funds, or any other nonoperating funds.*

The receipt of these resources is recorded by debiting the appropriate asset account and crediting the appropriate fund balance account.

To illustrate the accounting procedures followed in recognizing the realization of nonoperating inflows, we shall assume that Illustration University realizes the following resources designated for specified nonoperating purposes. These transactions are recorded in Figure 5.1 (see entry numbers with each transaction):

> The loan fund receives $400,000 including loan repayments amounting to $275,000 and additional funds in the amount of $125,000 (see Entry 5).

> Securities having a fair value of $2,000,000 were received as endowment resources (see Entry 6).

> Annuity funds amounting to $320,000 were received. The annuity payable is calculated to be $200,000 (see Entry 7).

> Cash amounting to $1,000,000 designated to be used for plant construction was received (see Entry 8).

> Plant funds also received $170,000, composed of revenue on investments held in the fund in the amount of $100,000 and $70,000 as a mandatory transfer from the unrestricted current fund to cover principal and interest payments on plant fund indebtedness (see Entry 9).

> Agency funds realized additional cash from depositors in the amount of $7,000 (see Entry 10).

Recognition of Nonoperating Expenditures

In the preceding section we dealt with the realization of nonoperating resource inflows. As these resources are received, they are recorded in their respective funds. As they are used, that fact must also be recorded in the appropriate funds. The following assumed transactions involving nonoperating expenditures are reflected in the transactions worksheet for Illustration University:

> From annuity fund resources $250,000 was paid to meet the period obligations for annuities payable (see Entry 11).

> Construction was completed on buildings in the amount of $800,000, and equipment was purchased amounting to $300,000 from plant fund resources (see Entry 12).

> The university retired $100,000 worth of plant fund bonds and paid $50,000 in interest on bonds outstanding (see Entry 13).

Transfers Between Funds

Transfers between funds may be characterized as either mandatory or non-mandatory. *Mandatory transfers* are transfers required by contract or by external directive. In our illustration we find mandatory transfers covering principal and interest on plant fund bonds ($70,000) recorded as part of Entry 9.

Transfers made by the action of management rather than in response to external requirements are characterized as *nonmandatory transfers.* For example, within this classification fall resources designated to be transferred from unrestricted funds to specified nonoperating funds by the governing board of an institution. *Because these allocations are not required by a donor or outside agency, they should be labeled as nonmandatory or other transfers.* In our illustration, $700,000 of resources transferred from unrestricted funds to plant funds ($200,000) and endowment funds ($500,000) are reflected as other transfers in Entry 14.

Auxiliary Activity Transactions

Colleges and universities typically carry on a number of activities not directly related to their primary educational function. Dormitories, intercollegiate athletics, and bookstores are examples of such auxiliary activities.

Because it is important to know the extent to which these activities support themselves or how much they contribute to the educational function of the college or university, separate income and expenditure accounts generally are maintained for each of these activities. The long-term assets and long-term obligations associated with these activities may be recorded in a separate fund, but usually they are included in the plant fund accounts. Current assets and obligations may also be carried in a separate balance sheet for auxiliary funds, but they generally are included in the balance sheet for the current funds group.

A statement of assumed income and expenditures for intercollegiate athletics, one form of auxiliary activity, is shown in Figure 5.2. The income and expenditure totals in this statement reflect the revenue from auxiliary services (see Entry 3) and expenditures (see Entry 15) for auxiliary services shown in the worksheet.

Other entries included in the transactions worksheet but not described previously are as follows:

Entry 16—Receipt of restricted educational and general revenue in the amount of $107,000. This included gifts and grants in the amount of $100,000.

Entry 17—Payment of educational and general expenditures from restricted funds in the amount of $307,000 ($200,000 for instruction and research and $107,000 for student aid).

FIGURE 5.2   Model College: Intercollegiate Athletics Statement of Income and Expenditures—for Fiscal Period

Income		
Football	$ XXXXXX	
Basketball	XXXXXX	
Etc.	XXXXXX	$2,000,000
Expenditures		
Administration	XXXXXX	
Publicity	XXXXXX	
Maintenance of plant	XXXXXX	
Football	XXXXXX	
Basketball	XXXXXX	
Etc.	XXXXXX	1,600,000
Excess of income over expenditures		$ 400,000

Entry 18—Loan funds amounting to $60,000 are invested. Loans are also made to students from this fund in the amount of $330,000.

Entry 19—Endowment cash amounting to $450,000 is invested.

Entry 20—Plant fund cash, restricted to being used to retire debt of the fund amounting to $100,000, is deposited with the trustees.

Entry 21—Excess of unrestricted revenues over expenditures amounting to $280,000 is transferred to unrestricted fund balance account.

After recording the described transactions illustrated in Figure 5.2, formal financial statements could be prepared for Illustration University from data shown in the last four columns of the worksheet. Because we assume a highly simplified situation for the purpose of illustrating how the various typical transactions should be recorded, we have not presented those statements. Instead, in the following section we illustrate and describe statements for Model College that include more of the accounts typically found in formal financial statements for colleges and universities.

FINANCIAL STATEMENTS

The financial statements for a college or university should include:

1. Balance sheets for each fund group included in the accounting records. These are generally combined into one balance sheet similar in form to the one shown in Figure 5.3.

2. A statement of current fund revenues, expenditures, and other changes showing revenues by sources and expenditures by func-

tional classifications. This statement may be presented in a form similar to that shown in Figure 5.4.

3. Statements of changes in fund balances for each fund group. These statements can be presented in a combined statement similar to the one shown in Figure 5.5.

4. Various supporting schedules, including a separate statement of revenues and expenditures for each auxiliary activity. A condensed supporting schedule showing income and expenditures for intercollegiate athletics is shown in Figure 5.2.

These statements show that although the accounting records of colleges and universities are generally maintained on a fund-entity basis similar to that discussed in Chapters 3 and 4 for governmental units, some of the accounting and reporting practices used by these institutions are significantly different from those used for governmental units. These differences can be summarized as follows:

1. Fund entities carry different names to accommodate the operational characteristics of educational institutions.

2. The accounting records of colleges and universities place greater emphasis on endowment fund entities that include nonspendable resources than do governmental units.

3. The plant fund combines liquid resources designated for the acquisition of plant assets with the elements included in the two account groups used for governmental entities.

4. Less emphasis is placed on strictly enforced appropriation control in budgeting, and budgetary data are less likely to be shown in the published financial reports of colleges and universities than in reports for governmental units.

5. Auxiliary activities, roughly comparable to self-sustaining funds for governmental units, generally are accounted for on a *departmental rather than a fund entity* basis. This arrangement, while requiring separately designated nominal accounts, does not require separate self-balancing accounting entities for resources associated with auxiliary activities.

6. Logically, as a quasi-nonprofit enterprise relying on use-based charges, more emphasis is placed on the matching of revenues and expenditures in the financial reports for colleges and universities than is the case in the governmental area.

7. Fund entity accounting practices do underlie college and university accounting practices, but the financial reports place their primary emphasis on statements combining the individual fund entity data.

FIGURE 5.3 Model College Balance Sheet, End of Fiscal Period

Assets	Current Year	Prior Year	Liabilities and Fund Balances	Current Year	Prior Year
Current Funds			*Current Funds*		
Unrestricted			Unrestricted		
Cash	$ 210,000	110,000	Accounts payable	$ 125,000	100,000
Investments	450,000	360,000	Accrued liabilities	20,000	15,000
Accounts receivable, less allowance of $18,000 both years	228,000	175,000	Students' deposits	30,000	35,000
			Due to other funds	158,000	120,000
Inventories, at lower of cost (first-in, first-out basis) or market	90,000	80,000	Deferred revenue	30,000	20,000
			Fund balance	643,000	455,000
Prepaid expenses and deferred charges	28,000	20,000			
Total unrestricted	1,006,000	745,000	Total unrestricted	1,006,000	745,000
Restricted			Restricted		
Cash	145,000	101,000	Accounts payable	14,000	5,000
Investments	175,000	165,000	Fund balances	446,000	421,000
Accounts receivable, less allowance of $8,000 both years	68,000	160,000			
Unbilled charges	72,000	—			
Total restricted	460,000	426,000	Total restricted	460,000	426,000
Total current funds	1,466,000	1,171,000	Total current funds	1,466,000	1,171,000

Loan Funds

Cash	30,000	20,000
Investments	100,000	100,000
Loans to students, faculty, and staff, less allowance of $10,000 current year—$9,000 prior year	550,000	382,000
Due from unrestricted current funds	3,000	—
Total loan funds	683,000	502,000

Endowment and Similar Funds

Cash	100,000	101,000
Investments	13,900,000	11,800,000
Total endowment and similar funds	14,000,000	11,901,000

Annuity and Life Income Funds

Annuity funds		
Cash	55,000	45,000
Investments	3,260,000	3,010,000
Total annuity funds	3,315,000	3,055,000
Life income funds		
Cash	$ 15,000	15,000
Investments	2,045,000	1,740,000
Total life income funds	2,060,000	1,755,000
Total annuity and life income funds	5,375,000	4,810,000

Loan Funds

Fund balances		
U.S. Government grants refundable	50,000	33,000
University funds		
Restricted	483,000	369,000
Unrestricted	150,000	100,000
Total loan funds	683,000	502,000

Endowment and Similar Funds

Fund balances		
Endowment	7,800,000	6,740,000
Term endowment	3,840,000	3,420,000
Quasi-endowment—unrestricted	2,360,000	1,741,000
Total endowment and similar funds	14,000,000	11,901,000

Annuity and Life Income Funds

Annuity funds		
Annuities payable	2,150,000	2,300,000
Fund balances	1,165,000	755,000
Total annuity funds	3,315,000	3,055,000
Life income funds		
Income payable	$ 5,000	5,000
Fund balances	2,055,000	1,750,000
Total life income funds	2,060,000	1,755,000
Total annuity and life income funds	5,375,000	4,810,000

continued on next page

FIGURE 5.3 (*continued*)

Plant Funds

Assets	Current Year	Prior Year	Liabilities and Fund Balances	Current Year	Prior Year
Unexpended			Unexpended		
Cash	275,000	410,000	Accounts payable	10,000	—
Investments	1,285,000	1,590,000	Notes payable	100,000	—
Due from unrestricted current funds	150,000	120,000	Bonds payable	400,000	—
			Fund balances		
			Restricted	1,000,000	1,860,000
			Unrestricted	200,000	260,000
Total unexpended	1,710,000	2,120,000	Total unexpended	1,710,000	2,120,000
Renewal and replacement			Renewal and replacement - Fund balances		
Cash	5,000	4,000	Restricted	25,000	180,000
Investments	150,000	286,000	Unrestricted	235,000	200,000
Deposits with trustees	100,000	90,000			
Due from unrestricted current funds	5,000	—			
Total renewal and replacement	260,000	380,000	Total renewal and replacement	260,000	380,000
Retirement of indebtedness			Retirement of indebtedness Fund balances		
Cash	50,000	40,000	Restricted	185,000	125,000
Deposits with trustees	250,000	253,000	Unrestricted	115,000	168,000
Total retirement of indebtedness	300,000	293,000	Total retirement of indebtedness	300,000	293,000

Investment in plant			Investment in plant		
Land	500,000	500,000	Notes payable	790,000	810,000
Land improvements	1,000,000	1,110,000	Bonds payable	2,200,000	2,400,000
Buildings	25,000,000	24,060,000	Mortgages payable	400,000	200,000
Equipment	15,000,000	14,200,000	Net investment in		
Library books	100,000	80,000	plant	38,210,000	36,540,000
Total investment in			Total investment in		
plant	41,600,000	39,950,000	plant	41,600,000	39,950,000
Total plant funds	43,870,000	42,743,000	Total plant funds	43,870,000	42,743,000

Agency Funds			Agency Funds		
Cash	50,000	70,000	Deposits held in		
Investments	60,000	20,000	custody for others	110,000	90,000
Total agency funds	$ 110,000	90,000	Total agency funds	$ 110,000	90,000

FIGURE 5.4   Model College Statement of Current Funds Revenues, Expenditures, and Other Changes—for Fiscal Period

	Unrestricted	Current Year Restricted	Total	Prior Year Total
Revenues				
Educational and general				
Student tuition and fees	$2,600,000		2,600,000	2,300,000
Governmental appropriations	1,300,000		1,300,000	1,300,000
Governmental grants and contracts	35,000	425,000	460,000	595,000
Gifts and private grants	850,000	380,000	1,230,000	1,190,000
Endowment income	325,000	209,000	534,000	500,000
Sales and services of educational departments	90,000		90,000	95,000
Organized activities related to educational departments	100,000		100,000	100,000
Other sources (if any)				
Total educational and general	5,300,000	1,014,000	6,314,000	6,080,000
Auxiliary enterprises	2,200,000		2,200,000	2,100,000
Expired term endowment	40,000		40,000	
Total revenues	7,540,000	1,014,000	8,554,000	8,180,000
Expenditures and mandatory transfers				
Educational and general				
Instruction and departmental research	2,820,000	300,000	3,120,000	2,950,000
Organized activities related to educational departments	140,000	189,000	329,000	350,000
Sponsored research		400,000	400,000	500,000
Other separately budgeted research	100,000		100,000	150,000
Other sponsored programs		25,000	25,000	50,000
Extension and public service	130,000		130,000	125,000
Libraries	250,000		250,000	225,000

	Col 1	Col 2	Col 3	Col 4
Student services	200,000		200,000	195,000
Operation and maintenance of plant	220,000		220,000	200,000
General administration	200,000		200,000	195,000
General institutional expense	250,000		250,000	250,000
Student aid	90,000	100,000	190,000	180,000
Educational and general expenditures	4,400,000	1,014,000	5,414,000	5,370,000
Mandatory transfers for				
Principal and interest	90,000		90,000	50,000
Renewals and replacements	100,000		100,000	80,000
Loan fund matching grant	2,000		2,000	
Total educational and general	4,592,000	1,014,000	5,606,000	5,500,000
Auxiliary enterprises				
Expenditures	1,830,000		1,830,000	1,730,000
Mandatory transfers for				
Principal and interest	250,000		250,000	250,000
Renewals and replacements	70,000		70,000	70,000
Total auxiliary enterprises	2,150,000		2,150,000	2,050,000
Total expenditures and mandatory transfers	6,742,000	1,014,000	7,756,000	7,550,000
Other transfers and additions/(deductions)				
Excess of restricted receipts over transfers to revenues		45,000	45,000	40,000
Refunded to grantors		(20,000)	(20,000)	
Unrestricted gifts allocated to other funds	(650,000)		(650,000)	(510,000)
Portion of quasi-endowment gains appropriated	40,000		40,000	
Net increase in fund balances	$ 188,000	25,000	213,000	160,000

FIGURE 5.5   Model College Statement of Changes in Fund Balances, for Fiscal Period

	Current Funds		Loan
	Unrestricted	*Restricted*	**Funds**
Revenues and other additions			
Educational and general revenues	$ 5,300,000		
Auxiliary enterprises revenues	2,200,000		
Expired term endowment revenues	40,000		
Expired term endowment—restricted			
Gifts and bequests—restricted		370,000	100,000
Grants and contracts—restricted		500,000	
Governmental appropriations—restricted			
Investment income—restricted		224,000	12,000
Realized gains on investments—unrestricted			
Realized gains on investments—restricted			4,000
Interest on loans receivable			7,000
U.S. government advances			18,000
Expended for plant facilities (including $100,000 charged to current funds expenditures)			
Retirement of indebtedness			
Accrued interest on sale of bonds			
Matured annuity and life income funds restricted to endowment			
Total revenue and other additions	7,540,000	1,094,000	141,000
Expenditures and other deductions			
Educational and general expenditures	4,400,000	1,014,000	
Auxiliary enterprises expenditures	1,830,000		
Indirect costs recovered		35,000	
Refunded to grantors		20,000	10,000
Loan cancellations and write-offs			1,000
Administrative and collection costs			1,000

[handwritten annotation: increase in fund balance]

Endowment and Similar Funds	Annuity and Life Income Funds	Plant Funds			
		Unex-pended	Renewal and Re-placement	Retire-ment of Indebted-ness	Investment in Plant
		50,000			
1,500,000	800,000	115,000		65,000	15,000
		50,000			
10,000		5,000	5,000	5,000	
109,000					
50,000		10,000	5,000	5,000	
					1,550,000
					220,000
				3,000	
10,000					
1,679,000	800,000	230,000	10,000	78,000	1,785,000
				1,000	

continued on next page

FIGURE 5.5 (*continued*)

	Current Funds		Loan Funds
	Unrestricted	*Restricted*	**Funds**
Adjustment of actuarial liability for annuities payable			
Expended for plant facilities (including noncapitalized expenditures of $50,000)			
Retirement of indebtedness			
Interest on indebtedness			
Disposal of plant facilities			
Expired term endowments ($40,000 unrestricted, $50,000 restricted to plant)			
Matured annuity and life income funds restricted to endowment			
Total expenditures and other deductions	6,230,000	1,069,000	12,000
Transfers among funds— additions/(deductions)			
Mandatory			
Principal and interest	(340,000)		
Renewals and replacements	(170,000)		
Loan fund matching grant	(2,000)		2,000
Unrestricted gifts allocated	(650,000)		50,000
Portion of unrestricted quasi-endowment funds, investment gains appropriated	40,000		
Total transfers	(1,122,000)		52,000
Net increase/(decrease) for the year	188,000	25,000	181,000
Fund balance at beginning of year	455,000	421,000	502,000
Fund balance at end of year	$ 643,000	446,000	683,000

Endowment and Similar Funds	Annuity and Life Income Funds	Plant Funds			
		Unex-pended	Renewal and Re-placement	Retire-ment of Indebted-ness	Investment in Plant
	75,000				
		1,200,000	300,000		
				220,000	
				190,000	
					115,000
90,000					
	10,000				
90,000	85,000	1,200,000	300,000	411,000	115,000
				340,000	
			170,000		
550,000		50,000			
(40,000)					
510,000		50,000	170,000	340,000	
2,099,000	715,000	(920,000)	(120,000)	7,000	1,670,000
11,901,000	2,505,000	2,120,000	380,000	293,000	36,540,000
14,000,000	3,220,000	1,200,000	260,000	300,000	38,210,000

SUMMARY

The accounting practices followed by colleges and universities were compared with those followed by governmental entities. In that comparison, we observed that both types of organizations follow fund-accounting practices designed primarily to reflect inflows and outflows of spendable resources. Resource inflows for colleges and universities fall into two general categories—operating and nonoperating. Nonoperating resource inflows were defined as those inflows that are externally restricted to use for nonoperating purposes. We also illustrated the journal entries required to account for typical college and university transactions.

We observed that fund entities for colleges and universities carry designations that are different from those used in governmental accounting to accommodate differences in operating characteristics. For example, because colleges and universities typically hold significant resources externally designated to be preserved and invested for the production of revenue, they make extensive use of endowment fund entities.

In the last part of the chapter, we illustrated the financial statements typically included in the annual reports of colleges and universities and pointed out some of the differences between these statements and the statements for governmental entities.

APPENDIX A: P. 312

QUESTIONS FOR CLASS DISCUSSION

5.1. Describe the more significant differences between the operations of a municipal unit and those of a college.

5.2. Compare and contrast the accounting characteristics recommended for the current funds group for colleges and universities with those of the general fund for governmental units.

5.3. Explain the difference between a fund and a fund group.

5.4. Outline the important characteristics of endowment fund accounting.

5.5. (a) To which segment of governmental operating activities are the auxiliary activities of colleges and universities most closely related? (b) What similarities and differences exist in the accounting and reporting practices followed in the two areas?

5.6. Compare and contrast the financial statements prepared for colleges and universities with those prepared for governmental units.

5.7. Compare and contrast the plant funds group used for colleges and universities with the account groups used by governmental units.

5.8. Explain how the accrual basis recommended for college and university accounting differs from the pure accrual basis used in the profit area.

5.9. The current funds accounting entity includes both unrestricted current funds and restricted current funds. Explain the difference between the resources included in these two segments of current funds.

5.10. Describe the nature of the restrictions normally associated with resources included in annuity and life income funds.

5.11. Define an agency fund.

5.12. Describe the accounting procedures followed in recording the receipt by a college or university of securities designated for the construction of a building on campus.

5.13. What types of assets and liabilities would you normally expect to find in the plant fund accounting entity for a college or university?

5.14. List the financial statements you would expect to find in the published financial report for a college or university.

5.15. Explain the difference between pure endowment funds and quasi-endowment funds.

EXERCISES

5.1. Flowers College receives a $25,000 endowment from an alumnus. The donor stipulates that income from the investment of these funds is to be used to provide scholarships for worthy accounting students. The funds are invested in securities that yield an income of $1,250 during the first year. At that time, scholarships amounting to $1,000 are awarded. Journalize all transactions relating to the endowment, designating the funds in which the entries are recorded.

5.2. A wealthy alumna of Beeville College gives her alma mater $500,000 for the construction of a new business school. During the ensuing year, the building is completed at a cost of $600,000. The extra cost is met from current fund—general resources. Record these transactions in the appropriate funds.

5.3. During its registration period, Compton University receives $800,000 in cash, $200,000 in notes, and $100,000 from scholarship funds to cover tuition of students. Record these facts in the appropriate funds.

5.4. At the end of its first month of operations, Compton University (see Exercise 5.3) pays faculty salaries amounting to $80,000. How should this fact be recorded?

5.5. Excell University has a general endowment fund amounting to $25,000,000. During the current year, the university realizes an 8 percent return on its endowment resources, which is received in cash. Record the receipt of the revenue and the transfer of cash to current funds.

5.6. Excell University (see Exercise 5.5) purchases $50,000 worth of laboratory equipment for use by its physics department. The purchase is made from current fund resources. Record the transaction in the appropriate funds.

5.7. The administration of a university decides to transfer $300,000 from its excess of revenues over expenditures in the current fund to a quasi-endowment fund. Record this transaction in the appropriate funds.

5.8. A university has, among others, the following transactions during the current operating period:

(a) Received tuition and fees in the amount of $4,000,000.

(b) Received unrestricted gifts totaling $300,000.

(c) A general endowment fund earned income in the amount of $500,000.

(d) Instructional salaries amounting to $200,000 were paid.

(e) Equipment costing $25,000 was purchased for the chemistry laboratory from current fund resources.

(f) Library salary expenditures were incurred in the amount of $50,000.

(g) General administrative expenses amounting to $60,000 were paid.

(h) Securities designated by the donor to be used as endowment resources and valued at $200,000 were received.

(i) An alumnus contributed $500,000 in cash, which he specified should be used for the construction of a classroom building.

(j) One phase of the classroom building construction is completed and payment in the amount of $200,000 was made to cover that part of the contract.

(k) A student organization deposited $5,000 with the university. These funds were left with the university for safekeeping and are subject to withdrawal by the student organization.

Required:

1. Journalize each of the preceding transactions.
2. Indicate the fund or funds in which each of the transactions would be recorded.

5.9. A university accountant has asked you to help prepare the university's current fund operating budget. Although capacity enrollment for the university is considered to be 10,000 students, the enrollment for the next year is expected to be in the vicinity of 9,000 students. The following operating data are considered appropriate for the university when operating at full capacity.

Tuition and fees		$40,000,000
Instructional salaries and other fixed expenditures	$35,000,000	
Variable expenditures	4,000,000	39,000,000
Excess of revenues over expenditures		$ 1,000,000

Required:

1. Prepare a budget for the anticipated operating level of 9,000 students.
2. What actions do you think the university should take in light of the projected budgetary data? Explain fully.

5.10. A university borrowed $500,000 to assist in the construction of a classroom building. They anticipate receiving future contributions to cover the cost of construction.

Required:

1. Journalize the borrowing transaction.
2. Identify the fund in which the transaction would be recorded. Explain.

5.11. A university receives $200,000 that is externally restricted to be used for loans to students. During the year, loans are granted in the amount of $60,000, of which $20,000 is repaid before the end of the period. Interest received from loans amounts to $4,000.

Required:

1. Journalize the preceding transactions.
2. Identify the fund in which the transactions would be recorded.
3. Prepare a balance sheet for the fund at the end of the period.

5.12. A university receives cash contributions in the amount of $300,000 that are designated to be used as general endowment resources. All cash in the fund is invested in securities. During the period, the university receives $15,000 as interest and dividend income from the securities. Cash equal to the income is made available to be used for general operations.

Required:

1. Journalize the preceding transactions.
2. Identify the fund or funds in which the transactions would be recorded.

3. Prepare a balance sheet for the endowment fund at the end of the period.

PROBLEMS

5.1. Comprehensive problem covering recording procedures for various transactions discussed and illustrated in Chapter 5. Alma Mater University begins its current year operations with the following account balances:

Unrestricted assets and liabilities
Cash	$ 200,000
Investments	600,000
Accounts receivable	50,000
Vouchers payable	80,000
Amounts due to other funds	20,000

Restricted assets and liabilities
Cash	120,000
Investments	160,000
Vouchers payable	20,000

Loan funds
Cash	40,000
Investments	200,000
Loans to students	600,000

Endowment funds
Cash	100,000
Investments (including $6,000,000 of quasi-endowment funds)	30,000,000

Annuity funds
Cash	80,000
Investments	8,000,000
Annuities payable	5,000,000

Plant funds
Unexpended
Cash	300,000
Investments	4,000,000
Notes payable	200,000
Bonds payable	1,000,000

Retirement of indebtedness
Cash	100,000
Deposits with trustees	600,000

Investment in plant
Land	1,000,000
Buildings	40,000,000

Equipment	24,000,000
Library books	800,000
Bonds payable	4,000,000

Agency funds

Cash	80,000
Investments	160,000

During the year the university has the following transactions:

(a) Received unrestricted revenues as follows:

Tuition and fees	$16,000,000
Governmental appropriations	6,000,000
Gifts	2,000,000
Other revenues	400,000

(b) Received endowment income amounting to $3,000,000, including $400,000 for specifically designated instruction and research.

(c) Received revenue from auxiliary enterprises in the amount of $4,000,000.

(d) Incurred expenditures of unrestricted resources as follows:

Instruction and research	$22,000,000
Libraries (including $200,000 for books)	600,000
Student services	400,000
Plant operations	2,000,000
General administration	600,000
Other expenditures	100,000

(e) The loan fund received $800,000, including loans repayments in the amount of $550,000 and additional funds in the amount of $250,000.

(f) Securities having a fair value of $4,000,000 were received as endowment funds.

(g) Annuity fund revenues amounting to $640,000 were received.

(h) Cash amounting to $2,000,000 designated to be used for plant construction was received.

(i) Plant funds realized $340,000 as revenue from investments held by the fund. Of this amount, $140,000 was earmarked for retirement of indebtedness.

(j) Agency funds realized cash from depositors in the amount of $14,000.

(k) Obligations for annuities payable in the amount of $500,000 were paid from annuity fund resources.

(l) Construction was completed on buildings in the amount of $1,600,000, and equipment was purchased at a cost of $600,000 from plant fund resources.

(m) University retired $200,000 worth of plant funds (unexpended) bonds at par value and paid $100,000 in interest on bonds outstanding. Bond retirement was paid from deposits with trustees.

(n) The university, by action of its trustees, transferred $1,400,000 of resources from unrestricted funds to plant funds and endowment funds. Of this amount, $400,000 went to the plant fund and $1,000,000 was transferred to endowment.

(o) The university paid expenditures in the amount of $3,200,000 relating to auxiliary activities.

(p) The university received $214,000 of restricted educational revenue. This included gifts and grants in the amount of $200,000.

(q) Educational and general expenditures paid from restricted funds amounted to $614,000. This included $400,000 for instruction and research and $214,000 for student aid.

(r) Loan funds in the amount of $120,000 were invested.

(s) New loans to students from the loan fund amounted to $660,000.

(t) Endowment cash in the amount of $900,000 was invested in securities.

(u) Plant fund cash restricted to being used to retire debt amounting to $200,000 was deposited with a trustee.

(v) The excess of unrestricted revenues over expenditures and other changes was transferred to the unrestricted fund balance account.

Required:

1. Prepare a transactions worksheet similar to the one illustrated in Exhibit 5.1 and record the preceding transactions in it.
2. Complete the worksheet and prepare financial statements for Alma Mater University.

5.2. The current funds trial balances for Apex University is shown next.

	Current Unrestricted Funds		Current Restricted Funds	
Cash	$ 105,000		$ 60,000	
Investments	40,000		30,000	
Accounts payable		$ 55,000		$ 12,000
Tuition and fees		1,200,000		
Gifts		300,000		150,000
Auxiliary activities revenue		500,000		
Endowment income		200,000		25,000
Instructional expenditures	1,300,000			
Student aid	75,000		125,000	
Research expenditures			40,000	
Operating expenditures	600,000			
Library expenditures			10,000	
Auxiliary activities expenditures	480,000			
Fund balance		345,000		78,000
Total	$2,600,000	$2,600,000	$265,000	$265,000

Required:

Prepare financial statements for the current funds.

5.3. (AICPA Adapted.) Select the best answer for each of the following:

1. A city realized large capital gains and losses on securities in its library endowment fund. In the absence of specific instructions from the donor or state statutory requirements, the general rule of law holds that these amounts should be charged or credited to
   - (a) general fund income
   - (b) general fund principal
   - (c) trust fund income
   - (d) trust fund principal
   - (e) none of the above

2. A university receives a cash gift in the amount of $500,000, which the donor specifies shall be used in constructing a classroom building. This gift should be recorded as
   - (a) gift revenue in the unrestricted current fund
   - (b) gift revenue in the restricted current fund
   - (c) an increase to cash and fund balance in the plant fund
   - (d) quasi-endowment in the endowment fund

3. The board of trustees of a college directs the controller to transfer $400,000 in cash from current funds unrestricted to endowment funds. This should be recorded as a nonmandatory transfer in current funds and
   - (a) as revenue in the endowment fund
   - (b) as quasi-endowment added to cash and fund balance in the endowment fund
   - (c) subtracted from expenditures in the statement of revenues and expenditures
   - (d) added to revenues in the statement of revenues and expenditures

4. A university borrows $1,000,000 to build a dormitory. This transaction should be recorded
   - (a) as a debit to cash in the current fund and a credit to mortgage note
   - (b) as a temporary addition to endowment fund so that it can be invested while the dormitory is being constructed
   - (c) as an addition to plant fund cash and a credit to mortgage payable in the plant fund
   - (d) in an agency fund until required in constructing the dormitory

5. A university receives a government grant designated to be used in carrying out a specified research project. When received, this grant should be recorded

(a) as a revenue in the current funds—unrestricted statement of revenues and expenditures
(b) as an addition to agency fund cash and the agency fund balance
(c) in a special purpose fund
(d) as revenue in the current funds—restricted statement of revenues and expenditures

6. During the years ended June 30, 19X2 and 19X3, Sonata University conducted a cancer research project financed by a $2,000,000 gift from an alumnus. This entire amount was pledged by the donor on July 10, 19X1, although he paid only $500,000 at that date. The gift was restricted to the financing of this particular research project. During the two-year research period, Sonata's related gift receipts and research expenditures were as follows:

	Year ended June 30	
	19X2	*19X3*
Gift receipts	$1,200,000	$ 800,000
Cancer research expenditures	900,000	1,100,000

How much gift revenue should Sonata report in the restricted column of its statement of current fund revenues, expenditures, and other changes for the year ended June 30, 19X3?

(a) $0
(b) $800,000
(c) $1,100,000
(d) $2,000,000

7. On January 2, 19X2, John Reynolds established a $500,000 trust, the income from which is to be paid to Mansfield University for general operating purposes. The Wyndham National Bank was appointed by Reynolds as trustee of the fund. What journal entry is required on Mansfield's books?

	Dr.	*Cr.*
(a) Memorandum entry only		
(b) Cash	$500,000	
Endowment fund balance		$500,000
(c) Nonexpendable endowment fund	$500,000	
Endowment fund balance		$500,000
(d) Expendable funds	$500,000	
Endowment fund balance		$500,000

8. For the fall semester of 19X1, Cranbrook College assessed its students $2,300,000 for tuition and fees. The net amount realized was only $2,100,000 because of the following revenue reductions:

Refunds occasioned by class cancellations and student withdrawals	$ 50,000
Tuition remissions granted to faculty members' families	10,000
Scholarships and fellowships	140,000

How much should Cranbrook report for the period for unrestricted current funds revenues from tuition and fees?

(a) $2,100,000
(b) $2,150,000
(c) $2,250,000
(d) $2,300,000

9. The current funds group of a not-for-profit private university includes which of the following subgroups?

	Term endowment funds	Life income funds
(a)	no	no
(b)	no	yes
(c)	yes	yes
(d)	yes	no

10. Tuition waivers for which there is no intention of collection from the student should be classified by a not-for-profit university as

	Revenue	Expenditure
(a)	no	no
(b)	no	yes
(c)	yes	yes
(d)	yes	no

11. For the spring semester of 19X4, Lane University assessed its students $3,400,000 (net of refunds), covering tuition and fees for educational and general purposes. However, only $3,000,000 was expected to be realized, because scholarships totaling $300,000 were granted to students, and tuition remissions of $100,000 were allowed to faculty members' children attending Lane. How much should Lane include in educational and general current funds revenues from student tuition and fees?

(a) $3,400,000
(b) $3,300,000
(c) $3,100,000
(d) $3,000,000

12. The following funds were among those on Kery University's books at April 30, 19X4:

Funds to be used for acquisition of additional properties for
university purposes (unexpended at April 30, 19X4) $3,000,000
Funds set aside for debt-service charges and for retirement
of indebtedness on university properties   5,000,000

How much of the above-mentioned funds should be included in
plant funds?

(a) $0
(b) $3,000,000
(c) $5,000,000
(d) $8,000,000

5.4. A university has, among others, the following transactions during the
current operating period:

(a) Received state appropriations in the amount of $3,000,000.
(b) Received unrestricted gifts totaling $100,000.
(c) A scholarship endowment fund earned income in the amount of
$500,000. Scholarships are to be awarded out of current funds-
restricted.
(d) Instructional salaries amounting to $200,000 were paid.
(e) Equipment costing $25,000 was purchased for the chemistry labo-
ratory from current fund resources.
(f) Library salary expenditures were incurred in the amount of
$60,000.
(g) General administrative expenses amounting to $60,000 were paid.
(h) Securities valued at $200,000 designated by the donor to be con-
verted to cash and used to acquire plant assets were received.
(i) An alumna contributed $500,000 in cash, which she specified
should be invested as endowment. Revenue from the endowment
is to be used to provide scholarships.
(j) One phase of a classroom building construction was completed,
and payment in the amount of $200,000 was made to cover that
part of the contract.
(k) A student organization deposited $5,000 with the university.
These funds were left with the university for safekeeping and
are subject to withdrawal by the student organization.

Required:

1. Journalize each of the preceding transactions.
2. Indicate the fund or funds in which the transactions would be
recorded.

5.5. You are asked to help the university controller prepare the university's
current fund operating budget. Capacity enrollment for the university
is considered to be 20,000 students. Enrollment for the next year is
expected to be approximately 16,000 students. When operating at
capacity, the university would expect to have the following revenues
and expenditures:

Tuition and fees	$80,000,000
Instructional salaries and other fixed expenditures	70,000,000
Variable expenditures	8,000,000

Required:

1. Prepare an operating budget for the next school year.
2. What actions would you recommend the university take in light of the projected budgetary data?

5.6. The accounting system for State College includes the following funds:
   (a) current funds unrestricted
   (b) current funds restricted
   (c) endowment and similar funds
   (d) plant funds

The accounting system also includes the following account titles for each of the various funds whose resources, obligations, or operations require them.

Account Titles:

(A) Cash
(B) Other assets
(C) Vouchers payable
(D) Fund balance
(E) Revenues
(F) Expenditures
(G) Transfers
(H) Bonds payable

Transactions:

(a) State University received tuition and fees in the amount of $6,000,000.
(b) The general endowment fund earned income in the amount of $300,000.
(c) Faculty salaries amounting to $400,000 were paid.
(d) The college received a contribution of $500,000 to be used in constructing a new building.
(e) The college transferred $500,000 of resources from unrestricted funds to endowment funds.
(f) The college received $200,000 of restricted revenue.
(g) Education and general expenditures paid from restricted funds amounted to $100,000.
(h) Securities having a fair value of $1,000,000 were received as endowment funds.
(i) State College retired $100,000 worth of plant fund bonds from plant fund cash.

Required:

On a worksheet, label the first four pairs of columns with the names of the four types of funds contained in State College's accounting records. Then label individual lines of the worksheet a through i, with each line representing one of the transactions we have listed. Enter the letters reflecting the accounts to be debited and credited in each of the various funds as a result of each of the transactions.

5.7. (AICPA adapted.) A partial balance sheet of Rapapo State University as of the end of its fiscal year ended July 31, 19X2, is presented below.

Rapapo State University
Current Funds Balance Sheet
July 31, 19X2

Assets		*Liabilities and Fund Balances*	
Unrestricted:		Unrestricted:	
Cash	$200,000	Accounts payable	$100,000
Accounts receivable—		Due to other funds	40,000
tuition and fees,		Deferred revenue—	
less allowance for		tuition and fees	25,000
doubtful accounts		Fund balance	435,000
of $15,000	360,000		
Prepaid expenses	40,000		
Total unrestricted	600,000	Total unrestricted	600,000
Restricted:		Restricted:	
Cash	10,000	Accounts payable	5,000
Investments	210,000	Fund balance	215,000
Total restricted	220,000	Total restricted	220,000
Total current funds	$820,000	Total current funds	$820,000

The following information pertains to the year ended July 31, 19X3:

(a) Cash collected from students' tuition totaled $3,000,000. Of this amount, $362,000 represented accounts receivable outstanding at July 31, 19X2; $2,500,000 was for current year tuition; and $138,000 was for tuition applicable to the semester beginning in August 19X3.

(b) Deferred revenue at July 31, 19X2, was earned during the year ended July 31, 19X3.

(c) Accounts receivable at July 31, 19X2, which were not collected during the year ended July 31, 19X3, were determined to be uncollectible and were written off against the allowance account. At July 31, 19X3, the allowance account was estimated at $10,000.

(d) During the year, an unrestricted appropriation of $60,000 was made by the state. This state appropriation was to be paid to Rapapo sometime in August 19X3.

(e) During the year, unrestricted cash gifts of $80,000 were received from alumni. Rapapo's board of trustees allocated $30,000 of these gifts to the student loan fund.

(f) During the year, investments costing $25,000 were sold for $31,000. Restricted fund investments were purchased at a cost of $40,000. Investment income of $18,000 was earned and collected during the year.

(g) Unrestricted general expenses of $2,500,000 were recorded in the voucher system. At July 31, 19X3, the unrestricted accounts payable balance was $75,000.

(h) The restricted accounts payable balance at July 31, 19X2, was paid.

(i) The $40,000 due to other funds at July 31, 19X2, was paid to the plant fund as required.

(j) One quarter of the prepaid expenses at July 31, 19X2, expired during the current year and pertained to general education expense. There was no addition to prepaid expenses during the year.

Required:

1. Prepare journal entries in summary form to record the foregoing transactions for the year ended July 31, 19X3. Label each entry to correspond with the letter indicated in the description of its respective transaction. Your answer sheet should be organized as follows:

| | | Current Funds | | | |
| | | Unrestricted | | Restricted | |
Entry no.	Accounts	Debit	Credit	Debit	Credit

2. Prepare a statement of changes in fund balances for the year ended July 31, 19X3.

ACCOUNTING FOR HOSPITALS

6

Hospitals have many operating characteristics that are similar to those of colleges and universities. Institutions in both areas exist for the purpose of providing a socially desirable service, and a significant portion of the costs of their services is paid by recipients of the service or by organizations obligated to them, such as Medicare, Medicaid, Blue Cross, or a private insurance carrier, in the case of hospitals. Both hospitals and schools are partially supported by contributions from constituents, endowments, and/ or taxes. Both require a large investment in plant per unit of service performed, and they have a similar combination of groups interested in their financial reports. However, with the adoption of cost-based formulas for payment of hospital costs by obligated third parties, properly supported cost data has become very important to those institutions. As a result, hospital accounting procedures place a strong emphasis on the development of appropriate cost data for the various services they provide.

In spite of operational similarities, the recommended accounting practices set out in *Chart of Accounts for Hospitals* (see Appendix B) are significantly different from those followed by colleges and universities. The procedures set out in this publication are, with two exceptions, considered by the American Institute of Certified Public Accountants to be compatible with generally accepted accounting principles. These two exceptions, cited in *Hospital Audit Guide,* are as follows[1]:

1. carrying property, plant, and equipment at current replacement cost and basing depreciation on these values
2. carrying long-term security investments at current market value.

[1] *Hospital Audit Guide,* 3rd ed. (New York: American Institute of Certified Public Accountants, 1980), p. 4.

As we observed in the opening paragraph of this chapter, the accounting practices of hospitals have been directly influenced by the environment in which those institutions operate. That, to some extent, explains the first of these two exceptions. Hospitals want to carry various fixed assets at current replacement cost primarily because of the emphasis on cost recovery in billing hospital services. Depreciation included in those recoverable costs is a device for recovering the portions of long-term assets consumed in providing services. In a period of inflation, the only way this recovery can occur is to base depreciation on current replacement cost rather than on historical cost. Hospitals also favor carrying investments in securities at current market values, because this method is considered to provide a better indicator of the earning power of the investments and of the stewardship responsibilities of management. Such an arrangement also facilitates the procedures followed in accounting for pooled investments in hospital endowment funds.

The relationship of accounting practices to the environment in which hospitals operate is further demonstrated by the provisions of AICPA Statement of Position (SOP) 81–2. In that statement the AICPA, recognizing the increasing trend toward the creation of separate organizations to raise and hold contributed resources for hospitals, has more specifically defined "other related organizations" whose financial statements should be combined with those of their related hospitals.

In many respects, accounting practices for hospitals more closely resemble those followed for business enterprises than those followed for colleges and universities.

In this chapter, we relate the accounting practices followed by hospitals to those previously described for governmental units and colleges and universities. We shall consider:

1. the basis of accounting used

2. the extent to which fund-accounting techniques are used

3. the general format within which hospital financial statements are presented

4. cost allocation procedures followed in arriving at the fees to be charged for patient services

5. hospital budgetary practices.

BASIS OF ACCOUNTING

One of the most significant differences between the accounting practices followed by hospitals and those followed by colleges and universities is that hospitals use the *full accrual basis of accounting,* which includes a distinction between capital and revenue items and the related recognition of depreciation as an expense. The hospital publication states that the accrual basis is used "to ensure completeness, accuracy, and meaningfulness in accounting data."[2]

The use of the full accrual basis suggests less emphasis on appropriation control of expenses and more emphasis on control through cost data than is commonly found in accounting for either governmental units or colleges and universities. Budgets, which are used extensively, fit into much the same place operationally as do budgets for profit entities. Planned operations are expressed in the form of a flexible budget capable of being adjusted in response to changes in the level of operations.

Hospital accounting procedures are, nevertheless, similar to those used by other nonprofit enterprises in that *they also follow fund accounting practices.* Thus, hospital accounting records reflect the unusual combination of the full accrual basis of accounting within the fund-accounting format.

USE OF FUND-ACCOUNTING TECHNIQUES

As we have observed, the use of fund-accounting techniques is recommended for hospitals just as it is for governmental units and colleges and universities. The major emphasis here, however, is on dividing all resources into unrestricted and restricted categories. Unrestricted funds is the accounting entity used to account for all resources, including plant assets, available for use at the discretion of management for operating purposes. It follows then that *all resources received without external restrictions on their use flow through the unrestricted funds-accounting entity.*

Consistent with these general operating practices, hospital accounting records typically show the following major fund sections or groups of accounts:

1. unrestricted funds, sometimes characterized as the general fund or operating fund

2. restricted funds, including subdivisions for
   (a) specific purpose funds
   (b) plant replacement and expansion funds
   (c) endowment funds.

This arrangement normally requires a two-tier balance sheet—one for unrestricted funds and the second for restricted funds. The restricted funds section then includes subdivisions for the last three types of funds. This type of balance sheet is shown in Figure 6.1 (pages 220–221).

[2] *Chart of Accounts for Hospitals* (Chicago: American Hospital Association, 1976), p. 9.

Unrestricted Funds

The unrestricted funds accounting entity, sometimes categorized as the general fund or operating fund, serves the hospital in much the same way as the unrestricted current fund serves the college or university. As you can observe in Figure 6.1, the balance sheet for unrestricted funds includes both current and noncurrent assets and liabilities. A fund balance account reflects the difference between total assets and total liabilities.

The statement of revenues and expenses includes revenue classifications for patient service revenue, other operating revenue, and nonoperating revenue (Figure 6.2, page 222). The six major functional or departmental categories recommended for operating expenses are:

1. nursing services

2. other professional services

3. general services

4. fiscal services

5. administrative services

6. provision for depreciation.

These classifications are used in the statement of revenues and expenses for Sample Hospital shown in Figure 6.2.

The distinction between capital and revenue expenditures and the recognition of depreciation within a fund-accounting system require some record-keeping techniques that are different from those used in business or government. Because "property, plant, and equipment" is carried among the assets of unrestricted funds, we may need to transfer resources from unrestricted funds to plant replacement and expansion funds, and to transfer funds accumulated in the plant replacement and expansion fund to unrestricted funds for acquiring plant, property, and equipment. These transfers are illustrated in the statement of changes in fund balances for Sample Hospital (Figure 6.3, page 223).

Restricted Funds

As we mentioned earlier, restricted funds, resources fall into three subcategories[3]:

1. specific purpose funds

2. funds for plant replacement and expansion

3. endowment funds.

[3] Ibid., p. 10.

FIGURE 6.1 Sample Hospital Balance Sheet, December 31, 19X3, with Comparative Figures for 19X2

Unrestricted Funds

Assets	Current Year	Prior Year
Current		
Cash	$ 133,000	$ 33,000
Receivables	1,382,000	1,269,000
Less estimated uncollectibles and allowances	(160,000)	(105,000)
	1,222,000	1,164,000
Due from restricted funds	215,000	—
Inventories (if material, state basis)	176,000	183,000
Prepaid expenses	68,000	73,000
Total current assets	1,814,000	1,453,000
Other		
Cash	143,000	40,000
Investments	1,427,000	1,740,000
Property, plant, and equipment	11,028,000	10,375,000
Less accumulated depreciation	(3,885,000)	(3,600,000)
Net property, plant, and equipment	7,143,000	6,775,000
Total	$10,527,000	$10,008,000

Liabilities and Fund Balances	Current Year	Prior Year
Current		
Notes payable to banks	$ 227,000	$ 300,000
Current installments of long-term debt	90,000	90,000
Accounts payable	450,000	463,000
Accrued expenses	150,000	147,000
Advances from third-party payors	300,000	200,000
Deferred revenue	10,000	10,000
Total current liabilities	1,227,000	1,210,000
Deferred revenue—third-party reimbursement	200,000	90,000
Long-term debt		
Housing bonds	500,000	520,000
Mortgage note	1,200,000	1,270,000
Total long-term debt	1,700,000	1,790,000
Fund balance	7,400,000	6,918,000
Total	$10,527,000	$10,008,000

Restricted Funds

Assets

Specific purpose funds		
Cash	$ 1,260	
Investments	200,000	
Grants receivable	90,000	
Total specific purpose funds		$ 291,260
Plant replacement and expansion funds		
Cash	$ 10,000	
Investments	800,000	
Pledges receivable, net of estimated uncollectible	20,000	
Total plant replacement and expansion funds		$ 830,000
Endowment funds		
Cash	$ 50,000	
Investments	6,100,000	
Total endowment funds		$ 6,150,000

Liabilities and Fund Balances

Specific purpose funds		
Due to unrestricted funds	$ 215,000	$ —
Fund balances		
Research grants	15,000	30,000
Other	61,260	41,000
	76,260	71,000
Total specific purpose funds	$ 291,260	$ 71,000
Plant replacement and expansion funds		
Fund balances		
Restricted by third-party payors	$ 380,000	$ 150,000
Other	450,000	950,000
Total plant replacement and expansion funds	$ 830,000	$ 1,100,000
Endowment funds		
Fund balances		
Permanent endowment	$ 4,850,000	$ 2,675,000
Term endowment	1,300,000	1,300,000
Total endowment funds	$ 6,150,000	$ 3,975,000

FIGURE 6.2 Sample Hospital Statement of Revenues and Expenses, Year Ended December 31, 19X3, with Comparative Figures for 19X2

	Current Year	Prior Year
Patient service revenue	$8,500,000	$8,000,000
Allowances and uncollectible accounts (after deduction of related gifts, grants, subsidies, and other income—$55,000 and $40,000)	(1,777,000)	(1,700,000)
Net patient service revenue	6,723,000	6,300,000
Other operating revenue (including $100,000 and $80,000 from specific purpose funds)	184,000	173,000
Total operating revenue	6,907,000	6,473,000
Operating expenses		
Nursing services	2,200,000	2,000,000
Other professional services	1,900,000	1,700,000
General services	2,100,000	2,000,000
Fiscal services (CONTROLLER)	375,000	360,000
Administrative services (including interest expense of $50,000 and $40,000)	400,000	375,000
Provision for depreciation	300,000	250,000
Total operating expenses	7,275,000	6,685,000
Loss from operations	(368,000)	(212,000)
Nonoperating revenue		
Unrestricted gifts and bequests	228,000	205,000
Unrestricted income from endowment funds	170,000	80,000
Income and gains from board-designated funds	54,000	41,000
Total nonoperating revenue	452,000	326,000
Excess of revenues over expenses	$ 84,000	$ 114,000

These funds include resources carrying external restrictions, such as endowment funds and funds designated for plant replacement or enlargement. *Management-designated restrictions on otherwise unrestricted funds should be accounted for within unrestricted funds.*

Specific Purpose Funds.   Assets of specific purpose funds consist of *donor-restricted resources that are expected to be used for specified operating purposes.* These funds are similar to "current funds—restricted" for colleges and universities and "special revenue funds" for governmental units. Cash and investments are the assets most generally found in this type of fund. Investments held as part of specific purpose fund assets should be distinguished from the permanent investments held among the assets of endowment funds. These assets represent the temporary investment of funds to be used later for

FIGURE 6.3   Sample Hospital Statement of Changes in Fund Balances, Year Ended December 31, 19X3, with Comparative Figures for 19X2

	Current Year	Prior Year
Unrestricted Funds		
Balance at beginning of year	$6,918,000	$6,242,000
Excess of revenues over expenses	84,000	114,000
Transferred from plant replacement and expansion funds to finance property, plant, and equipment expenditures	628,000	762,000
Transferred to plant replacement and expansion funds to reflect third-party payor revenue restricted to property, plant, and equipment replacement	(230,000)	(200,000)
Balance at end of year	$7,400,000	$6,918,000
Restricted Funds		
Specific purpose funds		
Balance at beginning of year	$ 71,000	$ 50,000
Restricted gifts and bequests	35,000	20,000
Research grants	35,000	45,000
Income from investments	35,260	39,000
Gain on sale of investments	8,000	—
Transferred to		
Other operating revenue	(100,000)	(80,000)
Allowances and uncollectible accounts	(8,000)	(3,000)
Balance at end of year	$ 76,260	$ 71,000
Plant replacement and expansion funds		
Balance at beginning of year	$1,100,000	$1,494,000
Restricted gifts and bequests	113,000	150,000
Income from investments	15,000	18,000
Transferred to unrestricted funds (described above)	(628,000)	(762,000)
Transferred from unrestricted funds (described above)	230,000	200,000
Balance at end of year	$ 830,000	$1,100,000
Endowment funds		
Balance at beginning of year	$3,975,000	$2,875,000
Restricted gifts and bequests	2,000,000	1,000,000
Net gain on sale of investments	175,000	100,000
Balance at end of year	$6,150,000	$3,975,000

specified operating purposes. In contrast, endowment fund investments are nonexpendable assets.

The use of the assets of a specific purpose fund usually appears in the accounting reports as "other operating income" in the statement of revenues and expenses (see Figure 6.2). Transfers out of specific purpose funds are reflected as "transfers to other operating revenues" in the statement of changes in fund balances for the specific purpose fund (see Figure 6.3). Expenses funded by these restricted resources are also recorded as part of the expenses shown in the statement of revenues and expenses.

Plant Replacement and Expansion Funds.   Assets of these funds include *resources restricted by donors to be used for additions to property, plant, and equipment.* The resources of this type of fund often include, in addition to cash and investments, pledges receivable. These are included as assets after providing for estimated losses in collecting them. As resources from this fund are used for plant replacement and expansion, the transfer is reflected in the statement of changes in fund balances (see Figure 6.3).

Endowment Funds.   Endowment funds for hospitals are similar to those held by colleges and universities. The accounting practices and even the account names are essentially the same.

Maintenance of the principal balance is an important aspect of endowment fund operations, and accounting records for these funds are organized to show that this objective has been achieved. The assets of endowment funds typically include cash and investments. The fund balance account may include only permanent endowment, or it may include subdivisions for permanent endowment and term endowment. Term endowment funds are resources that may be expended when a specified event has occurred or a stated period has passed. Income from endowment may be restricted or unrestricted depending on the endowment agreement.

The transfer of cash represented by earnings from endowment fund assets requires appropriate entries in the accounts of the funds involved. Unrestricted endowment fund earnings are transferred to unrestricted funds, where they are recognized in the statement of revenues and expenses as unrestricted income from endowment funds. The earnings from restricted endowment funds may be transferred to specific purpose funds to be held until spent for the designated purpose.

FINANCIAL STATEMENTS

In many respects, the organization of financial statements for a hospital is similar to that of college and university statements. The use of a combined balance sheet with sections for unrestricted funds and restricted funds, subdivided into the three fund groups as discussed earlier, is recommended. A balance sheet prepared in this manner is illustrated in Figure 6.1. The operating statement for a hospital generally is characterized as a statement of revenues and expenses and is presented in the general format shown in Figure 6.2. In addition to these two statements, a statement of changes in fund balances (see Figure 6.3) is prepared to account for the differences between the beginning-of-the-period and end-of-the-period fund balances for each fund group.

Consistent with the requirement for business enterprises, a statement of changes in financial position is prepared for the unrestricted fund (Figure 6.4). Each financial statement should be accompanied by appropriate footnotes describing some elements of the statement in more detail. Such footnotes are expected to meet the same standards of disclosure as those met by the financial statements of business enterprises.

COST ALLOCATION PROCEDURES

In an enterprise that depends on user- or buyer-based fees, it is important to be able to relate the costs of individual units of goods and/or services to the fees (revenue) realized from them. A manufacturing enterprise is concerned with matching the cost of producing each of its various products with the revenues realized from its sale. Thus, their cost allocation procedures are designed to allocate all manufacturing expenses to the units being produced. Material and labor costs are charged directly to job orders or to processes out of which they are subsequently allocated to the units produced. Overhead costs are charged to the units of product by using an overhead application rate related to some prime cost base, such as direct labor hours or direct labor dollars. Cost allocation procedures, designed to allocate service department costs to producing departments on the basis of benefits received, are important elements in determining the overhead application rates for the various producing departments. The end result of these procedures is a total manufacturing cost per unit that can then be matched against the sale price per unit to determine the margin realized on each of the various products or classes of products.

In service enterprises rendering different types of services, both direct and indirect costs should be allocated to the various functions being performed in a manner similar to that just described. The functional unit costs can then be compared with the prices billed for the various services.

Hospitals depending on user-based charges fall into this category of resource conversion entities. Their cost allocation procedures are similar to those found in profit-oriented service enterprises. As hospital services are used, the patient is charged for each of the various types of services provided on what is expected to be a cost-related basis. The costs of operating the hospital, therefore, should be *allocated to the revenue-producing centers* recognized in customer billing. The first step in the allocation process is to establish departmental cost centers. The cost of operating each depart-

FIGURE 6.4 **Sample Hospital Statement of Changes in Financial Position of Unrestricted Fund, Year Ended December 31, 19X3, with Comparative Figures for 19X2**

	Current Year	Prior Year
Funds Provided		
Loss from operations	$ (368,000)	$ (212,000)
Deduct (add) items included in operations not requiring (providing) funds		
Provision for depreciation	300,000	250,000
Increase in deferred third-party reimbursement	110,000	90,000
Revenue restricted to property, plant, and equipment replacement transferred to plant replacement and expansion fund	(230,000)	(200,000)
Funds required for operations	(188,000)	(72,000)
Nonoperating revenue	452,000	326,000
Funds derived from operations and nonoperating revenues	264,000	254,000
Decrease in board-designated funds	210,000	—
Property, plant, and equipment expenditures financed by plant replacement and expansion funds	628,000	762,000
Decrease in working capital	—	46,000
	$1,102,000	$1,062,000
Funds Applied		
Additions to property, plant, and equipment	$ 668,000	$ 762,000
Reduction of long-term debt	90,000	90,000
Increase in board-designated funds	—	210,000
Increase in working capital	344,000	—
	$1,102,000	$1,062,000
Changes in Working Capital		
Increase (decrease) in current assets		
Cash	$ 100,000	$ (50,000)
Receivables	58,000	75,000
Due from restricted funds	215,000	(100,000)
Inventories	(7,000)	16,000
Prepaid expenses	(5,000)	1,000
	361,000	(58,000)
Increase (decrease) in current liabilities		
Note payable to banks	(73,000)	50,000
Accounts payable	(13,000)	10,000
Accrued expenses	3,000	2,000
Advances from third-party payors	100,000	40,000
Deferred revenue	—	2,000
	17,000	104,000
Increase (decrease) in working capital	$ 344,000	$ (46,000)

ment includes both direct and allocated charges. Direct expenses, representing resources and services used entirely by the department, should be coded in such a way that they will be accumulated directly in the departmental expense control accounts. General expenses of the hospital should be allocated to the various departments, as far as practicable, on the basis of the benefits each department receives from them. This requires the accountant to identify bases of allocation that are representative of the benefits realized by the revenue-producing departments. Building insurance, for example, might be distributed to the various departments on the basis of square footage of floor space.

Within the conceptual arrangement calling for all operating costs to be allocated to revenue-producing departments, non-revenue-producing departments, such as building maintenance, are designated as *supporting departments*. The costs of supporting departments should be allocated to revenue-producing departments on the basis of some measure of benefits received. All operating costs can thus be accumulated in those cost centers.

After completing the cost allocation process we have described, managers can periodically compare the various service revenues with the costs of providing those services. This can be done on either an aggregate or a unit basis. The cost allocation process should be carried out for both budgeted and actual costs. This can best be done on a worksheet similar to the one shown in Figure 6.5, on which budgeted costs for Hypothetical Hospital are allocated to its four revenue-producing departments.

BUDGETARY PRACTICES FOR HOSPITALS

We have observed that the hospital budgetary process must be responsive to the anticipated level of operations. To achieve this responsiveness, it is generally desirable to develop a flexible budget for each revenue-producing department. This requires the separation of departmental costs into fixed and variable elements, which can then be projected within a format similar to that shown for Hypothetical Hospital Department 1 in Figure 6.6. Such a budget allows us to project the cost of providing a unit of service at a number of possible levels of operations. Management must then make a judgment at the beginning of each period as to the probable level of operations for the period. After that judgment has been made, the operating plan, including operating cost goals and service billing prices, can be established for each revenue producing department. As you relate the data in Figure 6.6 to those in Figure 6.5, you will observe that management is projecting an 80 percent level of operations for Department 1 during the next period.

Because the primary billing unit for many hospital services is a day of room occupancy, the level of operations in hospitals typically is expressed in terms of the rate of room occupancy. The flexible budgets setting out

FIGURE 6.5 Hypothetical Hospital Cost Allocation Worksheet

| | Revenue-Producing Cost Centers | | | | Supporting Cost Centers | | | |
	Dept. 1	Dept. 2	Dept. 3	Dept. 4	Dept. 5	Dept. 6	Dept. 7	Total
Direct expenses	$400,000	$ 800,000	$300,000	$600,000	$200,000	$ 80,000	$100,000	$2,480,000
Allocated expenses	80,000	120,000	100,000	150,000	40,000	30,000	30,000	550,000
Total	$480,000	$ 920,000	$400,000	$750,000	$240,000	$110,000	$130,000	$3,030,000
Allocation of Dept. 6 costs[1]	20,000	60,000	10,000	20,000		$110,000		
Allocation of Dept. 7 costs[2]	60,000	30,000	25,000	15,000			$130,000	
Allocation of Dept. 5 costs[3]	100,000	50,000	30,000	60,000	$240,000			
Total	$660,000	$1,060,000	$465,000	$845,000				$3,030,000
Billing units	66,000	10,600	93,000	42,250				
Cost per unit of service	$10	$100	$5	$20				

[1] Department 6 costs are building-related costs allocated on basis of square footage as follows: Dept. 1—4,000; Dept. 2—12,000; Dept. 3—2,000; Dept. 4—4,000.

[2] Department 7 costs are employee-related costs allocated on basis of number of employees as follows: Dept. 1—60; Dept. 2—30; Dept. 3—25; Dept. 4—15.

[3] Department 5 costs are equipment-related costs allocated on basis of cost of equipment in each department as follows: Dept. 1—$1,000,000; Dept. 2—$500,000; Dept. 3—$300,000; Dept. 4—$600,000.

FIGURE 6.6   Hypothetical Hospital Flexible Budget Department 1

Level of Operations (Related to Capacity)	70%	80%	90%	100%
Direct expenses (variable)	$262,500	$300,000	$337,500	$375,000
Direct expenses (fixed)	100,000	100,000	100,000	100,000
Allocated general expenses (fixed)	80,000	80,000	80,000	80,000
Allocated service dept. expenses				
Dept. 6 (fixed)	20,000	20,000	20,000	20,000
Dept. 7 (semifixed)	55,000	60,000	65,000	70,000
Dept. 5 (fixed)	100,000	100,000	100,000	100,000
Total expenses	$617,500	$660,000	$702,500	$745,000
Billing units	57,750	66,000	74,250	82,500
Cost per unit of service	$10.69	$10.00	$9.46	$9.03

the anticipated operating costs at various room occupancy levels is therefore an important instrument in planning future operations and establishing billing rates based on the anticipated costs of providing room occupancy–related hospital services. Flexible budgets for other revenue-producing departments, such as x-ray services, should be prepared and related to various possible levels of operations for those departments.

Budgets are developed and used in the plan phase of the plan-operate-evaluate-plan cycle. However, they should also be used to evaluate operations and guide managerial action at the end of the period. To illustrate that point, let us assume that Department 1 (see Figure 6.6) actually operates at an 85 percent level during the period when it was budgeted at an 80 percent level (see Figure 6.5). Expenses actually incurred during the period are shown in Figure 6.7, along with an analysis of the *variances from the adjusted budget allowances* for the period. Management should pursue the possible causes of unfavorable variances suggested in the notes at the bottom of the analysis.

Historically, Medicare and various other health insurance programs have paid hospitals for treatments of their clients on the basis of the costs of providing those treatments. Such health care costs, representing a significant percentage of the federal budget, have been increasing over the past several years at an annual rate of about 15 percent. Partly because of that experience, cost-based reimbursement has been criticized for encouraging inefficiency. Critics have reasoned that the greater the cost of hospital care, the more the hospitals received in payment from insurers. Also, wide variations in the costs of treating similar diagnoses from hospital to hospital and region to region have been cited as evidence of the inefficiency of cost-based reimbursement. From this historical background and these observations, Congress, as part of its Tax, Equity, and Fiscal Responsibility Act of 1982, developed a proposal for reimbursing hospitals for treatment

**FIGURE 6.7   Hypothetical Hospital Budget Analysis Schedule
              Department 1**

	Actual Expenses	Budget Allocation	Variances
Direct expenses (variable)	$320,000	$318,750	$1,250—Unfavorable[1]
Direct expenses (fixed)	101,000	100,000	1,000—Unfavorable[2]
Allocated general expenses (fixed)	78,000	80,000	2,000—Favorable
Allocated service dept. expenses			
Dept. 6 (fixed)	20,500	20,000	500—Unfavorable[3]
Dept. 7 (semifixed)	65,000	62,500	2,500—Unfavorable[4]
Dept. 5 (fixed)	101,500	100,000	1,500—Unfavorable[5]
Total	$686,000	$681,250	$4,750—Unfavorable

[1] This unfavorable variance should be explained by the Dept. 1 supervisor. It appears that he or she failed to control the variable costs properly in relationship to the actual level of operations. Individual items of expense should be reviewed.
[2] This variance suggests that the departmental supervisor has "overspent" his or her allocation for fixed expenses.
[3,5] These variances have probably been caused by inadequate cost controls in service depts. 6 and 5. Costs should be reviewed with departmental supervisors.
[4] This variance could have been caused either by Dept. 1 having too many employees or by inadequate cost controls in Dept. 7.

of Medicare patients on the basis of a Medicare Prospective Payment Plan.[4] Within less than one year from the submission of that proposal, the Medicare program has evolved from a cost-based, retrospective reimbursement system to a system that pays hospitals on the basis of predetermined prices for treating diagnosis-related groups (DRGs) of patients. The new system, called Medicare Prospective Payment, became effective with each hospital's first cost-recording period beginning on or after October 1, 1983.

The Medicare Prospective Payment System classifies patients into 467 DRGs based on major diagnostic categories defined by the affected body system. The classification is further broken down by principal and secondary diagnoses requiring operating room procedures, age, sex, discharge disposition, and complications. The use of DRGs makes it necessary for hospitals to understand the nature of their "product lines" and to give special attention to measuring, monitoring, and controlling the efficiencies of the services they provide.

The new system places a hospital financially at risk for the costs of services it provides. Those institutions that incur costs less than the fixed

[4] Material relating to Medicare Prospective Payment System summarized from *Medicare Prospective Payment System—Hospital Management Responses to Social Security Amendments of 1983* (Arthur Andersen & Co., 1983).

payment rates will be permitted to keep the savings. Hospitals with costs in excess of the predetermined rates will have to absorb the difference. This forces hospitals to manage available resources effectively by controlling length of stay, use of ancillary services, and the mix of patients treated. To be successful in the new competitive environment, hospitals must be concerned with the *efficiency* as well as the *quality* of the services they provide.

With this radical change in the system of reimbursing hospitals for Medicare payments, we are likely to see other health care insurance programs adopt similar reimbursement programs. If hospitals are to continue to operate effectively in the new reimbursement environment, they are going to *have to give special attention to their accounting and financial reporting practices.* Ultimately hospitals will have to develop detailed profit and loss reports by DRGs to facilitate the identification and correction of inefficiencies. Their information systems will need to be improved. For example, it may be necessary, as a result of operating information accumulated under the new reimbursement plan, for some hospitals to scale down from full-service institutions and to identify a particular market niche that is suitable for them. In the long run, hospitals may need to seek additional revenue sources through such things as the sale of services (either excess capacity or specialized services) to other hospitals. Promotion of such things as pharmacy services and sales to nonpatients and the expansion of fund raising and auxillary activities will also have to be considered as operating alternatives.

Although the hospital is at risk for the costs of the services it provides under the new prospective payment system, *physicians make most of the decisions that affect hospital resource consumption,* particularly in terms of length of stay and use of ancillary services. Therefore, hospitals will need to involve physicians in the management and control of hospital resources. More emphasis will have to be given to improving productivity in the operations of hospitals.

SUMMARY

Although hospitals have many characteristics in common with colleges and universities, there are significant differences, as well as some similarities, in their accounting practices. Hospitals use the pure accrual basis of accounting, including the recognition of depreciation within the framework of fund-accounting techniques.

The primary emphasis in fund designations is on the separation of unrestricted and restricted resources. Unrestricted funds include all resources available for discretional use by management, along with the obligations associated with operations. Fixed assets used in operations are also included in unrestricted funds. Restricted funds include specific purpose funds, plant replacement and expansion funds, and endowment funds.

Because hospital charges generally are based on the cost of services rendered, and because most hospital bills are paid by insurance companies, Medicare, or other agencies on behalf of the patient, much attention is given to cost allocation and cost determination procedures. In the last part of this chapter, we described and illustrated the procedures followed in allocating service department costs to revenue-producing departments. This procedure produces the cost per unit of service, which can be used as a basis for billing patients for services.

QUESTIONS FOR CLASS DISCUSSION

6.1. It has been said that hospitals place less emphasis on fund-accounting techniques than do either governmental units or colleges. Do you agree? Explain.

6.2. Contrast the basis of accounting for hospitals with that for (a) colleges. (b) governmental units.

6.3. The distinction between capital and revenue items coupled with the use of fund entities in the hospital area creates certain accounting problems. (a) What are these problems? (b) How are they solved?

6.4. Compare and contrast the funds and fund groups recommended for hospitals with those suggested for governmental and college entities.

6.5. (a) Define specific purpose funds as used in hospital accounting. (b) Which fund in college and university accounting most closely resembles the specific purpose fund in hospital accounting?

6.6. Explain the relationship between various hospitalization insurance programs and the strong emphasis on development of cost data in hospital accounting procedures.

6.7. Describe the two principal subdivisions normally found in a hospital balance sheet.

6.8. What are the principal sources of revenue normally found in a hospital's statement of revenues and expenses?

6.9. Describe the typical functional classifications found in the operating expenses section of a hospital statement of revenues and expenses.

6.10. Describe the fund entities included in the restricted funds portion of a hospital balance sheet.

EXERCISES

6.1. The Good Turn Hospital inaugurates a building fund campaign. All funds received are to be used for the addition of a new wing.

Funds received during the campaign amount to $250,000. Construction is completed during the year at a cost of $275,000. Unrestricted funds resources are used to meet the extra construction costs. Record all transactions in the appropriate funds.

6.2. The new wing (see Exercise 6.1) is to be depreciated at the rate of 4 percent per year. Record the first year's depreciation.

6.3. The Good Turn Hospital sells used equipment for $4,000. The accounting records show that the equipment originally cost $10,000. Accumulated depreciation amounts to $7,200. Make all journal entries required by this transaction.

6.4. The following account balances appear in the unrestricted funds portion of the statement of changes in fund balances for a hospital:

Transferred from plant replacement and expansion fund	$8,000
Transferred to plant replacement and expansion fund	$5,000

Indicate the related accounts likely to be found in the plant replacement and expansion fund portion of the statement of changes in fund balances. Discuss.

6.5. A hospital purchases $100,000 worth of equipment from its unrestricted funds. Record the transaction. Compare your answer to this exercise with your answer to Exercise 5.6 in Chapter 5. Justify the difference between the entries made to record the transaction for the two organizations.

6.6. General endowment funds for Community Hospital yield revenues in the amount of $25,000. Record this fact in the appropriate funds.

6.7. Central City Hospital estimates that the expense for a day of room occupancy at a 100 percent occupancy level for Department A is $25.75, of which $15.00 is fixed. Department A has 200 rooms.

Required:
1. Prepare a flexible budget showing the anticipated daily departmental costs for Department A at 70 percent, 80 percent, 90 percent, and 100 percent levels of occupancy.
2. Calculate the projected cost per day of room occupancy for Department A at each level of occupancy.
3. What causes the differences in the projected daily room occupancy costs at various levels of occupancy? Explain.

6.8. Central City Hospital (see Exercise 6.7) has actual expenses for Department A during the current year (365 days) of $1,850,000. These include fixed expenses of $1,095,000. The department had an occupancy rate of 92 percent for the year.

Required:

1. Prepare an analysis of the relationships between actual and budgeted expenses for Department A.
2. Comment on your findings in Part 1.

6.9. Community Hospital purchased a specialized piece of equipment from plant replacement and expansion fund cash on January 1, 19XX, for an installed cost of $125,000. The equipment had an estimated useful life of ten years, with estimated salvage value at the end of that time of $35,000. At the close of the calendar year the equipment had an estimated replacement cost new of $137,000 and a revised salvage value of $37,000.

Required:

1. Record the purchase of equipment.
2. Record depreciation of the equipment at the end of the year.
3. Comment on the implications of the end-of-year replacement cost for depreciation practices.

6.10. Mercy Hospital had a billing rate of $88 per day for a single-bed room in the maternity ward. The ward has sixty such beds and experiences a normal occupancy rate of 95 percent for year 19XX. The billing rate is set to cover user costs plus a share of the expected cost of "social services" rendered by the ward. An analysis of the accounts receivable attributable to the ward discloses the following reductions from operating revenues for the year:

Charity services	$378,200
Provision for uncollectible accounts	$106,000

A donation of $15,000, designated to cover charity cases, was also received.

Required:

1. Determine what the billing rate would be if no charity cases (including "bad" accounts) were accepted.
2. What amount is the average paying patient (average period of stay is 3 days) contributing to the coverage of charity cases? Explain.

PROBLEMS

6.1. The following is a comprehensive transaction and financial statements problem.

Hillview Hospital begins its year with the following account balances in its ledger:

Unrestricted Funds

Cash	$ 100,000
Receivables	1,000,000
Allowance for uncollectible accounts	120,000
Inventories of supplies	140,000
Prepaid fiscal services expenses	50,000
Property, plant, and equipment	8,000,000
Accumulated depreciation	3,000,000
Accounts payable	300,000
Accrued general services expenses	100,000
Bonds payable	1,200,000
Fund balance	4,570,000

Restricted Funds
Specific Purpose Funds

Cash	$ 1,000
Grants receivable	60,000
Fund balance	61,000

Plant Replacement and Expansion Funds

Cash	$ 8,000
Investments	600,000
Pledges receivable	50,000
Allowance for uncollectible pledges	10,000
Fund balance—restricted	248,000
Fund balance—other	400,000

Endowment Funds

Cash	$ 40,000
Investments	4,000,000
Fund balance	4,040,000

The following transactions occur during the year:

(a) Patient services are billed in the amount of $6,000,000.

(b) Allowances for charity cases are $500,000 (amount has been billed).

(c) Allowances for uncollectible accounts in the amount of $600,000 are provided.

(d) Receivables in the amount of $4,600,000 are collected.

(e) Receivables in the amount of $620,000 are written off as uncollectible.

(f) The following operating expenses are paid:

Salaries to nurses	$1,600,000
Salaries to other professionals	1,400,000
Salaries to administrators	300,000

(g) Other operating expenses are incurred as follows:

General services	$1,300,000
Fiscal services	250,000
Supplies	125,000

(h) Accounts payable in amount of $1,500,000 are paid.

(i) Unrestricted gifts available for general operations amounting to $225,000 are received.

(j) Income from endowment in the amount of $120,000 is realized.

(k) Otherwise unrestricted pledges toward plant replacement and expansion in the amount of $120,000 are received. It is anticipated that $15,000 of those pledges will be uncollectible.

(l) Pledges for plant replacement and expansion in the amount of $130,000 are collected.

(m) Fixed asset costing $40,000 and having a book value of $12,000 is sold for $15,000.

(n) Plant replacement and expansion fund investments with a book value of $100,000 are sold for $105,000. Income from plant fund investments in the amount of $40,000 is received.

(o) Fixed assets are purchased, using plant replacement and expansion funds, at a cost of $200,000.

(p) Securities for endowment valued at $500,000 are received.

(q) Depreciation for the year amounts to $250,000.

(r) Special purpose fund grants outstanding at the beginning of the year are collected.

(s) A new grant for a specified research project in the amount of $90,000 is received.

(t) Specific purpose projects are completed as part of unrestricted fund operations. These projects are charged at $48,000. The unrestricted fund is reimbursed by the specific purpose fund for these expenses.

(u) Other end-of-period adjustments should be recognized as required by the following end-of-year balances:

Supplies inventory	$120,000
Prepaid fiscal services expenses	70,000
Accrued general services expenses	75,000

Required:

1. Enter the beginning-of-period account balances in the first two columns of a worksheet.

2. Record the transactions for the period in the worksheet.

3. Complete the worksheet and prepare appropriate financial statements for Hillview Hospital.

6.2. The accounting records for Central Hospital include the following four self-balancing accounting entities:

(a) unrestricted funds

(b) specific purpose funds

(c) funds for plant replacement and expansion

(d) endowment funds

The following transactions occur during the fiscal period:

   (a) Patient services are billed in the amount of $3,000,000.

   (b) Receivables in the amount of $2,000,000 are collected.

   (c) Operating expenses are paid in the amount of $1,500,000.

   (d) Unrestricted gifts available for general operations are received amounting to $100,000.

   (e) Securities designated as endowment valued at $300,000 are received.

   (f) A grant is received for a specified research project in the amount of $50,000.

   (g) Part of the special project (see transaction (f)) was completed as part of unrestricted fund operations at a cost of $25,000. The unrestricted fund is reimbursed by the specific purpose fund for these expenses.

   (h) End-of-period adjustments include prepaid operating expenses in the amount of $35,000 and accrued operating expenses in the amount of $40,000.

   (i) A contribution externally designated for plant replacement and expansion in the amount of $300,000 is received.

   (j) Fixed assets to be used in operations are purchased from plant replacement and expansion fund cash at a cost of $150,000.

Required:

On a sheet of worksheet paper, label individual pairs of columns to show the types of fund entities included in the hospital accounting records. Then, journalize the ten transactions listed by recording the accounts debited and credited to the left of the four columns and entering the money amounts as debits and credits in the appropriate fund(s) columns.

6.3. A hospital purchases $50,000 worth of equipment from unrestricted funds and also spends $150,000 of plant replacement and expansion resources for fixed assets during the period.

Required:

Record these transactions. Indicate the fund(s) in which each entry is recorded.

6.4. New Hope Hospital estimates expense for a day of room occupancy when the hospital is fully occupied at $42.50, of which $15.00 is fixed. The hospital has 100 rooms.

Required:

1. Prepare a flexible budget showing the anticipated daily room cost at 70 percent, 80 percent, 90 percent, and 100 percent levels of occupancy.

2. Calculate the projected cost per day, per room for each level of occupancy.

6.5. (AICPA adapted.) These problems refer to the accounts of a large nonprofit hospital that properly maintains four funds: unrestricted, special purpose, endowment, and plant replacement. Select the best answer for each of the following items:

1. The endowment fund consists of several small endowments, each for a special purpose. The hospital treasurer has determined that it would be legally possible and more efficient to "pool" the assets and allocate the resultant revenue. The soundest basis on which to allocate revenue after assets are "pooled" and comply with the special purposes of each endowment would be to

   (a) determine market values of securities or other assets composing each endowment at the time of transfer to the pool and credit revenue to each endowment on that pro rata basis
   (b) determine book value of each endowment at the time of transfer to the pool and credit revenue to each endowment on that pro rata basis
   (c) apportion future revenue in the moving-average ratio that the various endowments have earned revenue in the past
   (d) ask the trustee who administers the pooled assets to make the determination since she is in a position to know which assets are making the greatest contribution

2. How should charity service, contractual adjustments, and bad debts be classified in the statement of revenues and expenses for a hospital?

   (a) All three should be treated as expenses.
   (b) All three should be treated as deductions from patient service revenues.
   (c) Charity service and contractual adjustments should be treated as revenue deductions, whereas bad debts should be treated as an expense.
   (d) Charity service and bad debts should be treated as expenses, whereas contractual adjustments should be treated as a revenue deduction.

3. Depreciation on some hospital fixed assets, referred to as "minor equipment," is not accounted for in the conventional manner. How is depreciation with respect to these assets accounted for?

   (a) ignored on the basis of immateriality
   (b) handled in essentially the same manner as would be the case if the assets were assigned to the activities of a city and were accounted for in its general fund
   (c) determined periodically by inventorying minor equipment and writing the assets down to their value at the inventory date
   (d) recognized only when minor equipment is replaced

4. To ensure the availability of money for improvements, replacement, and expansion of plant, it would be most desirable for the hospital to

   (a) use accelerated depreciation to provide adequate funds for eventual replacement

   (b) use the retirement or replacement system of depreciation to provide adequate funds

   (c) sell assets at the earliest opportunity

   (d) earmark cash in the operating fund for plant replacement in amounts at least equal to the periodic depreciation charges

6.6. (AICPA adapted.) Select the best answer to each of the following items:

1. A gift to a voluntary not-for-profit hospital that is not restricted by the donor should be credited directly to

   (a) fund balance

   (b) deferred revenue

   (c) operating revenue

   (d) nonoperating revenue

2. Depreciation should be recognized in the financial statements of

   (a) proprietary (for-profit) hospitals only

   (b) both proprietary (for-profit) and not-for-profit hospitals

   (c) both proprietary (for-profit) and not-for-profit hospitals, only when they are affiliated with a college or university

   (d) all hospitals, as a memorandum entry not affecting the statement of revenues and expenses

3. An unrestricted pledge from an annual contributor to a voluntary not-for-profit hospital made in December 19X1 and paid in cash in March 19X2 would generally be credited to

   (a) nonoperating revenue in 19X1

   (b) nonoperating revenue in 19X2

   (c) operating revenue in 19X1

   (d) operating revenue in 19X2

4. Glenmore Hospital's property, plant, and equipment (net of depreciation) consists of the following:

Land	$ 500,000
Buildings	10,000,000
Movable equipment	2,000,000

What amount should be included in the restricted fund grouping?

   (a) $0

   (b) $ 2,000,000

   (c) $10,500,000

   (d) $12,500,000

5. On July 1, 19X1, Lilydale Hospital's Board of Trustees designated $200,000 for expansion of outpatient facilities. The $200,000 is expected to be expended in the fiscal year ending June 30, 19X4. In Lilydale's balance sheet at June 30, 19X2, this cash should be classified as a $200,000

    (a) restricted current asset
    (b) restricted noncurrent asset
    (c) unrestricted current asset
    (d) unrestricted noncurrent asset

6. Donated medicines that normally would be purchased by a hospital should be recorded at fair market value and should be credited directly to

    (a) other operating revenue
    (b) other nonoperating revenue
    (c) fund balance
    (d) deferred revenue

7. During the year ended December 31, 19X1, Melford Hospital received the following donations stated at their respective fair values:

Employee services from members of a religious group	$100,000
Medical supplies from an association of physicians. These supplies were restricted for indigent care and were used for such purpose in 19X1	30,000

    How much revenue (both operating and nonoperating) from donations should Melford report in its 19X1 statement of revenues and expenses?

    (a) $0
    (b) $ 30,000
    (c) $100,000
    (d) $130,000

8. Which of the following would normally be included in other operating revenues of a voluntary not-for-profit hospital?

    (a) unrestricted interest income from an endowment fund
    (b) an unrestricted gift
    (c) donated services
    (d) tuition received from an educational program

9. On May 1, 19X4, Lila Lee established a $50,000 endowment fund, the income from which is to be paid to Waller Hospital for general operating purposes. Waller does not control the fund's principal. Lee appointed Anders National Bank as trustee of this fund. What journal entry is required on Waller's books?

	Debit	Credit
(a) Memorandum entry only	—	—
(b) Nonexpendable endowment fund	$50,000	
Endowment fund balance		$50,000
(c) Cash	50,000	
Endowment fund balance		50,000
(d) Cash	50,000	
Nonexpendable endowment fund		50,000

10. Which of the following would be included in the unrestricted funds of a not-for-profit hospital?

    (a) Permanent endowments
    (b) Term endowments
    (c) Board designated funds originating from previously accumulated income
    (d) Plant expansion and replacement funds

Items 11 through 12 are based on the following data:

Under Abbey Hospital's established rate structure, the hospital would have earned patient service revenue of $6,000,000 for the year ended December 31, 19X3. However, Abbey did not expect to collect this amount because of charity allowances of $1,000,000 and discounts of $500,000 to third-party payors. In May 19X3, Abbey purchased bandages from Lee Supply Co. at a cost of $1,000. However, Lee notified Abbey that the invoice was being cancelled and that the bandages were being donated to Abbey. At December 31, 19X3, Abbey had board-designated assets consisting of $40,000 in cash and $700,000 in investments.

11. For the year ended December 31, 19X3, how much should Abbey record as patient service revenue?

    (a) $6,000,000
    (b) $5,500,000
    (c) $5,000,000
    (d) $4,500,000

12. For the year ended December 31, 19X3, Abbey should record the donation of bandages as

    (a) A $1,000 reduction in operating expenses
    (b) nonoperating revenue
    (c) other operating revenue of $1,000
    (d) a memorandum entry only

13. A gift to a voluntary not-for-profit hospital that is not restricted by the donor would be credited directly to

    (a) fund balance
    (b) deferred revenue
    (c) operating revenue
    (d) nonoperating revenue

6.7. (AICPA adapted.) The following selected information was taken from the books and records of Glendora Hospital (a voluntary hospital) as of and for the year ended June 30, 19X2:

(a) Patient service revenue totaled $16,000,000, with allowances and uncollectible accounts amounting to $3,400,000. Other operating revenue aggregated $346,000 and included $160,000 from specific purpose funds. Revenue of $6,000,000 recognized under cost reimbursement agreements is subject to audit and retroactive adjustment by third-party payors. Estimated retroactive adjustments under these agreements have been included in allowances.

(b) Unrestricted gifts and bequests of $410,000 were received.

(c) Unrestricted income from endowment funds totaled $160,000.

(d) Income from board-designated funds aggregated $82,000.

(e) Operating expenses totaled $13,370,000 and included $500,000 for depreciation computed on the straight-line basis. However, accelerated depreciation is used to determine reimbursable costs under certain third-party reimbursement agreements. Net cost reimbursement revenue amounting to $220,000, resulting from the difference in depreciation methods, was deferred to future years.

(f) Also included in operating expenses are pension costs of $100,000, in connection with a noncontributory pension plan covering substantially all of Glendora's employees. Accrued pension costs are funded currently. Prior service cost is being amortized over a period of twenty years. The actuarially computed value of vested and nonvested benefits at year-end amounted to $3,000,000 and $350,000, respectively. The assumed rate of return used in determining the actuarial present value of accumulated plan benefits was 8 percent. The plan's net assets available for benefits at year-end was $3,050,000.

(g) Gifts and bequests are recorded at fair market values when received.

(h) Patient service revenue is accounted for at established rates on the accrual basis.

Required:

1. Prepare a formal statement of revenues and expenses for Glendora Hospital for the year ended June 30, 19X2.

2. Draft the appropriate disclosures in separate notes accompanying the statement of revenues and expenses, referencing each note to its respective item in the statement.

6.8. (AICPA adapted.) The balance sheet for Dexter Hospital as of December 31, 19X1 is shown on page 244. During 19X2 the following transactions occurred:

(a) Gross charges for hospital services, all charged to accounts receivable, were as follows:

Room and board charges	$780,000
Charges for other professional services	321,000

(b) Deductions from gross earnings were as follows:

Provision for uncollectible receivables	$ 30,000
Charity service	15,000

(c) The operating fund paid $18,000 to retire mortgage bonds payable with an equivalent fair value. The operating fund will not be repaid.
(d) During the year the operating fund received general contributions of $50,000 and income from endowment fund investments of $6,500. The operating fund has been designated to receive income earned on endowment fund investments.
(e) New equipment costing $26,000 was acquired through use of plant replacement and expansion fund cash. An x-ray machine that originally cost $24,000 and that had a depreciated cost of $2,400 was sold for $500.
(f) Vouchers totaling $1,191,000 were issued for the following items:

Administrative service expenses	$120,000
Fiscal service expense	95,000
General service expense	225,000
Nursing service expense	520,000
Other professional service expense	165,000
Supplies	60,000
Expenses accrued at December 31, 19X1	6,000

(g) Collections on accounts receivable totaled $985,000. Accounts written off as uncollectible amounted to $11,000.
(h) Cash payments on vouchers payable during the year were $825,000.
(i) Supplies of $37,000 were issued to nursing services.
(j) On December 31, 19X2, accrued interest income on plant fund investments was $800.
(k) Depreciation of buildings and equipment was as follows:

Buildings	$ 44,000
Equipment	73,000

(l) On December 31, 19X2, an accrual of $6,100 was made for fiscal service expense on plant fund bonds.

Required:

1. Record the balance sheet as of December 31, 19X1, and the preceding transactions in a transactions worksheet.
2. Prepare financial statements for Dexter Hospital for the year ending December 31, 19X2.

Dexter Hospital Balance Sheet

Assets

Unrestricted Funds

Current		
Cash		$ 20,000
Accounts receivable	$ 37,000	
Allowance for uncollectible accounts	7,000	30,000
Supplies		14,000
Total current assets		$ 64,000
Other		
Equipment	$ 680,000	
Allowance for depreciation	134,000	$ 546,000
Buildings	$1,750,000	
Allowance for depreciation	430,000	1,320,000
Land		400,000
Total plant and equipment		$2,266,000
Total		$2,330,000

Restricted Funds—Plant Replacement and Expansion Fund

Cash	$ 53,800
Investments	71,200
Total	$ 125,000

Restricted Funds—Endowment Funds

Cash	$ 6,000
Investments	260,000
Total	$ 266,000

Liabilities and Fund Balances

Current		
Accounts payable		$ 16,000
Accrued expenses		6,000
Total current liabilities		$ 22,000
Long-term debt		
Mortgage bonds payable		150,000
Total liabilities		$ 172,000
Fund balance		$2,158,000
		$2,330,000

Fund balance	$ 125,000
Total	$ 125,000

Fund balance	$ 266,000
Total	$ 266,000

ACCOUNTING FOR OTHER NONPROFIT ORGANIZATIONS

7

A number of other organizations, such as school districts, churches, and health and welfare agencies, are classified as nonprofit organizations. The operational characteristics of these organizations are similar in many respects to those of the organizations already discussed. No authoritative statement of principles has been formulated for churches. School district authorities, however, have adopted a statement that closely parallels the municipal statement. Accounting practices for health and welfare agencies are prescribed primarily by two publications: *Standards of Accounting and Financial Reporting for Voluntary Health and Welfare Organizations*[1] and *Audits of Voluntary Health and Welfare Organizations.*[2]

In this chapter, we briefly consider the accounting practices followed by (1) health and welfare organizations, (2) churches, and (3) selected other nonprofit organizations.

HEALTH AND WELFARE ORGANIZATIONS

Health and welfare agencies historically have exhibited less uniformity in their accounting and reporting practices than any other segment of the

---

[1] *Standards of Accounting and Financial Reporting for Voluntary Health and Welfare Organizations* (New York: National Health Council and National Social Welfare Assembly, 1975).

[2] *Audits of Voluntary Health and Welfare Organizations* (New York: American Institute of Certified Public Accountants, 1974).

nonprofit area. These organizations generally follow fund-accounting practices. However, the operations of some of these agencies require no fund
entities other than a general or current fund. In this case, fund-accounting
techniques are similar to accounting procedures followed by businesses.

As we describe and illustrate the accounting procedures followed by
health and welfare agencies, we shall:

1. briefly discuss the official literature defining their generally accepted accounting practices

2. demonstrate how a series of assumed typical transactions for Illustration Health and Welfare Agency should be recorded

3. present illustrative financial statements.

Literature Defining Generally Accepted Accounting Practices

The accounting practices for these organizations historically have often
involved use of the cash or modified cash basis rather than the full accrual
basis. Financial reports have been designed primarily to show the flows
of resources and the financial position of the organization relative to liquid
assets only. As a result, health and welfare organization financial reports
generally have been less comprehensive and complete than reports commonly presented for business entities or for many other nonprofit organizations.

To meet this obvious inadequacy in financial reporting, a joint study
was undertaken by the National Health Council and the National Social
Welfare Assembly, and the result was published in 1964.[3] For many years,
this constituted the most authoritative statement defining accounting practices in the health and welfare area. In general terms, this publication
sought to promote more informative and uniform financial reporting for
health and welfare organizations by establishing certain rules to govern
the content and form of financial statements.

The rules cited in this publication were based on the concept that
financial reports should reflect accountability of the organization to contributors, the public, and other interested parties. They clearly imply that
the reporting organization must recognize that it is "accountable" to its
constituents for operational efficiency as well as for dollars acquired and
spent.

Considerable attention was also given to the detailed implementation
of these rules in the organization and presentation of accounting data.

---

[3] *Standards of Accounting and Financial Reporting for Voluntary Health and Welfare
Organizations* (New York: National Health Council and National Social Welfare Assembly, 1964).

The various recommended financial statements were well illustrated in the last part of the book.

More recently, in 1974, the American Institute of Certified Public Accountants published its Industry Audit Guide, entitled *Audits of Voluntary Health and Welfare Organizations.* This publication sets out accounting practices that, if followed by these organizations, should significantly improve their financial reports. Basically, it recommends an accounting system that is a compromise between the system recommended for colleges and universities and that recommended for hospitals. For current or operating funds, the system closely follows the format prescribed for colleges and universities. It recognizes the need for using both a current unrestricted fund and a current restricted fund in accounting for these resources. The recommended procedures are also similar to those prescribed for college and universities in the use of a land, building, and equipment fund (often referred to as a plant fund) to accumulate the investments in fixed assets along with resources contributed for the acquisitions of such assets. Mortgages and other liabilities relating to fixed assets are also reflected in this fund. The procedures set out in this publication are similar to those for hospitals in their recommendation of the *accrual basis* with full cost determination, including a provision for depreciation.

To implement the concept of dollar accountability, this publication recommends the use of the following funds in accounting for the resources of health and welfare agencies[4]:

1. current unrestricted fund
2. current restricted fund
3. land, building, and equipment fund
4. endowment fund
5. custodian fund
6. loan and annuity fund.

Except for *custodian funds,* all these funds have been described in other sections of this book. These funds are similar to agency funds in the college and university area and are established to account for assets received by an organization to be held or disbursed according to the instructions of the person or organization providing the funds. Generally, revenue generated from investing the resources of a custodian fund must be used according to the wishes of the contributor of the original funds. Therefore, such resources are not shown as part of the health and welfare organization revenue or support. In 1975, *Standards of Accounting and Financial Reporting* was revised to conform to the AICPA Industry Audit Guide.

[4] *Audits,* pp. 2–3.

Typical Transactions Illustrated

We have noted that the accounting system for a health and welfare agency should be designed to disclose both dollar and operational accountability. It should *combine fund-oriented records with the full accrual basis of accounting.* We shall now illustrate how a series of typical health and welfare agency transactions would be recorded in a *transactions worksheet for Illustration Health and Welfare Agency* (Figure 7.1). Assumed beginning-of-period balances are

FIGURE 7.1   Illustration Health and Welfare Agency Transactions Worksheet for Period

	Beginning-of-Period Balances	
Current Funds		
Unrestricted		
Cash	2,500,000	
Pledges receivable net of allowances for collectibles	300,000	
Vouchers payable		150,000
Fund balances		
Designated by governing board for purchase of fixed assets		1,500,000
Undesignated		1,150,000
Total	2,800,000	2,800,000
Restricted		
Cash	15,000	
Fund balance		15,000
Total	15,000	15,000
Total for current funds	2,815,000	2,815,000
Land, Building, and Equipment Fund		
Cash	3,000	
Investments	100,000	
Pledges receivable net of allowances for uncollectibles	20,000	
Building and equipment	650,000	
Accumulated depreciation		250,000
Land	100,000	
Mortgage payable		40,000
Fund balances		
Expended		460,000
Unexpended		123,000
Total	873,000	873,000

shown in the first two columns of the worksheet. A series of assumed transactions, described next, is recorded in the third and fourth columns. Transaction numbers are shown in the worksheet to identify the entries required to record each of them. Operating statement and balance sheet data, derived from those two pairs of columns, are recorded in the last four columns. Financial statements similar to those shown in Figures 7.2, 7.3, and 7.4 (pages 254–259) could then be prepared from those data.

Transactions and Adjustments		Operating Statement Items	Balance Sheet	
		Current Funds		
(2) 2,900,000	(7) 20,000		2,790,000	
(3) 360,000	(9) 2,950,000			
(1) 3,000,000	(2) 2,900,000		400,000	
(9) 2,950,000	(4) 1,970,000			370,000
	(6) 1,200,000			
(7) 20,000				1,480,000
	(10) 190,000			1,340,000
			3,190,000	3,190,000
(1) 200,000	(5) 150,000		65,000	
	(10) 50,000			65,000
			65,000	65,000
			3,255,000	3,255,000
		Land, Building, and Equipment Fund		
(2) 80,000			83,000	
			100,000	
(1) 70,000	(2) 80,000		10,000	
(7) 20,000			670,000	
	(8) 35,000			285,000
			100,000	
				40,000
(10) 35,000	(7) 20,000			445,000
	10) 70,000			193,000
			963,000	963,000

continued on next page

FIGURE 7.1 (*continued*)

	Beginning-of-Period Balances	

Endowment Funds

Cash	8,000	
Investments	2,010,000	
Fund balance		2,018,000
Total	$2,018,000	$2,018,000

Operating Statement Accounts

Revenues
    Contribution revenue—unrestricted
    Contribution revenue—restricted
    Special events revenue
    Legacies and bequests
    Membership dues
    Investment (endowment) revenue
    Miscellaneous revenue
    Contributions to land building and equipment
        fund
    Contributions to endowment fund
Expenses
    Research expenses—restricted
    Research expenses

    Public education expenses

    Counseling service expenses

    Community service expenses

    General education expenses

Fund-raising expenses

Excess of revenues over expenses
    Unrestricted
    Restricted
    Land, building, and equipment fund
    Endowment fund
Total

Transactions and Adjustments			Operating Statement Items	Balance Sheet	

Endowment Funds

Transactions and Adjustments			Operating Statement Items	Balance Sheet	
(1)	5,000			13,000	
				2,010,000	
	(10)	5,000			2,023,000
				$2,023,000	$2,023,000

Operating Statement Accounts

Transactions and Adjustments			Operating Statement Items	
	(1)	3,000,000	3,000,000	
	(1)	200,000	200,000	
	(3)	120,000	120,000	
	(3)	80,000	80,000	
	(3)	20,000	20,000	
	(3)	100,000	100,000	
	(3)	40,000	40,000	
	(1)	70,000	70,000	
	(1)	5,000	5,000	
(5)	150,000		150,000	
(4)	600,000		601,500	
(8)	1,500			
(4)	520,000		526,000	
(8)	6,000			
(4)	300,000		305,500	
(8)	5,500			
(4)	550,000		561,000	
(8)	11,000			
(6)	550,000		556,000	
(8)	6,000			
(6)	650,000		655,000	
(8)	5,000			
(10)	190,000		190,000	
(10)	50,000		50,000	
(10)	35,000		35,000	
(10)	5,000		5,000	
			$3,635,000	$3,635,000

Assumed Transactions

1. Contributions received:

Unrestricted contributions	$3,000,000 (in pledges)
Restricted contributions	200,000 (in cash)
For building fund	70,000 (in pledges)
For endowment fund	5,000 (in cash)

2. Collected pledges as follows:

Unrestricted contributions	$2,900,000
Building fund	80,000

3. Other unrestricted revenues received in cash:

Special events (net of direct costs of $60,000)	$ 120,000
Legacies and bequests	80,000
Membership dues	20,000
Investment income	100,000
Miscellaneous	40,000

4. Program expenses incurred (handled through vouchers payable):

Research	$ 600,000
Public education	520,000
Counseling services	300,000
Community services	550,000

5. Program expenses paid from restricted resources:

Research	$ 150,000

6. Support and sustentation expenses (handled through vouchers payable):

General administration	$ 550,000
Fund raising	650,000

7. Other changes in fund balances:

Fixed assets acquired by use of unrestricted funds	$ 20,000

8. Depreciation of fixed assets allocated as follows:

Program services:

Research	$ 1,500
Public education	6,000
Counseling services	5,500
Community services	11,000

Support and sustentation:

General administration	6,000
Fund raising	5,000

9. Paid vouchers payable in amount of $2,950,000

10. Transferred excess of revenues over expenses to fund balance accounts

Financial Statements

After completing the transaction worksheet shown in Figure 7.1, we could prepare formal financial statements for Illustration Health and Welfare Agency from the data shown in the operating statement and balance sheet columns of that worksheet. However, because those statements would include only a limited number of accounts, we now present the financial statements for Model Voluntary Health and Welfare Service as they appear in the AICPA Audit Guide to show how formal financial statements for health and welfare agencies should be organized.

The all-inclusive, multiple-column operating statement, entitled "statement of support, revenue and expenses, and changes in fund balances" (Figure 7.4) reflects two principal categories of revenues. First and most significant is "public support." The second category is labeled "revenue" and includes such things as membership dues, program service fees, sales of materials, investment income, and gains on investment transactions. The expense section of the statement is divided into two major categories. One is labeled "program services" and includes expenses incurred in implementing the services of the organization. The second, described as "supporting services," includes the costs of managing the organization and raising funds. A third category, sometimes included, is entitled "payments to national organization."[5]

One of the significant aspects of financial reporting in the health and welfare area is the need for distinguishing between the *sustentation costs,* shown as supporting services expenses in the illustrated operating statement, and *service implementation costs,* also referred to as program service expenses. We may think of sustentation costs as the *expenses incurred in keeping the organization in operation.* They include such things as fund-raising costs and administrative outlays that are not directly related to carrying out the services the entity was organized to provide. These can be thought of as overhead costs associated with sustaining the entity. On the other hand, service implementation costs include the outlays made to furnish the services the organization was created to provide. The third subdivision sometimes found in the expenses section—entitled "payments to national organization"—indicates the extent to which local contributions are being used to finance the national operations of the agency.

Although the term *sustentation costs* can be defined with some degree of clarity, it is often much more difficult in actual practice to identify the outlays that it includes. For example, one of the services expected of the American Cancer Association is that of educating the public concerning the detection of cancer symptoms. The cost of printing and distributing literature that contains this information and also invites the public to contribute to the organization is difficult to allocate between sustentation and service implementation costs except on an arbitrary basis. That is one of the reasons why the *Standards* publication gives considerable attention to these allocation procedures.[6] Nevertheless, discerning potential contributors are always interested in knowing how many cents out of each dollar of their contributions are actually being used to provide the intended ser-

[5] Ibid. (Exhibit A).
[6] Ibid., pp. 61–67.

**FIGURE 7.2 Model Voluntary Health and Welfare Service
Statement of Functional Expenses for Fiscal Period**

		19X2 Program Services			
	Research	Public Health Education	Professional Education and Training	Community Services	Total
Salaries	$ 45,000	$291,000	$251,000	$269,000	$ 856,000
Employee health and retirement benefits	4,000	14,000	14,000	14,000	46,000
Payroll taxes, etc.	2,000	16,000	13,000	14,000	45,000
Total salaries and related expenses	51,000	321,000	278,000	297,000	947,000
Professional fees and contract service payments	1,000	10,000	3,000	8,000	22,000
Supplies	2,000	13,000	13,000	13,000	41,000
Telephone and telegraph	2,000	13,000	10,000	11,000	36,000
Postage and shipping	2,000	17,000	13,000	9,000	41,000
Occupancy	5,000	26,000	22,000	25,000	78,000
Rental of equipment	1,000	24,000	14,000	4,000	43,000
Local transportation	3,000	22,000	20,000	22,000	67,000
Conferences, conventions, meetings	8,000	19,000	71,000	20,000	118,000
Printing and publications	4,000	56,000	43,000	11,000	114,000
Awards and grants	1,332,000	14,000	119,000	144,000	1,609,000
Miscellaneous	1,000	4,000	6,000	4,000	15,000
Total expenses before depreciation	1,412,000	539,000	612,000	568,000	3,131,000
Depreciation of buildings and equipment	2,000	5,000	6,000	10,000	23,000
Total expenses	$1,414,000	$544,000	$618,000	$578,000	$3,154,000

Manage- ment and General	Fund Raising	Total	Total Expenses 19X2	19X1
$331,000	$368,000	$ 699,000	$1,555,000	$1,433,000
22,000	15,000	37,000	83,000	75,000
18,000	18,000	36,000	81,000	75,000
371,0000	401,000	772,000	1,719,000	1,583,000
26,000	8,000	34,000	56,000	53,000
18,000	17,000	35,000	76,000	71,000
51,000	23,000	38,000	74,000	68,000
13,000	30,000	43,000	84,000	80,000
30,000	27,000	57,000	135,000	126,000
3,000	16,000	19,000	62,000	58,000
23,000	30,000	53,000	120,000	113,000
38,000	13,000	51,000	169,000	156,000
14,000	64,000	78,000	192,000	184,000
—	—	—	1,609,000	1,448,000
16,000	21,000	37,000	52,000	64,000
567,000	650,000	1,217,000	4,348,000	4,004,000
7,000	4,000	11,000	34,000	32,000
$574,000	$654,000	$1,228,000	$4,382,000	$4,036,000

19X2 Supporting Services

FIGURE 7.3 Model Voluntary Health and Welfare Service Balance Sheets, December 31, 19X2, and 19X1

Assets	19X2	19X1
Current Funds, Unrestricted		
Cash	$2,207,000	$2,530,000
Investments		
For long-term purposes	2,727,000	2,245,000
Other	1,075,000	950,000
Pledges receivable less allowance for uncollectibles		
of $105,000 and $92,000	475,000	363,000
Inventories of educational materials at cost	70,000	61,000
Accrued interest, other receivables, and prepaid expenses	286,000	186,000
Total	$6,840,000	$6,335,000
Current Funds, Restricted		
Cash	$ 3,000	$ 5,000
Investments	71,000	72,000
Grants receivable	58,000	46,000
Total	$ 132,000	$ 123,000
Land, Building, and Equipment Fund		
Cash	$ 3,000	$ 2,000
Investments	177,000	145,000
Pledges receivable less allowance for uncollectibles of		
$7,500 and $5,000	32,000	25,000
Land, buildings, and equipment at cost less accumulated		
depreciation of $296,000 and $262,000	516,000	513,000
Total	$ 728,000	$ 685,000
Endowment Funds		
Cash	$ 4,000	$ 10,000
Investments	1,944,000	2,007,000
Total	$1,948,000	$2,017,000

Liabilities and Fund Balances	19X2	19X1
Current Funds, Unrestricted		
Accounts payable	$ 148,000	$ 139,000
Research grants payable	596,000	616,000
Contributions designated for future periods	245,000	219,000
Total liabilities and deferred revenues	989,000	974,000
Fund balances		
Designated by the governing board for		
Long-term investments	2,800,000	2,300,000
Purchases of new equipment	100,000	—
Research purposes	1,152,000	1,748,000
Undesignated, available for general activities	1,799,000	1,313,000
Total fund balance	5,851,000	5,361,000
Total	$6,840,000	$6,335,000

Current Funds, Restricted

	19X2	19X1
Fund balances		
Professional education	$ 84,000	$ —
Research grants	48,000	123,000
Total	$ 132,000	$ 123,000

Land, Building, and Equipment Fund

	19X2	19X1
Mortgage payable, 8% due 19XX	$ 32,000	$ 36,000
Fund balances		
Expended	484,000	477,000
Unexpended—restricted	212,000	172,000
Total fund balance	696,000	649,000
Total	$ 728,000	$ 685,000

Endowment Funds

	19X2	19X1
Fund balance	$1,948,000	$2,017,000
Total	$1,948,000	$2,017,000

FIGURE 7.4 Model Voluntary Health and Welfare Service Statement of Support, Revenue, and Expenses and Changes in Fund Balances—Year Ended December 31, 19X2, with Comparative Totals of 19X1

| | 19X2 | | | | Total All Funds | |
| | Current Funds | | Land, Building, and Equipment Fund | Endowment Fund | | |
	Unrestricted	Restricted			19X2	19X1
Public support and revenue						
Public support						
Contributions (net of estimated uncollectible pledges of $195,000 in 19X2 and $150,000 in 19X1)	$3,764,000	$162,000	$ —	$ 2,000	$3,928,000	$3,976,000
Contributions to building fund	—	—	72,000	—	72,000	150,000
Special events (net of direct costs of $181,000 in 19X2 and $163,000 in 19X1)	104,000	—	—	—	104,000	92,000
Legacies and bequests	92,000	—	—	4,000	96,000	129,000
Received from federated and nonfederated campaigns (which incurred related fund-raising expenses of $38,000 in 19X2 and $29,000 in 19X1)	275,000	—	—	—	275,000	308,000
Total public support	$4,235,000	$162,000	$ 72,000	$ 6,000	$4,475,000	$4,655,000
Revenue						
Membership dues	17,000	—	—	—	17,000	12,000
Investment income	98,000	10,000	—	—	108,000	94,000
Realized gain on investment transactions	200,000	—	—	25,000	225,000	275,000
Miscellaneous	42,000	—	—	—	42,000	47,000
Total revenue	$ 357,000	$ 10,000	—	$ 25,000	$ 392,000	$ 428,000
Total support and revenue	$4,592,000	$172,000	$ 72,000	$ 31,000	$4,867,000	$5,083,000

Expenses						
Program services						
Research	1,257,000	155,000	2,000	—	1,414,000	1,365,000
Public health education	539,000	—	5,000	—	544,000	485,000
Professional education and training	612,000	—	6,000	—	618,000	516,000
Community services	568,000	—	10,000	—	578,000	486,000
Total program services	$2,976,000	$155,000	$ 23,000	—	$3,154,000	$2,852,000
Supporting services						
Management and general	567,000	—	7,000	—	574,000	638,000
Fund raising	642,000	—	12,000	—	654,000	546,000
Total supporting services	$1,209,000	—	$ 19,000	—	$1,228,000	$1,184,000
Total expenses	$4,185,000	$155,000	$ 42,000	—	$4,382,000	$4,036,000
Excess (deficiency) of public support and revenue over expenses	$ 407,000	$ 17,000	$ 30,000	$ 31,000		
Other changes in fund balances						
Property and equipment acquisitions from unrestricted funds	(17,000)	—	17,000	—		
Transfer of realized endowment fund appreciation	100,000	—	—	(100,000)		
Returned to donor	—	(8,000)	—	—		
Fund balances, beginning of year	5,361,000	123,000	649,000	2,017,000		
Fund balances, end of year	$5,851,000	$132,000	$696,000	$1,948,000		

vices, and the accounting procedures for these organizations must be designed to meet that need.

One of the important changes reflected in the 1975 *Standards* publication is recognition of the need to record and report depreciation as an expense. This publication, as well as the AICPA publication, recommends the disclosure of depreciation expense in the statement of functional expenses (see Figure 7.2).

The balance sheet for voluntary health and welfare agencies generally is presented within a format similar to that used for colleges and universities (see Figure 7.3). However, the *Standards* publication also suggests the possibility of using an alternate columnar format listing the assets, liabilities, and fund balances of each fund in a separate column, with the totals accumulated in an extreme right column.[7]

ACCOUNTING FOR CHURCHES

Churches generally operate exclusively by appropriation control. Fund-accounting practices usually are followed. Typically, general or current fund expenditures are planned by the pastor and officers to provide a specific program of services. The budgetary process is, in that way, similar to that followed by governmental units.

The proposed service plan or budget generally is presented to the congregation for acceptance, modification, or rejection. Once approved by the membership, the budget becomes the operating plan for the church during the ensuing fiscal period. Contributions are solicited to carry out the program, and expenditures are controlled within the limits of budgetary allowances.

As a result of their strong emphasis on appropriation control and dollar accountability, churches often use the *cash* or *modified cash basis* of reporting. Both revenues and expenditures are related to the budget plan. Although budgetary data can be recorded in the accounts as illustrated for governmental entities, the more common practice is to relate actual and budgetary amounts to each other only in the periodic statements of revenues and expenditures. Figure 7.5 (pages 262–263) shows the form and some of the account titles that are typically used in reporting the revenues and expenditures for a church.

The *relationship of benevolences to total budgeted expenditures* is generally considered an important element to be disclosed in the operating statement. This is consistent with the basic operating philosophy of most churches, which calls for each church to seek to help others as well as to sustain its own program of ministering to its members.

The general or current fund balance sheet for a church typically dis-

[7] Ibid. (Exhibit D).

closes only appropriate assets and claims against those assets. Fixed assets and long-term obligations may be disclosed in a separate plant fund balance sheet, but they are more often completely omitted from the financial reports.

The following illustration shows how two assumed transactions should be recorded in a transactions worksheet (Figure 7.6, page 264) and how financial statements may be prepared from the worksheet data (Figures 7.7 and 7.8, page 265). The statement of revenues and expenditures shows only control account balances in the expenditures section. In actual practice these would be subdivided as shown in Figure 7.5.

Assumed Transactions

1.	Receipts for period	
	Church school offering	$ 100
	Plate offering	200
	Pledges	$10,000
	Miscellaneous	200
2.	Disbursements for period	
	Benevolences	$ 1,500
	Christian education	200
	Music program	100
	Staff salaries	4,000
	Includes payroll taxes amounting to $100 and withholding taxes of $200	
	Current expenditures	1,000
	Building expenditures	1,500

SELECTED OTHER NONPROFIT ORGANIZATIONS

In September 1978, the AICPA issued a statement of position on accounting principles and recording practices for certain other nonprofit organizations.[8] This statement is intended to define accounting practices for nonprofit organizations other than those already covered by existing AICPA audit guides. By implication, therefore, it prescribes accounting practices for organizations such as churches, schools, museums, and foundations. Like the audit guides, it outlines procedures that should be followed if the organization is to have its financial statements recognized as being prepared in accordance with generally accepted accounting principles. It

[8] *Statement of Position on Accounting Principles and Reporting Practices for Certain Nonprofit Organizations* (New York: American Institute of Certified Public Accountants, 1978).

FIGURE 7.5   Model Church Statement of Revenues and Expenditures, Last Month of Fiscal Year

	Amount		Budget		
	This Month	*Year to Date*	*This Month*	*Year to Date*	*Year to Date Over or (Under)*
Revenues					
Church school offering					
Plate offering					
Pledges for 19X1					
Pledges for 19X2					
Miscellaneous					
Total revenues					
Expenditures					
Benevolences					
Christian education					
Literature					
Church school supplies					
Conference and camp fund					
Outside speakers and leaders					
Parties and recreation					
Miscellaneous					
Subtotal					
Music					
Staff					
Minister					
Minister of education					
Secretary					
Janitor and maid					
Subtotal					
Current expenses					
Printing and office supplies					

FIGURE 7.5 (*continued*)

	Amount		Budget		
	This Month	Year to Date	This Month	Year to Date	Year to Date Over or (Under)
Custodian supplies					
Miscellaneous					
Subtotal					
Building					
Insurance (real estate and auto)					
Utilities					
Maintenance					
Subtotal					
Debt retirement					
Total expenditures					
Revenues over (under) expenditures					

is not, however, an authoritative pronouncement. Also, in many instances, such recognition is not necessary for these organizations. As a result, churches and many of the other organizations already mentioned probably will continue to use the dollar accountability reporting practices we have already described.

The more significant requirements of the AICPA statement are as follows:

1. The full accrual basis of accounting should be used.

2. Separate funds should be used for financial reporting purposes only to disclose the nature and amounts of *significant externally restricted* resources.

3. Financial reports should include a balance sheet, a statement of activity or operations, and a statement of changes in financial position.

4. Combined statements should be prepared for all financially inter-related segments of an organization.

FIGURE 7.6 Illustration Church Transactions Worksheet—for Period

	Beginning-of-Period Balances		Transactions		Operating Statement Items		Balance Sheet Items	
Cash in bank	11,800		(1) 10,500	2,000			14,300	
Petty cash	500						500	
Payroll taxes payable		100		(2) 100				200
Withholding taxes payable		200		(2) 200				400
Fund balance		12,000						12,000
Revenues from church school				(1) 100		100		
Revenues from plate offering				(1) 200		200		
Revenues from pledges				(1) 10,000		10,000		
Miscellaneous revenues				(1) 200		200		
Expenditures								
Benevolences			(2) 1,500		1,500			
Christian education			(2) 200		200			
Music program			(2) 100		100			
Staff salaries			(2) 4,000		4,000			
Current operations			(2) 1,000		1,000			
Building costs			(2) 1,500		1,500			
Totals	12,300	12,300	18,800	18,800	8,300	10,500	14,800	12,600
Excess of revenues over expenditures					2,200			2,200
Totals	12,300	12,300	18,800	18,800	10,500	10,500	14,800	14,800

FIGURE 7.7 Illustration Church Statement of Revenues and Expenditures—for Period

	Actual Amounts	Budget Amounts	Actual Over or (Under)
Revenues			
Church school offering	$ 100	$ 150	$(50)
Plate offering	200	225	(25)
Pledges	10,000	9,800	200
Miscellaneous	200	300	(100)
Total revenues	$10,500	$10,475	$ 25
Expenditures			
Benevolences	$ 1,500	$ 1,500	$ 0
Christian education	200	250	(50)
Music	100	75	25
Staff salaries	4,000	4,000	0
Current operations	1,000	1,100	(100)
Building costs	1,500	1,500	0
Total expenditures	$ 8,300	$ 8,425	$(125)
Excess of revenues over expenditures	$ 2,200	$ 2,050	$ 150

FIGURE 7.8 Illustration Church Balance Sheet—End of Period

Assets		Liabilities and Fund Balance		
Cash in bank	$14,300	Payroll taxes payable	$ 200	
Petty cash	500	Withholding taxes payable	400	$ 600
Total assets	$14,800	Fund balance		
		Beginning-of-period balance	$12,000	
		Excess of revenues over expenditures for period	2,200	14,200
		Total liabilities and fund balance		$14,800

5. Pledges receivable should be recorded when they are received. Appropriate provision should be made for probable losses in collecting the pledges. Revenue from pledges should be recognized in the year that the donor intended the resources to be used. If that is not clear, they should be recognized as revenue in the year the donors indicate the pledges will be paid. That means that the credit offsetting the recognition of a pledge receivable can be to either deferred pledge income or pledge income, depending on the stipulations associated with the pledge.

6. Current gifts with restricted uses should be recorded by crediting deferred income in the operating fund rather than by creating a separate current funds restricted accounting entity. Restricted grants should be handled in the same manner.

7. Certain specified criteria must be met before donated and contributed services may be recognized as revenue.

8. Expenses should be reported according to functional or program classifications similar to the way they are reported for health and welfare agencies.

9. Sustentation expenses (management and general expenses plus fund-raising expenses) should be separately disclosed.

10. Investments may be reflected in the financial statement at either market value or the lower of cost or market value. Valuation adjustments should be handled in accordance with FASB Statement 12.

11. Fixed assets should be capitalized, and depreciation should be recognized periodically, except on structures used primarily as houses of worship or that are inexhaustible, such as landmarks, monuments, cathedrals, or historical treasures.

Private foundations constitute a unique segment of the nonprofit area, requiring specialized accounting procedures. In 1977, Price Waterhouse & Company conducted a survey of the financial reporting and accounting practices followed by these enterprise units.[9] The study showed that approximately two-thirds of the large foundations used the accrual basis of accounting; the other one-third essentially reported on the cash basis. Furthermore, of the fifty foundations surveyed, forty-seven presented a balance sheet or an equivalent statement of position. The financial report also generally included a statement of income, expenses, and changes in fund balance or an equivalent operating statement plus a statement of changes in fund balance. Only five of the fifty foundations surveyed presented a statement of changes in financial position.

SUMMARY

Health and welfare organizations historically have followed accounting practices emphasizing dollar accountability similar to those described for colleges and universities. Recent publications, however, clearly imply a need for reflecting operational accountability, with an emphasis on the

[9] *A Survey of Financial Accounting and Reporting Practices of Private Foundations* (New York: Price Waterhouse & Co., 1977).

disclosure of full costs, by calling for the use of the accrual basis of accounting including the recognition of depreciation expense and a careful distinction between sustentation, or overhead costs, and service-implementation expenses.

Churches operate within a system of appropriation control similar to that followed in the governmental area. As a result, the operating reports of these organizations emphasize the relationships between budgeted revenues and actual revenues and between budgeted expenditures and actual expenditures. Church balance sheets typically disclose only appropriable resources (often only cash) and the short-term obligations against those resources.

In the last part of this chapter we briefly discussed the significant requirements of the AICPA Statement of Position regarding accounting practices for certain other nonprofit organizations.

QUESTIONS FOR CLASS DISCUSSION

7.1. (a) How are the financial operations of a church similar to and different from those of a college or university? (b) Do the differences justify a greater emphasis on appropriation control practices in accounting for churches? Justify your position.

7.2. What is the common underlying operational objective of all organizations studied in Chapters 3, 4, 5, 6, and 7?

7.3. The pastor of a church believes that his congregation should raise a budget of $200,000. A deacon, who also operates a large business establishment, states that the church should determine its needs before it begins to talk about the amount to be solicited for the budget. The pastor replies that an infinite amount of resources is needed to further the cause of Christianity. Therefore, he suggests that the congregation should first consider its giving potential and then apportion that among the various needs. Discuss the implications of these two points of view.

7.4. Discuss briefly the importance of the relationship between the sustentation expenses of a health and welfare agency and its service-implementation expenses.

7.5. Compare and contrast the accounting system recommended in *Audits of Voluntary Health and Welfare Organizations* with the systems recommended for colleges and universities and for hospitals.

7.6. What kinds of resources would you expect to see included in the custodian fund for a health and welfare agency?

7.7. Discuss the importance of distinguishing between benevolences and local church expenditures in the statement of revenues and expenditures for a church.

EXERCISES

7.1. A health and welfare agency realized revenues from its annual solicitation campaign in the amount of $50,000. The direct cost of the funds solicitation campaign was $8,000. Annual administrative costs amount to $15,000. It is estimated that the administrative staff spends one-third of its time soliciting funds for the organization. All resources left after paying for the fund drive and administrative costs are used directly to implement services of the organization. Calculate the sustentation expenses for the organization. What portion of each dollar contributed is used for sustaining the organization? What portion of each dollar contributed is used for service implementation?

7.2. Discuss the significance of the data developed in Exercise 7.1.

7.3. A voluntary health and welfare organization solicits and receives pledges for construction of a new building in the amount of $80,000. It is estimated that 5 percent of the pledges will be uncollectible. Record the preceding data in the accounts of the health and welfare agency.

7.4. A health and welfare agency receives cash in the amount of $10,000 that is designated to be used in financing specified research. Record the receipt of these funds.

7.5. A church treasurer receives the morning offering of her church. The offering includes pledge envelopes containing checks and cash in the amount of $900 plus currency in the amount of $50. Journalize the receipt of these revenues in the accounting records of the church.

7.6. The church treasurer in Exercise 7.5 writes checks covering the following items:

Staff salaries	$ 500
Church school literature	80
Printing and office supplies	100
Furnishings and equipment	3,000

Journalize these disbursements.

7.7. The National Health Agency has a $400,000 building with an expected life of forty years and no salvage value. Depreciation is not to be funded.

Required:

1. Record the depreciation for the current year, indicating the fund(s) in which the entry would be recorded.

2. What will be the final disposition of depreciation expense recognized in Part 1?

7.8. The budget for First Church shows estimated revenues of $7,000 from pledges, $350 from plate offerings, and $50 from miscellaneous contributions for the month of January 19XX. Actual revenues for the month were $6,500 from pledges, $375 from plate offerings, and $50 from miscellaneous sources. The budget also reflected planned expenditures for the month of $110 for music program, $4,000 for staff salaries, $1,500 for current operating expenditures, and $1,500 for building maintenance. Actual expenditures for January were:

Staff salaries	$4,000
Current operations	1,450
Music program	150
Building maintenance costs	1,500

Required:

Prepare a statement of revenues and expenditures for January 19XX to be presented to the board of deacons.

7.9. The Activist Health Agency has a $200,000 building with an expected life of forty years. Estimated salvage value at the end of that time is expected to be $20,000. Depreciation is not to be funded.

Required:

Record the depreciation for the current year as recommended by AICPA Audit Guide.

7.10. The American Health Society has received contributions of $10,000. The society spent $2,000 in soliciting the donations and $8,000 in service-implementation costs.

Required:

1. Record the above transactions.
2. What observations can be made from these transactions regarding the operations of the society?

PROBLEMS

7.1. This is a comprehensive problem illustrating the procedures for recording the various transactions of health and welfare organizations discussed and illustrated in this chapter.

The Social Service Health and Welfare Agency shows the following balances in its accounting records at the beginning of the year:

Unrestricted current funds assets and liabilities:

Cash	$1,250,000
Pledges receivable (net of allowance for uncollectible accounts)	150,000
Vouchers payable	75,000

(Note: Fund balance includes $750,000 designated by the governing board for the purchase of fixed assets.)

Restricted current fund assets:

Cash	7,500

Land, buildings, and equipment fund assets and liabilities:

Cash	1,500
Investments	50,000
Pledges receivable (net of allowance for uncollectible accounts)	10,000
Building and equipment	325,000
Allowance for depreciation	125,000
Land	100,000
Mortgage payable	40,000

Endowment fund assets:

Cash	4,000
Investments	1,005,000

The agency had the following transactions during the year:

(a) Received contributions as follows:

Unrestricted in the form of pledges (net of uncollectible amounts)	$1,500,000
Restricted (in cash)	100,000
For building fund (in pledges)	35,000
For endowment fund (in cash)	2,500

(b) The following pledges were collected:

Unrestricted pledges	$1,450,000
Building fund pledges	40,000

(c) Other unrestricted revenues were received in cash as follows:

Revenues from special events (net of direct costs)	$ 60,000
Legacies and bequests	40,000
Membership dues	10,000
Investment income	50,000
Miscellaneous revenues	20,000

(d) Program expenses incurred:

Research	$ 300,000
Public education	260,000
Medical services	150,000
Community information services	75,000

(e) Research expenses paid from restricted resources amounted to $ 75,000

(f) Support sustentation expenses incurred (handled through vouchers payable):

General administration	$ 275,000

Fund-raising expenses		325,000

(g) Fixed assets costing $10,000 were acquired by the use of unrestricted resources

(h) Depreciation of fixed assets was allocated as follows:

Research	$	750
Public education		3,000
Medical services		2,750
Community information services		5,500
General administration		3,000
Fund raising		2,500

(i) Paid vouchers payable in the amount of $1,425,000.

(j) Transferred excesses of revenues over expenses to fund balance accounts.

Required:

1. Prepare a transactions worksheet similar to the one illustrated in Figure 7.1 and record the preceding transactions in it.
2. Prepare the appropriate financial statements for Social Service Health and Welfare Agency.

7.2. Hillcrest Blood Bank, a nonprofit organization handling all of operations through one operating fund, shows the following balance sheets as of June 30, 19X1, and June 30, 19X2, and the statement of cash receipts and disbursements for the year ended June 30, 19X2.

Hillcrest Blood Bank Balance Sheet

	June 30, 19X1	June 30, 19X2
Assets		
Cash	$ 2,712	$ 3,093
U.S. treasury bonds	15,000	16,000
Accounts receivable—sales of blood:		
Hospitals	1,302	1,448
Individuals	425	550
Inventories:		
Blood	480	640
Supplies and serum	250	315
Furniture and equipment, less depreciation	4,400	4,050
Total assets	$24,569	$26,096
Liabilities and surplus		
Accounts payable—supplies	$ 325	$ 275
Fund balance	24,244	25,821
Total liabilities and fund balance	$24,569	$26,096

Hillcrest Blood Bank Statement of Cash Receipts and Disbursements for the Year Ended June 30, 19X2

Balance, July 1, 19X1			
Cash in bank			$ 2,712
Receipts			
From hospitals:			
Hillcrest Hospital	$7,702		
Good Samaritan Hospital	3,818	$11,520	
Individuals		6,675	
From other blood banks		602	
From sales of serum and supplies		2,260	
Interest on bonds		525	
Gifts and bequests		4,928	
Total receipts			26,510
Total to be accounted for			$29,222
Disbursements:			
Laboratory expense:			
Serum	$3,098		
Salaries	3,392		
Supplies	3,533		
Laundry and miscellaneous	277	$10,300	
Other expenses and disbursements:			
Salaries	$5,774		
Dues and subscriptions	204		
Rents and utilities	1,404		
Blood testing	2,378		
Payments to other blood banks for blood given to members away from home	854		
Payments to professional blood donors	2,410		
Other expenses	1,805		
Purchase of U.S. treasury bond	1,000	15,829	
Total disbursements			26,129
Balance, June 30, 19X2			$ 3,093

Required:

1. Prepare a transactions worksheet for the Hillcrest Blood Bank that develops data for an accrual-based operating statement and end-of-period balance sheet.
2. Prepare appropriate accrual-based financial statements.
3. Assume now that the treasury bonds represent endowment funds and that Hillcrest follows accounting practices prescribed for health and welfare agencies. Prepare a balance sheet as of June 30, 19X2.

7.3. First Church began its 19X1 operations with a cash balance of $5,000. It also had vouchers payable in the amount of $3,090 outstanding. (All vouchers payable are for current expense items.) During the year the following actions and transactions occurred:

(a) A budget calling for estimated revenues of $105,000 and antici-
pated expenditures of $105,000 was adopted by the congregation.
Estimated revenues were subdivided into pledge revenues of
$101,000 and other anticipated offerings and gifts in the amount
of $4,000. Anticipated expenditures are subdivided into the follow-
ing seven categories:

Benevolences	$ 15,000
Christian education	6,200
Music	600
Staff	48,800
Current expenses	8,700
Building maintenance	13,700
Debt retirement	12,000
Total	$105,000

(b) Cash receipts for the year were as follows:

Pledge offering	$ 98,000
Other offerings and gifts	5,000
Total	$103,000

(c) Cash disbursements for the year were as follows:

Benevolences	$ 12,000
Christian education	6,000
Staff	50,000
Current expenses	8,500
Building maintenance	14,000
Debt retirement	12,000
Total	$102,500

(d) Unpaid vouchers (all for current expenses) at the end of the year
amount to $2,700.

Required:

1. Record the year's transactions in a transactions worksheet. It
should be organized to develop a statement of revenues and expenditures for the year and an end-of-year balance sheet.
2. Prepare a statement of revenues and expenditures showing the
relationship between the budgeted and actual operations.
3. Comment on the data shown in the statement prepared in Part
2, above.

7.4. Service Health and Welfare Agency trial balance as of December 31,
19X1, is shown next.

Service Health and Welfare Agency Trial Balance— December 31, 19X1

Current Funds—Unrestricted

Cash	$ 220,000	
Investments	270,000	
Pledges receivable	105,000	
Prepaid expenses	21,000	
Accounts payable		$ 15,000
Fund balance—undesignated		567,000
Contributions		375,000
Legacies and bequests		10,000
Investment income		9,000
Fund-raising expense	60,000	
Management and general	55,000	
Research expenses	125,000	
Public health education expense	65,000	
Community services expense	55,000	
Total	$ 976,000	$ 976,000

Current Funds—Restricted

Cash	$ 300	
Pledges receivable	15,700	
Fund balance		$ 15,000
Contributions		16,000
Designated research expense	15,000	
Total	$ 31,000	$ 31,000

Land, Building, and Equipment Fund

Cash	$ 3,000	
Investments	18,000	
Land, building, and equipment	80,000	
Allowance for depreciation		$ 30,000
Mortgage payable		3,000
Fund balance—expended		47,000
Fund balance—unexpended		20,700
Depreciation expense	8,000	
Contributions		7,000
Interest income		1,600
Interest expense	300	
Total	$ 109,300	$ 109,300
Grand total	$1,116,300	$1,116,300

Required:

1. Prepare appropriate financial statements for Service Health and Welfare Agency for the year ending December 31, 19X1. Building and equipment expenses should be distributed as follows:

Fund raising	10%
Management and general	15%
Research	20%
Public health education	35%
Community services	20%

2. What portion of each dollar of public support and revenue has been spent for supporting services and for program services?

7.5. (AICPA adapted.) Select the best answer to each of the following items:

1. A voluntary health and welfare organization received a pledge in 19X0 from a donor specifying that the amount pledged be used in 19X2. The donor paid the pledge in cash in 19X1. The pledge should be accounted for as
   (a) a deferred credit in the balance sheet at the end of 19X0 and as support in 19X1
   (b) a deferred credit in the balance sheet at the end of 19X0 and 19X1 and as support in 19X2
   (c) support in 19X0
   (d) support in 19X1 and *no* deferred credit in the balance sheet at the end of 19X0

2. A reason for a voluntary health and welfare organization to adopt fund accounting is that
   (a) Restrictions have been placed on certain of its assets by donors.
   (b) It provides more than one type of program service.
   (c) Fixed assets are significant.
   (d) Donated services are significant.

3. Which basis of accounting should a voluntary health and welfare organization use?
   (a) cash basis for all funds
   (b) modified accrual basis for all funds
   (c) accrual basis for all funds
   (d) accrual basis for some funds and modified accrual basis for other funds

Items 4 and 5 are based on the following data:

Community Service Center is a voluntary welfare organization funded by contributions from the general public. During 19X3, unrestricted pledges of $900,000 were received, half of which were payable in 19X3, with the other half payable in 19X4 for use in 19X4. It was estimated that 10 percent of these pledges would be uncollectible.

In addition, Selma Zorn, a social worker on Community's permanent staff, earning $20,000 annually for a normal work load of 2,000 hours, contributed an additional 800 hours of her time to Community at no charge.

4. How much should Community report as net contribution revenue for 19X3 with respect to the pledges?
   (a) $0
   (b) $405,000
   (c) $810,000
   (d) $900,000

5. How much should Community record in 19X3 for contributed service expense?
   (a) $8,000
   (b) $4,000
   (c) $800
   (d) $0

6. Cura Foundation, a voluntary health and welfare organization supported by contributions from the general public, included the following costs in its statement of functional expenses for the year ended December 31, 19X3:

Fund raising	$500,000
Administrative (including data processing)	300,000
Research	100,000

   Cura's functional expenses for 19X3 program services included
   (a) $900,000
   (b) $500,000
   (c) $300,000
   (d) $100,000

7.6. The accounting records for a voluntary health and welfare agency include the following funds:
   (a) current unrestricted funds
   (b) current restricted funds
   (c) land, building, and equipment funds
   (d) endowment funds

The following transactions occur during the fiscal period:
   (a) Unrestricted contributions in the form of pledges in the amount of $750,000 are received.
   (b) Building fund pledges in the amount of $70,000 are received.
   (c) Revenues from special events in the amount of $30,000 are received.

(d) Support or sustentation expenses in the amount of $200,000 are incurred.

(e) Fixed assets costing $20,000 are acquired by the use of unrestricted resources.

(f) Research expenses are paid from unrestricted resources (to be reimbursed from restricted funds) in the amount of $35,000.

(g) Externally restricted funds in the amount of $300,000 to be used for endowment purposes are received.

(h) Cash restricted to use in the acquisition of building and equipment in the amount of $30,000 is spent to acquire a special piece of equipment to be used by the agency.

(i) Program expenses paid during the period amount to $400,000.

(j) Funds in the amount of $50,000 externally designated to be used for research activities are received.

Required:

On a sheet of worksheet paper, label individual pairs of columns to reflect the different fund entities included in the accounting records of the health and welfare agency. Then, record each of the ten transactions listed above to the left of the columns labeled by fund names and reflect the amounts in the debit and credit columns for the appropriate funds(s).

INTERPRETING NONPROFIT ORGANIZATION FINANCIAL STATEMENTS

8

The accounting systems we have described and illustrated are designed to record, classify, and accumulate financial data that can be used by those interested in the operations of various nonprofit enterprises. The interested parties fall into two general groups—internal managers who use the financial data to make day-by-day operating decisions, and those outside the organization who have a constituency, regulatory, or credit interest in the organization. Published financial reports are made available to the external groups to be used in making various support and credit decisions. In this chapter we explain how the accounting data may be analyzed and used by externally interested parties.

Externally interested parties play an important role in promoting the operating efficiency and effectiveness of nonprofit organizations. They do so by exercising appropriate supervision of internal managers and by providing or withdrawing their support of the enterprise on the basis of their judgments regarding the entity's operating effectiveness. Most nonprofit organizations have a board of trustees or a legislative body elected by constituents that monitors the activities of the internal managers. The constituents may also become directly involved to the point of challenging the actions taken by the elected boards or by withholding financial support from the organization. The voter support of Proposition 13 in California in 1978 and other taxpayer revolts in the United States are examples of direct constituency reaction to the operations of governmental units. Creditors of nonprofit organizations are concerned with the same things (perceived ability to meet interest and principal payments) in the nonprofit area as they are in the profit area. All of these externally interested parties should be prepared to analyze and use the published financial data of these organizations in making support decisions.

We shall begin our discussion by showing how published financial data may be used by externally interested parties in *monitoring the fiduciary responsibility of internal managers.* After that we shall turn to a more specific consideration of the *procedures to be followed in analyzing and interpreting the financial data* for externally interested parties. In the last portion of the chapter, we shall *describe and illustrate some specific analytical techniques* followed in evaluating the operations of different types of nonprofit entities, along with some of the actions that externally interested parties might take in response to the analytical data.

As we begin the analytical process, it is helpful to recall that the accounting data are created by transactions that show what has happened to an entity as a result of operating events. In the analytical process, then, we attempt to relate the financial data back to summarizations of those underlying events. For example, we record expenses or expenditures as services are provided during an operating period. Logically, then, one of the analytical procedures will call for relating each type of expenditure to some measure of the units of services provided during that period. This procedure helps users of the data in evaluating the resource conversion activities of a nonprofit organization.

EVALUATING THE FIDUCIARY RESPONSIBILITY OF INTERNAL MANAGERS

Internal managers are expected to carry out the resource conversion activities of an enterprise in accordance with the perceived desires of the owners in the case of profit entities or the *contributing constituency* in the case of nonprofit organizations. Those resource conversion activities are expected to be carried out in an efficient and effective manner. In addition, all enterprise units operate within certain socially imposed constraints, and internal managers are also expected to operate in compliance with those constraints. External boards, in discharging their responsibility to their constituencies, are thus concerned with evaluating the efficiency and effectiveness of operations and the extent of compliance with externally imposed constraints. They use the financial data in making those evaluations.

Both the efficiency and the effectiveness of profit enterprises can be evaluated by judging the extent to which the long-term profit objective has been achieved. Past profit achievements, along with calculations reflecting the probable liquidity and stability of the enterprise, are used to judge the extent to which that goal is being achieved. In the profit area, compliance largely involves adherence to legally imposed constraints on operations. The recent emphasis on the elimination of corrupt practices in international corporate activities and the identification of unsafe products of domestic companies represent extensions of the concept of compliance beyond those specifically prescribed by regulatory agencies. Thus, to an increasing degree we find managers (both internal and external) of profit enterprises being held accountable for ethical operations and proper treatment of customers in addition to their responsibility for operational efficiency and effectiveness.

The internal managers of nonprofit enterprises are expected to carry out the resource conversion activities efficiently and effectively, just as are managers of profit enterprises. Because nonprofit organizations have a service objective rather than a profit objective, however, it is much more difficult to judge whether resource conversion activities have been carried out efficiently. In most instances it is impossible to measure objectively the benefits produced by the services rendered and thus permit efforts to be matched against achievements as we can in the profit area. Nevertheless, the governing boards and constituencies of nonprofit organizations are expected to evaluate the efficiency and effectiveness of internal manager's resource conversion activities and to react appropriately to their findings. That requires a critical evaluation of cost data in relation to services rendered.

Compliance in the nonprofit area is partially determinable by relating the acquisitions and uses of resources to externally imposed constraints and to budgetary plans for resource flows. The accounting system, using separate funds for externally restricted resources and appropriation control techniques within funds, provides the required information for that evaluation. The other fiduciary responsibilities of the internal managers of nonprofit organizations to their governing boards and constituencies are essentially the same as those of the internal managers of profit enterprises to their boards of directors and owners. However, we shall observe in the following pages that the devices used in evaluating their efforts are significantly different.

ANALYSIS AND INTERPRETATION OF FINANCIAL DATA

We shall begin our description of the analysis and interpretation of financial data by exploring the implications for the analytical process of the three basic concerns—efficiency, effectiveness, and compliance—discussed in the preceding section. After that we shall describe how the financial data of profit enterprises may be analyzed and interpreted to show the extent to which those basic concerns have been met. In the last part of this section, we shall develop general analytical techniques that can be applied in interpreting the financial statements of nonprofit entities.

Basic Concerns

The *efficiency* with which resource conversion activities are carried out can best be measured by *relating efforts to achievements.* In the profit area we do this in the income statement by relating revenues earned to expenses incurred in earning those revenues, thus determing the net income from operations. To supplement this, we also divide the costs of producing goods or services by the output achieved to calculate unit costs that reflect the effort-achievement relationship. Other things being the same, a lower cost per unit is more efficient than a higher cost per unit. We also relate effort to achievement when we compute the relationship between net income and invested capital. Therefore, in evaluating the efficiency of operations, *we must strive to develop effort-achievement relationships that can be compared with standards or with past period data.*

Enterprise units operate *effectively* when they achieve their operating objectives. An enterprise unit may operate effectively—that is, achieve its operating objectives—without operating efficiently. For example, in seeking to kill a fly, we might use a sledgehammer to thoroughly meet our operating objective. However, this would not be an efficient way of accomplishing that objective. Therefore, *effectiveness must be evaluated separately from efficiency.* The analytical process should be designed to produce data that will help externally interested parties evaluate both the extent to which objectives have been achieved and how efficiently that achievement has been carried out.

The third basic concern of externally interested parties is to determine if the enterprise unit has *complied with legal and/or other externally imposed requirements.* For profit enterprises this involves operating within the constraints of the law and the charter under which the entity was created. Breaches of compliance often result in legal action against the enterprise unit. Boards of directors, creditors, and other constituents of profit enterprises are always vitally concerned with contingent obligations evidenced by lawsuits and other information indicating possible conflict with the law or regulatory agencies. Nonprofit organizations must adhere to these legal constraints and also must comply with specific limitations on resource use imposed by external constraints and budgetary actions. This is sometimes referred to as *fiscal accountability.* As we have observed, the records of these organizations should be organized to disclose the extent to which internal managers have complied with those constraints.

Analysis of Profit Enterprise Financial Statements

In Chapter 1 we explained how the universe of enterprise units could be beneficially classified into pure profit, quasi-profit, quasi-nonprofit, and pure nonprofit enterprises. Since the analytical procedures associated with the interpretation of certain quasi-nonprofit enterprises will include some elements of profit enterprise analytical procedures along with elements of pure nonprofit analysis, it is important to understand the basic procedures for analyzing pure profit as well as pure nonprofit enterprise statement data.

The *operational efficiency and effectiveness* of profit enterprises is basically measured through an evaluation of effort-achievement relationships. In analyzing the published financial statements, we begin by observing the relationship between revenues and the expenses incurred in realizing them. From that we get the net income figure (an achievement), which can be related to efforts expended in the form of invested resources. This key measurement can be reflected in terms of earnings per share or in terms of a percentage return on equity capital. Also, in measuring the effectiveness with which assets of the firm have been used, we can calculate the rate of return on total assets by dividing net income by total assets. Another indication of overall efficiency and effectiveness of operations can be secured by measuring relationships among various elements of the income statement. The gross margin percentage is important in evaluating the competitiveness of the environment in which the firm operates, and the percentage relationship between net operating income and sales is important in evaluating operating effectiveness. The latter tells us what portion of the sales dollar the company is able to keep to cover income taxes and to increase equity capital.

If a profit enterprise is to continue to operate effectively and efficiently, it must also be able to meet its current obligations as they mature. Furthermore, the working capital position of the firm must provide adequate operational flexibility. The current ratio, calculated by dividing current assets by current liabilities, generally is used as the starting point in measuring *current liquidity*. That ratio should, however, be supplemented by other ratios measuring the liquidity of current assets. These include the acid-test or quick-assets ratio, the turnover of receivables, and the turnover of inventory. The acid-test ratio is calculated by dividing cash plus near-cash assets, such as marketable securities and receivables, by current liabilities. Receivables turnover is calculated by dividing sales on account by average accounts receivable, and inventory turnover is determined by dividing cost of sales by average inventory. High ratios or turnovers point toward greater liquidity; lower figures indicate a less satisfactory current liquidity position. In making an overall judgment regarding current liquidity, however, it is important to observe that a lower than normal current ratio can be compensated for by high acid-test and high turnover ratios. The analyst must look at these ratios as a group to evaluate the overall current liquidity of the firm.

The constituents of a business entity who are considering long-term ownership or credit commitments are also concerned with the firm's long-term outlook for overcoming economic adversity. We generally refer to this as a firm's prospects for *long-term stability and liquidity*. To meet this test, a firm must show a capability for absorbing reasonable financial reverses without becoming insolvent. One of the key ratios in measuring probable long-term stability and liquidity is the debt-to-equity-capital ratio. A profit enterprise using debt capital is said to be *trading on its equity*. Other things being equal, a firm relying heavily on debt capital would have more risk of insolvency in a period of economic adversity than would a firm that was financed entirely through equity capital. Another way of measuring the extent of trading on the equity is to calculate the ratio of equity capital to total assets. Again, other things being equal, a high ratio would suggest a greater probability of the firm being able to weather economic adversity. To supplement the equity-capital-to-total-assets ratio, we frequently calculate the number of times fixed interest has been earned by dividing the net income before income taxes and interest expense by the amount of annual interest charges. Here, too, other things being equal, a larger number indicates a greater margin of safety. Another calculation that will help evaluate the effectiveness of trading on the equity is to compare the average interest rate on debt capital with the rate of return on total assets. We have already observed that the rate of return on total assets can be calculated by dividing net income by total assets. If that percentage is significantly higher than the average interest rate being paid on debt capital, we have a clear indication that the firm is experiencing success in its efforts to trade on the equity. This type of relationship justifies, to some extent, the use of debt capital, because such debt financing is directly beneficial to those holding owner equity interests in the firm.

As we have previously observed, externally interested parties are always concerned with the extent to which enterprise units have complied with legal or other externally imposed requirements. In the profit area, failure to comply normally would be evidenced by legal proceedings against the firm or, possibly, by questions being raised by regulatory agencies such as the Securities and Exchange Commission. Externally interested parties are therefore concerned with identifying any such evidence of noncompliance.

Analysis of Nonprofit Organization Statements

In analyzing the financial statements of pure nonprofit organizations, external parties are concerned with evaluating the same basic characteristics as in the profit area. They want to evaluate the efficiency and effectiveness of operations and to determine the extent to which fiscal and other compliance responsibilities have been met. Due to differences in operating objectives and organizational characteristics, however, the relationships and ratios used for analytical purposes are significantly different.

Because of the direct relationship between ownership and control in the profit area, we can expect the board of directors to act in the best interests of stockholder constituents. But this relationship does not necessarily prevail in the nonprofit area. The natural bias of legislative bodies and boards controlling nonprofit enterprises is typically in the direction of *enlargement and expansion of organizational activities without appropriate regard for the affordability of programs proposed*. Furthermore, nonprofit organizations have no externally imposed "self-cleansing" force similar to the need for earning a profit in the profit area. No profit enterprise can continue to exist indefinitely without meeting its operating objective of earning a profit. Nonprofit enterprises, on the other hand, can continue to operate as long as the constituency can be prevailed on to support it. These characteristics can cause nonprofit organizations to enlarge their services beyond a reasonable level of social need.

There is also a natural inclination for internal managers to enlarge the operations of the enterprise to justify greater salary benefits. That inclination, coupled with the frequent tendency of the governing boards to have the same bias, means that constituents must be prepared to give more attention to entity operations than is necessary in the profit area. This is particularly true when boards tend to become rubber-stamp oversight bodies ready to approve any actions proposed by internal managers.

Even though we recognize these external control weaknesses, we begin our analysis by developing those data that a constituency-oriented board ought to use. However, we recognize that these data should also be of value to the constituents as they make decisions regarding initiation or continuance of support.

The basic technique for measuring the efficiency of any organization is to relate its outputs to its inputs. In the profit area we do this by matching revenues and expenses and by relating net income to equity investments. The primary problem in measuring this relationship for a pure nonprofit entity is that we seldom have an objective quantitative measurement of outputs. If we could objectively determine the present value of the services provided by such an organization, we could develop a ratio of those values to the cost of providing the services, or we could quantitatively match those two sets of data to arrive at efficiency indicators. Inputs can be easily measured as the accrual-based costs of providing the services. Therefore, if objective values were available for the service output, it would be relatively easy to develop cost-benefit analyses that would allow us to evaluate the efficiency of operations.

Because we seldom have an objective determination of the values of services rendered by a pure nonprofit organization, it is important that externally interested parties have available at least a description of the services provided by the organization over the operating period being evaluated. This can take the form of tonnage of waste processed by the waste disposal department of a city or the number of degrees granted by a college or university. *These data can be used as surrogates for the value of output.* By using such data along with the accrual-based cost data as input information, interested parties can calculate the unit functional costs of services rendered. Those costs can then be compared with past period data, similar costs for other entities, or predetermined standards to gain some insight into operating efficiency.

The type of measurements cited in the preceding paragraph gives no consideration to the quality of services rendered. Although this may be relatively unimportant in evaluating a waste disposal service, it can be extremely important in evaluating the output of a college or university. Because of this need, selected input data are sometimes used as surrogates for measuring the quality of output. Accrediting agencies for colleges and universities, for instance, evaluate the qualitative aspects of the school's operations by looking at such things as the amounts spent on instructional costs per student and the faculty-student ratio, with the implicit assumption that a higher cost of input per student should produce a higher quality program.

Further insight into operating efficiency can sometimes be achieved by *relating overhead costs to toal expenses or expenditures.* Overhead costs in this case are defined to include general administrative and fund-raising costs. An increase in the ratio of these costs to total costs is not always an indicator of less efficient operations, but it does show that the organization is spending a larger amount to sustain itself in relation to the implementation of services. Input changes in that direction should always be critically evaluated.

As we have observed, efficiency should ideally be evaluated by relating outputs to inputs. Effectiveness, on the other hand, can best be evaluated by relating outputs to the objectives of the organization. Obviously this requires that a clear statement, not only of the general objectives of an organization but also of the specific goals that were expected to be achieved during the operating period, be disclosed along with the financial statement data. *The measurement of effectiveness is not cost oriented.* It simply measures results against intentions. However, externally interested parties should be concerned with the affordability of the stated goals as well as whether the goals have been achieved. Ideally, the external board should strive for a balance between the satisfaction of perceived needs and the capability of the constituency to bear the financial load associated with meeting those needs.

Total accrual-based costs should also be related to total revenues and other operating inflows for the period to help judge the extent *of capital maintenance or erosion and whether reasonable generational equity is being preserved* with the present level of services. The incurrence of expenses in excess of revenues earned during the period erodes capital and shifts the tax or contribution burden for current services to future generations.

During the late 1960s and the 1970s, the proposed services of governmental units mushroomed with the stated objective of achieving the "perfect society." Little attention was given to the capability of our economy to support those services or to the question of generational equity. Even less attention has been given to the psychological influences of providing too many services on the basis of perceived need rather than requiring recipients to earn the right to have them. Among federally supported agencies we have seen the inclination to provide services beyond what can be financed from current taxes. The federal government has secured funds through debt financing and, as a result, has created a generational inequity by forcing future generations to pay for services currently being provided. Legislative bodies and governing boards in general ought to consider the responsibility of generational equity as they evaluate the overall effectiveness of nonprofit operations. They should be aware that these enterprise units have no external "self-cleansing" pressure similar to that found in the profit area. Recently much attention has been given to *zero-based budgeting* as a means of more efficiently establishing the operating objectives of governmental agencies and other nonprofit enterprises. Strictly speaking, that budgetary process calls for complete justification of all expense or expenditure requests starting from a zero base each period. For that reason, most attempts to implement it have failed. As a result, one publication has suggested that, although zero-based budgeting may be impractical, *zero-based review of ongoing programs* is highly desirable in establishing future operating objectives.[1] This calls for the use of zero-based budgeting in establishing operating plans less frequently than every year, such as possibly every five years.

Externally interested parties should also evaluate the extent to which internal management has complied with specified operating plans. Insofar as the financial operations are concerned, this is most directly determined by observing the use of appropriate fund entities and by relating actual to budgetary financial data. Because nonprofit organizations usually are controlled by specifying how resources may be used, the resource inflows and outflows of individual fund entities must be related to their stated objectives and general or operating fund inflows and outflows must be compared with the budgetary plan. It is especially important for external boards to determine that expenses or expenditures have been properly controlled within appropriation limits. This is done by comparing actual expenses or expenditures with those established when the budget was approved.

Because nonprofit organizations have no equity capital in the sense of ownership shares outstanding, they often must depend on debt financing for a large portion of their long-term resources. Because they are often unable to continue to exist without debt financing, the oversight board, as well as potential creditors, should be particularly interested in the "borrowing capability" of the enterprise unit. It is important for those groups to critically review the organization's overall debt position, the total valuation of property in relationship to the tax levies, the statement of tax collections, and the population being served by the entity. It is also important that they know who the larger taxpayers are and the nature of the area's economy. Internal managers should be expected to provide a statement of borrowing plans for a reasonable period in the future as well as a statement setting out the proposed capital improvement program and plans for the next few years.[2]

---

[1] Robert N. Anthony and Regina Herzlinger, *Management Control in Nonprofit Organizations* (Homewood, IL: Richard D. Irwin, 1975), p. 213.

[2] Hugh C. Sherwood, *How Corporate Municipal Debt Is Rated* (New York: John Wiley and Sons, 1976), pp. 115–116.

APPLICATION OF ANALYTICAL TECHNIQUES

We have observed that many of the resource conversion units that fall within our broad definition of nonprofit organizations are more realistically quasi-nonprofit enterprises realizing a significant amount of resource inflows from user-based charges. Therefore, when we analyze and interpret the financial statements of these organizations, we must selectively employ analytical procedures from both the profit and nonprofit areas. To illustrate that point we shall briefly explore the analytical procedures that should be applied to the financial statements of governmental units, colleges and universities, hospitals, and health and welfare agencies.

Analysis of Governmental Financial Statements

In analyzing published financial statements, we must always recognize the limitations inherent in those data. When we analyze governmental financial statements, we must be aware that they are conventionally prepared on the *modified accrual rather than the full accrual basis* of accounting and that we will *seldom have an objectively determinable measure of output* for them. The first of these two shortcomings could be overcome by converting the expenditure-based financial data to the full accrual basis. Also, we can partially compensate for the lack of an objectively determined value for output by insisting on *nondollar quantitative data relating to the services provided*. Primary attention will be focused on the general or operating fund data as we carry out the analytical process.

In recognition of the weaknesses cited in the preceding paragraph, the external users of the financial data will want to begin their analyses by calculating the amount of expenditures or expenses per service unit or per citizen served. These data should be compared with the budgeted amount per unit, prior period amount per unit, and/or amount per unit for similar operating entities to help judge how efficiently resources were used as they were converted to services.

In evaluating the effectiveness of operations, it is important to begin by comparing some measure of the actual services provided with the operating goals established at the beginning of the period. From that comparison we can learn the extent to which period operating objectives have been met. It is also important to give attention to the quality of service provided by the entity. As observed earlier in this chapter, accrediting and regulatory agencies, with the benefit of exposure to the operations of many similar entities, typically evaluate the quality of service by analyzing input data.

The legislative body or governing board should be concerned with providing *an optimum level and quality of service* that *properly balances needs and affordability*. The level of need is generally determinable from the voice of the electorate. An objective analysis of the relationships between taxes and the bases on which the taxes are assessed can provide some insight in judging affordability. The legislative board is expected to consider these factors as they establish service objectives. Failure to react to them properly can cause constituency action to overrule them; quite obviously, the property owners of California, in their so-called taxpayer revolt of 1978 through Proposition 13, said that they could not afford the current level of services unless the services could be provided more efficiently. Other similar actions also suggest that legislative bodies may have failed to give adequate attention to the question of affordability. Total service expenses or expenditures for the period should also be compared with revenues realized for use during the period to help decide whether the appropriate level of services is being provided for the present generation of taxpayers.

As observed earlier, governmental units are legally bound to control operating expenditures within budgetary appropriations. Legislative bodies and governing boards are therefore responsible for ascertaining from the financial reports or by certification from auditors that the internal management of the governmental units has adhered to budgetary constraints imposed upon its spending.

Because governmental units depend heavily on debt financing in carrying out many of their activities, it is also important for externally interested parties—in particular, governing boards—to be concerned with the capability of the entity to meet interest payment and debt retirement obligations. This capability is determined primarily by the entity's ability to realize sufficient tax inflows to meet those obligations. Therefore, in decisions to incur long-term debt, it is important to recognize that interest and principal obligations will have to be met through increased taxes unless the expenditure of borrowed funds or other increases in values will increase the tax base sufficiently to provide for them.

Externally interested parties should also be aware that the modified accrual basis statements for these organizations will often fail to disclose significant amounts of liabilities incurred but not due to be paid until a later period. For example, obligations for future pension benefits, incurred during the working lives of employees, typically are not disclosed in governmental financial statements, even though the productive efforts of the employees' services have already been used. Long-term creditors must be aware of these future obligations as they judge whether credit should be extended and the terms under which it should be granted. These considerations are particularly important to investors who hold the long-term bonds of these entities. Bond rating agencies that provide evaluations of these securities for prospective investors are therefore also much interested in those data. Full accrual-based cost data can beneficially be used in making these and other analytical judgments.

We now illustrate the calculation of the various ratios and percentages discussed above for Model City's expenditure-based data (see page 81). We shall assume for purposes of our analysis that Model City has a population of 20,000 persons with incomes approximating the national average. The property tax rate has been based on an assessed value of \$36,250,000 (see Chapter 3), which we shall assume is approximately 40 percent of fair market value. Also recall that general fund expenditures were subclassified in Chapter 3 by the functions they performed, as follows (see Figure 3.2, page 81):

General fund expenditures (by functional categories)

General government	\$ 348,000
Police services	249,000
Sanitation services	160,000
Recreation services	175,000
Street-maintenance services	393,000
School services	375,000
Total direct functional expenditures	1,700,000
Transfers and miscellaneous	184,000
Total general fund expenditures and transfers	\$1,884,000
Other expenditures and encumbrances	
Capital projects expenditures	402,000
Special assessment fund expenditures	251,050
Trust fund expenditures	2,000
Total expenditures	\$2,539,050

For the purposes of our analysis we shall allocate nonfunctional labeled expenditures to functional categories as follows:

1. Transfers and miscellaneous items allocated to:

General government	\$ 37,000
Police services	26,000
Sanitation services	17,000
Recreation services	46,000
School services	58,000
Total	\$184,000

2. Capital projects and special assessment fund expenditures allocated to:

Street-maintenance services	\$644,050
School services	9,000
	\$653,050

3. Trust fund expenditures allocated to recreational services.

After we have made those allocations, total expenditures are classified by function, as follows:

General government	$ 385,000
Police services	275,000
Sanitation services	177,000
Recreation services	223,000
Street-maintenance services	1,037,050
School services	442,000
Total expenditures	$2,539,050

We can then develop the following analysis of the expenditure-based data:

Common Size and Expenditure per Capital Data

Items	Expenditures	Percent	Expenditures per Capita
General administration	$ 385,000	15.2	$ 19.25
Police services	275,000	10.8	13.75
Sanitation services	177,000	7.0	8.85
Recreation services	223,000	8.8	11.15
Street-maintenance services	1,037,050	40.8	51.85
School services	442,000	17.4	22.10
Total expenditures	$2,539,050	100.0	$126.95

Relationship Between Revenues and Expenditures

Excess of revenues over expenditures ($2,620,925 − $2,539,050)	$81,875
Ration of revenues to expenditures $2,620,925 ÷ $2,539,050	1.032

Other Analytical Information

General long-term debt per capita
 ($500,000 ÷ 20,000) = $25
Tax assessment to market value of property
 $1,460,000 ÷ $90,625,000 = 1.6%
Expenditures per person
 $2,539,050 ÷ 20,000 = $126.95

Analysis of College and University Financial Statements

Colleges and universities are quasi-nonprofit organizations. They have some of the basic characteristics of nonprofit entities but also realize a significant amount of their resource inflows from user-based charges in the form of tuition and fees. Therefore, in analyzing the financial statements of these institutions, we use some procedures from profit entity analysis along with other procedures used in evaluating pure nonprofit entities.

In judging the *operational efficiency* of a college or university, the analyst should begin by observing the relationship between operating revenues and operating outflows. Conventionally prepared financial statements will show most revenues as they are earned. Outflows, however, are reflected on an expenditure basis. Because we have not illustrated the conversion of those data to full accrual-based expenses, we shall use the expenditure basis outflow data for analytical purposes. It is important, however, for you to be aware of that limitation in our analysis.

Although a college or university may be justified in operating with an excess of expenditures over revenues for a certain year or a certain short span of years, it cannot operate that way and continue as a going concern over a long period of time. As a quasi-nonprofit organization, it is imperative that operating revenues, including contributions for that purpose, cover operating expenditures over a period of several years. Any annual excess of revenues over expenditures should also not be extreme because that would represent a student generational inequity bias against presently enrolled students. In summary, *we expect an efficiently operated institution to meet its operating expenditures from current operating revenues but at the same time to increase the quality of its services by increasing expenditures when revenues significantly exceed expenditures.*

In analyzing expenditures it is important to determine the percentages of expenditures associated with general administration and overhead, distinguished from such things as instruction and research. It is also important to relate instruction and other student-oriented expenditures to tuition and fees to determine the portion of total student costs being covered by user-based charges. We often use a *common-size operating statement* to disclose these and other relationships described. These data can also be presented in the form of "pie charts" similar to those shown in Exhibit 8.1. Total educational expenditures per credit hour and per degree granted are other data that are helpful in evaluating operating efficiency.

In evaluating the *effectiveness of operations* in the college and university area, it is important to know such nondollar quantitative data as the number of degrees granted, number of student credit hours provided, and the number of full-time-equivalent faculty members employed, including their degree qualifications. These data help us evaluate both the extent and the quality of educational services being rendered. Volumes of *College Blue Book*,[3] and the publication entitled *American Universities and Colleges*,[4] published to inform potential students of the general operating characteristics of various colleges and universities, include many of these data for most schools. We include ratios and percentages developed from such data in the illustrated analysis later in this chapter.

Operational effectiveness is also contingent on the capability of the

[3] See various volumes of *College Blue Book*, 16th ed. (New York: Macmillan Information, 1977).

[4] *American Universities and Colleges*, 11th ed. (Washington, DC: American Council on Education, 1973).

EXHIBIT 8.1

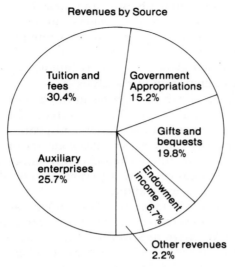

Revenues by Source

Tuition and fees 30.4%

Government Appropriations 15.2%

Gifts and bequests 19.8%

Auxiliary enterprises 25.7%

Endowment income 6.7%

Other revenues 2.2%

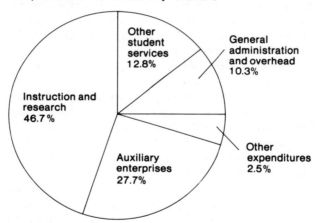

Expenditures and Transfers by Functions

Other student services 12.8%

General administration and overhead 10.3%

Instruction and research 46.7%

Other expenditures 2.5%

Auxiliary enterprises 27.7%

Source: Emerson O. Henke, *Introduction to Nonprofit Organization Accounting* (Boston: Kent Publishing Co., 1980), p. 428.

institution to continue to exist in the foreseeable future. The *current ratio* for unrestricted funds can be calculated to help evaluate current liquidity. The analyst will also be concerned with measures of the demand for the services of the institution. The relationship between admissions and applications can be quite important in making that judgment. A school that has significantly more qualified applications for admission than it is able to admit clearly shows a heavy demand for its educational services that should help sustain it in the event of economic adversity.

The amount and nature of nonoperating inflows for a college or university are also important factors in judging probability of continuance. An institution that consistently realizes significant resource inflows into endowment funds and plant funds shows a constituency committed toward improving and enlarging its program. On the other hand, failure to realize such resource inflows can cast a shadow on the probability of an institution continuing as a going concern in the future.

One of the most important factors in judging the effectiveness of college or university operations is the form of the accreditations and other recognitions granted to the institution. Various disciplines and schools of a typical college or university are periodically subjected to accreditation evaluations. Agencies performing these evaluations use much of the data described in the preceding paragraphs to arrive at an overall judgment of operating effectiveness.

Compliance is evaluated in the college and university area primarily by determining that externally imposed restrictions on the uses of resources have been properly honored. In some instances it may also be important to prove budgetary compliance, but this responsibility is generally delegated to internal managers.

To illustrate the analytical procedures described in the preceding pages, we now show how the financial statements of Model College presented in Chapter 5 (with certain assumptions added) should be analyzed by external users.

Assumptions regarding nondollar quantitative data for the current year are:

Enrollment—2,000 full-time-equivalent students
Faculty—100 full-time-equivalent teachers
Doctorally qualified faculty—60
Student credit hours—60,000
Degrees granted—400
Applications for admission—1,500
New students admitted—500

The analytical data for the current year are as follows:

1. Relationship between operating revenues and operating expenditures:

Excess of operating revenues over operating expenditures:

$$(\$8,554,000 - \$7,756,000) = \$798,000$$

Ratio of operating revenue to operating expenditures:

$$(8,554,000 \div 7,756,000) = 1.103$$

2. Structure of operating revenues:

Items	Percent
Educational and general	
Student tuition and fees	30.4
Government appropriations	15.2
Gifts and grants	19.8
Endowment income	6.7
Other revenues	2.2
Auxiliary enterprises	25.7
Total	100.0

3. Structure of operating expenditures:

Items	Percent
Educational and general	
Instruction and research	46.7
Other student services	12.8
General administration and overhead	10.3
Other expenditures	2.5
Auxiliary enterprises	27.7
Total	100.0

4. Student-oriented expenditures related to tuition and fees:

$$(\$3,760,000 \div 2,600,000) = 1.446$$

5. Educational expenditures per degree granted:

$$(5,414,000 \div 400) = \$13,535$$

6. Educational expenditures per student credit hour:

$$(5,414,000 \div 60,000) = \$90.23$$

7. Student faculty ratio:

$$(2,000 \div 100) = 20 \text{ to } 1$$

8. Doctorally qualified to fulltime-equivalent faculty members:

$$(60 \div 100) = 60\%$$

9. Current ratio:

$$(1,006,000 \div 363,000) = 2.77 \text{ to } 1$$

10. Ratio of applications for admissions to new students admitted:

$$(1,500 \div 500) = 3 \text{ to } 1$$

11. Nonoperating inflows (totals):

Fund	Amount	Percent Increase
Loan funds	141,000	26.1
Endowment funds	1,679,000	14.1
Annuity funds	800,000	31.9
Plant funds	2,103,000	5.3
Total	4,723,000	8.7

This structure of operating revenues and operating expenditures can also be displayed graphically in "pie charts," as in Exhibit 8.1 (page 292).

Analysis of Hospital Financial Statements

The operations of hospitals and colleges and universities are, in some respects, very similar. Both types of institutions, for example, require large investments in long-term assets. Both provide a variety of services, and both operate self-sustaining subentities. Both recover fees for some or all of their operating costs from persons served, third parties, or governmental units. For that reason, the analytical procedures for these two types of institutions are also quite similar in many respects.

In developing common-size data for hospitals, however, it is important to emphasize the *extent of allowances and uncollectible accounts* deducted from patient revenue. That shows the amount of patient services provided as a gratuitous service to the community. In analyzing hospital statements we are working with accrual-based (expense-oriented) rather than expenditure data. In this section we illustrate (with certain assumptions added) the calculation of selected ratios and percentages for Sample Hospital financial statements shown in Chapter 6.[5] Assumptions regarding nondollar quantitative data for current year are:

Rooms	150
Admissions	6,000
Average occupancy	120
Employees	450

The analytical data for the current year are as follows:

1. Relationships between operating revenues and operating expenses: Excess of operating revenues over operating expenses:

$$(\$6,907,000 - 7,275,000) = (\$368,000) \text{ loss}$$

[5] Data for most hospitals available in *Guide to the Health Care Field* (Chicago: American Hospital Association, 1977).

Ratio of operating revenues to operating expenses:

$$(6,907,000 \div 7,275,000) = .949$$

2. Structure of operating revenues:

Items	Percent
Patient service revenue	123.0
Allowances and uncollectible accounts	(25.7)
Other operating revenue	2.7
Net operating revenue	100.0

3. Structure of operating expenses:

Items	Percent
Nursing services	30.2
Other professional services	26.1
General services	28.9
Administrative and fiscal services	10.7
Depreciation expense	4.1
Total	100.0

4. Net patient service revenue:

Per available room ($6,723,000 ÷ 150)	$44,820
Per average occupancy ($6,723,000 ÷ 120)	$56,025
Per admission ($6,723,000 ÷ 6,000)	$ 1,121

5. Percentage occupancy:

$$(120 \div 150) = 80\%$$

6. Operating revenue per employee:

$$(\$6,907,000 \div 450) = \$15,349$$

7. Operating expenses:

Per available room ($7,275,000 ÷ 150)	$48,500
Per average occupancy ($7,275,000 ÷ 120)	$60,625
Per admission ($7,275,000 ÷ 6,000)	$ 1,213

8. Current ratio:

$$(\$1,814,000 \div \$1,227,000) = 1.5 \text{ to } 1$$

9. Nonoperating inflows:

Fund	Amount	Percent Increase
Specific purpose funds	113,260	159.5
Plant replacement funds	128,000	11.6
Endowment funds	2,175,000	54.7
Total	2,416,260	47.0

Analysis of Financial Statements for Health and Welfare Agencies

Because most health and welfare agencies are pure nonprofit organizations, we follow many of the same analytical procedures for them that are used in analyzing governmental financial statements. These organizations typically provide a number of related services that are distributed on the basis of perceived need for them. Therefore, externally interested parties will be concerned with having a profile of those services along with the sources of support for the organization. This can be provided by showing the portion of each dollar spent in implementing the different types of services. A common-size operating statement can be prepared to provide a revenue and expense profile (as shown in Figures 8.1 and 8.2). Functional unit cost data can be calculated as shown in Figure 8.2.

The amount spent for administrative and fund raising activities is also of critical importance to the constituents of health and welfare agencies. For that reason it is important to show, as part of the common-size data already mentioned, the portion of each contribution dollar spent in sustaining the organization.

In measuring the effectiveness of an entity's operations, it is important to have nondollar quantitative data summarizing the services performed by the agency over a period of time. Effectiveness can then be evaluated by relating actual achievements to the goals of the organization for the period.

Health and welfare agencies generally operate under an object-of-expense appropriation-controlled budget. They can also receive resources that are restricted to specified uses. Therefore, in evaluating the extent of compliance, it is important to determine whether the agency has operated within budgetary and externally imposed restrictions on the uses of funds.

To illustrate the most important elements of health and welfare agency financial statement analysis, we present a common-size operating statement

FIGURE 8.1 Model Voluntary Health and Welfare Service Common-Size Operating Statement 19X2

		Percent
Revenues by sources		
Public support		91.9
Revenues earned		8.1
Total		100.0
Expenses		
Sustentation		28.0
Service implementation		
Research	32.3	
Public health education	12.4	
Professional education and training	14.1	
Community services	13.2	72.0
Total		100.0

FIGURE 8.2 Model Voluntary Health and Welfare Service Functional Unit Cost Data, 19X2

Assumptions Regarding Services Rendered	
Research projects	100
Public health education (persons served)	10,000
Professional education and training (persons served)	600
Community services (population of community)	100,000

Service Implementation Services	Functional Cost Per Unit
Research	$14,140.00
Public health education	54.40
Professional education and training	1,030.00
Community services	5.78

along with functional unit cost data for Model Voluntary Health and Welfare Service financial statements shown in Chapter 7 (see Figures 8.1 and 8.2).

Actions in Response to Financial Statements Analysis

Externally interested parties provide resources for enterprise units either by purchasing ownership shares, paying taxes, making contributions, or extending credit to them. In the profit area, favorable impressions from the analytical data cause externally interested parties to seek to invest in the enterprise unit or lend money to it. Unfavorable impressions cause those parties to withdraw financial support by selling stock interests or refusing to lend additional resources to the enterprise unit.

In the nonprofit area, the noncreditor constituents are trying to decide whether they should provide support to the entity in the form of taxes or contributions. Favorable impressions regarding efficiency, effectiveness, and compliance encourage such support; unfavorable observations regarding these characteristics lead to decreased support, which can manifest itself in reduced contributions or taxpayer revolts. Creditors and potential creditors of nonprofit organizations look to the operating history and environmental characteristics to help them determine whether credit should be extended and, if so, the terms under which it should be granted.

SUMMARY

In this chapter we have explored the ways in which the published financial report data of nonprofit enterprises are used by externally interested parties. We began by reviewing the analytical procedures normally followed in evaluating the operations and financial positions of pure profit and pure nonprofit enterprises. We then described the analytical process and illustrated how some of those techniques can be applied in analyzing the financial statements of governmental entities, colleges and universities, hospitals, and health and welfare agencies.

We explained that externally interested parties are concerned primarily with evaluating the activities of internal managers. Basically, they want to know whether operations have been carried out efficiently and effectively and whether resources have been used in compliance with externally imposed constraints. Creditors are primarily concerned with whether or not interest and principal obligations can be met as they become due.

QUESTIONS FOR CLASS DISCUSSION

8.1. Compare the way consumable resources are distributed within a capitalistic economic system with the way they are distributed within a socialistic system.

8.2. How does profit motivation promote the efficient use of resources? Discuss.

8.3. How do externally interested parties help promote operating efficiency and effectiveness in the profit area? In the nonprofit area?

8.4. Explain why it is more difficult to evaluate the efficiency of enterprise unit operations in the nonprofit area than in the profit area.

8.5. What are the three basic concerns of governing boards and constituencies as they seek to evaluate the activities of an enterprise unit?

8.6. Explain the difference between efficiency and effectiveness as these terms are used in characterizing the operations of an enterprise unit. How are these terms related to the fundamental evaluation of effort-achievement relationships?

8.7. How do we evaluate the current liquidity of a profit-type enterprise unit?

8.8. What are some of the relationships that are generally considered in evaluating the operational effectiveness of a profit enterprise? Is it appropriate to use these in evaluating the operational effectiveness of a nonprofit enterprise? Explain.

8.9. Compare and contrast the relationship between the board of directors of a corporate business entity and the business entity with the relationship between a legislative body or board and the governmental entity that it serves.

8.10. Explain how the need for earning a profit in the profit area constitutes a "self-cleansing" force. Does such a force exist in the nonprofit area? Explain.

8.11. Can we always count on the governing board of a nonprofit entity to act in the best interests of the constituents? Discuss fully.

8.12. The basic technique for measuring the operating efficiency of any enterprise unit is to relate its outputs to its inputs. How can that be done in the profit area? In the nonprofit area?

8.13. Explain how functional cost data can be used as surrogates for output data in the nonprofit area.

8.14. Explain the conceptual difference between zero-based review and zero-based budgeting. What are these techniques intended to accomplish when they are applied in the management of a nonprofit entity?

8.15. Discuss the concerns of long-term creditors and potential long-term creditors as they consider loans to nonprofit enterprises.

EXERCISES

8.1. The balance sheet for an enterprise fund includes the following items for the ends of Year A and Year B:

	Year A	Year B
Current assets	$250,000	$275,000
Current liabilities	110,000	190,000
Utility plant and equipment	600,000	750,000
Bonds payable	650,000	625,000
Bond debt-service fund	35,000	45,000
Contribution from city	100,000	200,000
Retained earnings	25,000	55,000

Required:

1. Compute the current ratio for the fund at the end of each year.
2. Compute the change in net working capital during Year B.
3. Calculate the ratio of equity capital to long-term debt capital at the end of each year.
4. What was the net income of the enterprise fund for Year B? There have been no earnings distributions to the city out of the fund.
5. Comment on your findings in Parts 1, 2, 3, and 4.

8.2. The revenues and expenditures statement for a nonprofit entity includes the following items for the current and preceding years:

	Preceding Year	Current Year
Revenues	$1,000,000	$1,200,000
Expenditures		
Fund raising	200,000	270,000
Administration	150,000	225,000
Service implementation	625,000	675,000
Excess of revenues over expenditures	25,000	30,000

Required:

1. Calculate the percentage of revenues used to cover overhead expenditures. Comment on your findings.
2. Revenues for the current year were larger than they were last year. Show how the added revenue was used. Comment on your findings.
3. Prepare common-size statements of revenues and expenditures for each of the two years. What observations can be made from those statements?

8.3. A governmental entity shows revenues and expenditures for the current year of $1,425,000 and $1,410,000, respectively. When these data are converted to the full accrual basis, the entity shows revenues of $1,415,000 and expenses of $1,450,000.

Required:

1. Has the present generation of taxpayers paid for all the services they have provided for themselves during the current year? Explain.
2. Relate your findings to the concept of generational equity.

3. Has the entity maintained its "capital resources" during the current year? Explain.
4. What are some of the ways in which the tax burden for services can be shifted to future generations? Explain.

8.4. The following data are available for the same year relating to two universities (labeled A and B) providing similar educational services:

	University A	University B
Enrollment (full-time equivalent)	10,000	15,000
Student credit hours	300,000	400,000
Faculty (full-time equivalent)	500	600
Doctorally qualified faculty	400	300
Applications for admission	5,000	4,000
New students admitted	2,500	4,000

Required:

1. Develop appropriate analytical ratios for each school.
2. Comment on your findings regarding the similarities and differences in the operating characteristics of the two schools.

8.5. The operating statements for schools A and B (see Exercise 8.4) show the following educational revenue data, expressed on a common-size basis:

	A Percent	B Percent
Student tuition and fees	60.0	10.0
Governmental appropriations	0.0	80.0
Gifts and grants	20.0	5.0
Endowment income	20.0	5.0
Total	100.0	100.0

Required:

Describe the nature of each school's operations as disclosed by the preceding data.

8.6. The operating statements for schools A and B (see Exercises 8.4 and 8.5) also contain the following educational expenditure data, expressed on a common-size basis:

	A Percent	B Percent
Instruction and research	60.0	70.0
Other student services	20.0	5.0
General administration	10.0	15.0
Other educational expenditures	10.0	10.0
Total	100.0	100.0

Required:

What further insight into the general operations of the two schools is provided by these data?

8.7. The operating statements for schools A and B (see Exercises 8.4–8.6) also show the following educational revenue and expenditure data:

	A	B
Educational revenues	$40,000,000	$42,000,000
Educational expenditures	39,500,000	41,900,000
Excess of revenues over expenditures	$ 500,000	$ 100,000

Required:

1. Calculate the ratio of educational revenues to educational expenditures for each school.
2. Calculate the amount of educational expenditures per full-time student and per student credit hour for each school.
3. Calculate the amounts being spent for instruction and research by each school.
4. Calculate the amount of endowment income being realized by each school.
5. Comment on your findings.

8.8. The condensed operating statements for a hospital for the current year and preceding year are as follows:

	Preceding Year	Current Year
Patient service revenue	$6,000,000	$7,000,000
Allowances and uncollectible accounts (net of gifts covering these services)	1,200,000	1,500,000
Net patient revenue	$4,800,000	$5,500,000
Operating expenses	5,000,000	6,000,000
Loss from operations	$ (200,000)	$ (500,000)
Nonoperating revenues	250,000	475,000
Excess (deficiency) of revenues over expenses	$ 50,000	$ (25,000)
Other quantitative data		
Rooms	250	250
Average occupancy	225	235
Admissions	10,000	11,000
Employees	600	625

Required:

1. Calculate the following ratios and percentages for each year:
   (a) ratio of operating revenues to operating expenses
   (b) percentage of patient revenue representing direct community service by hospital each year

(c) percentage of room occupancy
(d) patient service revenue and operating expenses per available room, per average occupancy, and per admission
(e) operating revenue per employee
2. Comment on your findings.

8.9. The condensed operating statements for a health and welfare agency for the current year and preceding year are shown below:

	Preceding Year	Current Year
Revenues		
Public support	$85,000	$100,000
Revenues earned	5,000	8,000
Total	$90,000	$108,000
Expenses		
Sustentation	20,000	25,000
Service implementation		
Public health education	30,000	35,000
Research	14,000	18,000
Medical services	25,000	30,000
Total expenses	$89,000	$108,500
Excess (deficiency) of revenues over expenses	$ 1,000	$ (500)
Other data		
Community served	100,000	105,000
Persons provided medical service	10,000	11,000
Research projects	200	225

Required:

1. Prepare common-size operating statements for both years.
2. Calculate the functional cost per unit for each type of service rendered by the agency.
3. Comment on your findings.

PROBLEMS

8.1. The balance sheet and statement of revenues and expenditures for a well-known private church-related university are shown on pages 306 through 308.

The following nondollar quantitative data are also included in the annual report for the university:

	19X2	19X1
Enrollment	8,400	8,000
Faculty employed	400	380
Doctorally qualified faculty	300	250
Student credit hours	250,000	240,000
Degrees granted	1,800	1,700
Applications for admission	3,300	3,000
New students admitted	2,100	2,000

Required:

1. Develop analytical ratios and other data that can be used in evaluating the operations of the university.
2. Comment on your findings.

8.2. The various elements of the statements of expenditures, encumbrances, and transfers for Freemanville, a city of 50,000 persons, for 19X1 and 19X2 are shown below. The population has remained relatively stable over the two-year period. The primary source of general fund revenue is property taxes. The assessed valuation of property was $200,000,000 each year, which is approximately 50 percent of market value.

	19X1	19X2
General fund expenditures and encumbrances		
General government	$ 1,800,000	$ 1,900,000
Police services	1,200,000	2,500,000
Sanitation services	700,000	1,000,000
Recreation services	1,100,000	2,000,000
Street-maintenance services	2,000,000	2,500,000
School services	2,500,000	3,500,000
Transfers and miscellaneous	900,000	1,200,000
Total	$10,200,000	$14,600,000
Other expenditures and encumbrances		
Capital project expenditures	$ 900,000	$ 500,000
Special assessment expenditures	500,000	300,000
Trust fund expenditures	10,000	10,000
Total expenditures	$11,610,000	$15,410,000

General fund revenues amounted to $11,000,000 for 19X1 and $15,000,000 for 19X2.

    For the purposes of this problem you should allocate transfers and miscellaneous expenditures equally to each of the six service areas.

Required:

1. Analyze the general fund revenues and functional expenditure data as illustrated in the chapter.
2. Comment on your findings.

Balance Sheets, May 31, 19X2, and 19X1[1]

Assets

	19X2	19X1
Current Funds—Unrestricted		
Cash	$ 900	$ 500
Investments	2,200	2,400
Other assets	1,400	1,300
Total	$ 4,500	$ 4,200
Current Funds—Restricted		
Miscellaneous assets	$ 1,400	$ 1,200
Total	$ 5,900	$ 5,400
Loan Funds		
Notes receivable	$ 4,700	$ 4,700
Other assets	1,400	1,200
Total	$ 6,100	$ 5,900
Endowment Funds		
Investments—endowment	$28,000	$27,000
Investments—quasi-endowment	8,000	7,000
Total	$36,000	$34,000

Liabilities and Fund Balances

	19X2	19X1
Current Funds—Unrestricted		
Accounts payable	$ 700	$ 350
Other liabilities	3,600	3,670
Fund balances	200	180
Total	$ 4,500	$ 4,200
Current Funds—Restricted		
Fund balances	$ 1,400	$ 1,200
Total	$ 5,900	$ 5,400
Loan Funds		
Fund balances	$ 6,100	$ 5,900
Total	$ 6,100	$ 5,900
Endowment Funds		
Fund balances—endowment	$28,000	$27,000
Fund balances—quasi-endowment	8,000	7,000
Total	$36,000	$34,000

Annuity and Life Income Funds

Annuity funds invested	$ 4,200	$ 3,700	Annuities payable	$ 1,600	$ 1,300
Life income funds invested	2,400	2,500	Fund balances—annuities	2,600	2,400
			Fund balances—life income funds	2,400	2,500
Total	$ 6,600	$ 6,200	Total	$ 6,600	$ 6,200

Plant Funds

Cash	$ 600	$ 600	Notes and bonds payable	$ 4,500	$ 4,400
Investments	3,900	3,400	Advances from quasi-endowment	3,000	0
Land, buildings, and improvements	43,000	36,000	Other obligations	500	200
Equipment	9,500	8,000	Fund balances unexpended	(3,500)	(600)
			Fund balances—investment in plant	52,500	44,000
Total	$57,000	$48,000	Total	$57,000	$48,000

[1] All dollar amounts in thousands.

Statement of Revenues and Expenditures (All dollar amounts in thousands)

	Year Ending May 31, 19X2			Year Ending May 31, 19X1		
	Total	Unrestricted	Restricted	Total	Unrestricted	Restricted
Revenues						
Tuition and fees	$11,000	$11,000	0	$ 9,700	$ 9,700	0
Church-affiliated contributions	1,300	1,300	0	1,100	1,100	0
Endowment income	2,500	2,300	$ 200	1,900	1,600	$ 300
Government grants and contracts	900	100	800	1,000	100	900
Gifts	800	600	200	400	100	300
Other educational and general income	1,700	1,200	500	1,400	1,300	100
Total educational and general	18,200	16,500	1,700	15,500	13,900	1,600
Auxiliary enterprises	8,000	7,700	300	7,200	6,900	300
Total revenues	$26,200	$24,200	$2,000	$22,700	$20,800	$1,900
Expenditures						
Instruction and research	$ 8,500	$ 8,300	$ 200	$ 7,500	$ 7,200	$ 300
Library	1,200	1,100	100	1,100	1,000	100
Student services	1,300	1,000	300	1,000	900	100
Plant operations	1,700	1,700	0	1,300	1,300	0
General institutional expense	2,000	1,900	100	1,700	1,600	100
Student aid	1,100	400	700	1,100	400	700
Other educational and general expenditures	1,200	800	400	1,000	700	300
Total educational and general expenditures	$17,000	$15,200	$1,800	$14,700	$13,100	$1,600
Auxiliary activities	$ 8,000	$ 7,800	$ 200	$ 7,000	$ 6,700	$ 300
Total expenditures	$25,000	$23,000	$2,000	$21,700	$19,800	$1,900
Excess of revenues over expenditures	$ 1,200	$ 1,200	0	$ 1,000	$ 1,000	0
Transfers to endowment funds	$ 400	$ 400		$ 300	$ 300	
Transfers to plant fund	400	400		200	200	
Excess of revenues over expenditures and transfers	$ 400	$ 400		$ 500	$ 500	

8.3. The New Hospital balance sheets and statements of revenues and expenses for 19X1 and 19X2 are on pages 309 and 310.

You are also given the following nondollar quantitative data for the two years of operation:

	19X2	19X1
Rooms	75	75
Admissions	3,000	2,400
Average occupancy	60	50
Employees	225	225

Required:

1. Develop analytical ratios and other data that can be used in evaluating the operations of New Hospital over the two-year period.
2. Comment on your findings.

New Hospital Statement of Revenues and Expenses, Years Ending 12/31/19X1 and 19X2[1]

	19X2	19X1
Patient service revenue	$4,250	$4,000
Allowances and uncollectible accounts	(900)	(800)
Net patient service revenue	$3,350	$3,200
Other operating revenue	90	80
Total operating revenue	$3,440	$3,280
Operating expenses		
Nursing services	$1,100	$1,000
Other professional services	900	800
General services	1,100	1,000
Provision for depreciation	150	125
Other operating expenses	300	400
Total operating expenses	$3,550	$3,325
Loss from operations	$ (110)	$ (45)
Nonoperating revenue		
Unrestricted gifts and bequests	$ 114	$ 100
Endowment income	85	40
Total nonoperating revenue	$ 199	$ 140
Excess of revenues over expenses	$ 89	$ 95

[1] All dollar amounts in thousands

8.4. The statement of support, revenues, and expenses for a health and welfare agency (page 311) shows data relating to the agency's operations for 19X1 and 19X2:

New Hospital Balance Sheets, 12/31/19X1 and 12/31/19X2[1]

Unrestricted Funds

Assets	19X2	19X1	Liabilities and Fund Balances	19X2	19X1
Current			Current		
Cash	$ 65	$ 30	Accounts payable	$ 225	$ 230
Receivables	690	630	Notes payable	150	200
Inventories	85	90	Accrued expenses	200	175
Prepaid expenses	35	36	Total current liabilities	$ 575	$ 605
Total current assets	$ 875	$ 786	Long-term debt	$ 900	$1,000
Other			Fund balances	3,100	2,681
Property, plant, and equipment	$5,500	$5,000			
Accumulated depreciation	(1,800)	(1,500)			
Total	$4,575	$4,286	Total	$4,575	$4,286

Restricted Funds—Specific Purpose Funds

Assets	19X2	19X1	Liabilities and Fund Balances	19X2	19X1
Cash	$ 1	$ 1			
Investments	100	35			
Grants receivable	45	0	Fund balances	$ 146	$ 36
Total	$ 146	$ 36	Total	$ 146	$ 36

Plant Replacement and Expansion Funds

Assets	19X2	19X1	Liabilities and Fund Balances	19X2	19X1
Cash	$ 10	$ 225			
Investments	400	145			
Pledges receivable	10	180	Fund balances	$ 420	$ 550
Total	$ 420	$ 550	Total	$ 420	$ 550

Endowment Funds

Assets	19X2	19X1	Liabilities and Fund Balances	19X2	19X1
Cash	$ 25	$ 17			
Investments	3,100	2,000	Fund balances	$3,125	$2,017
Total	$3,125	$2,017	Total	$3,125	$2,017

[1] All dollar amounts in thousands

	19X2	19X1
Public support and revenue[1]		
Contributions	$ 2,200	$ 2,300
Revenues earned	145	215
Total revenues	$ 2,345	$ 2,515
Expenses		
Management and general	$ 300	$ 325
Fund-raising program expenses	325	270
Service No. 1	700	690
Service No. 2	275	240
Service No. 3	300	260
Service No. 4	290	245
Total expenses	$ 2,190	$ 2,030
Excess of public support and revenues		
over expenses	$ 155	$ 485
Additional nondollar quantitative data		
Units of Service No. 1	50	40
Units of Service No. 2	5,000	4,500
Units of Service No. 3	300	260
Units of Service No. 4	50,000	40,000

[1] All dollar amounts in thousands

Required:

1. Develop appropriate analytical data to be used in evaluating the operations of the health and welfare agency.
2. Comment on your findings.

Appendix A:
Selected Portions
of Fundamental Concepts
# of Financial Accounting
and Reporting for Colleges
and Universities[1]

FUND ACCOUNTING

To satisfy the requirement to account properly for the diversity of resources and their use, the principles and practices of "fund accounting" are employed. Within this concept, there have evolved certain principles of classification and presentation of accounting data as well as standard terminology for institutions of higher education.

Fund accounting is the manner of organizing and managing the accounting by which resources for various purposes are classified for financial accounting and reporting purposes in accordance with activities or objectives as specified by donors, with regulations, restrictions, or limitations imposed by sources outside the institution, or with directions issued by the governing board. In this respect, a clear distinction between funds which are externally restricted and those which are internally designated by action of the governing board should be maintained in the accounts and disclosed in the financial reports.

A fund is an accounting entity with a self-balancing set of accounts consisting of assets, liabilities, and a fund balance. Separate accounts are

[1] From *College and University Business Administration*, 4th ed. (Washington, DC, 1982), by permission of the National Association of College and University Business Officers (NACUBO).

312

maintained for each fund to insure observance of limitations and restrictions placed on use of resources. For reporting purposes, however, funds of similar characteristics are combined into fund groups. The fund groups generally found in an educational institution are as follows:

Current funds

Loan funds

Endowment and similar funds

Annuity and life income funds

Plant funds

Agency funds.

In addition to the foregoing fund groups, there may be additional fund groups unique to particular institutions, such as self-administered employee retirement funds. If there are such fund groups, they should be accounted for separately and reported in the annual financial statements.

Since each fund group is considered as a separate entity, there are numerous transactions among the fund groups, which must recognize this entity concept. When the movement of funds from one fund group to another is intended to be permanent, it should be recorded as a transfer between the fund entities. However, when the movement is intended to be temporary, the transaction should be recorded as an interfund borrowing. To be considered temporary, and therefore an interfund borrowing, there should be a definite plan of repayment within a defined period of time. A further indication that a borrower-lender relationship exists would be if interest were being paid by the borrowing fund group to the lending fund group.

When the current funds group is divided into two or more parts, such as unrestricted, auxiliary enterprises, and restricted categories, the permanent or temporary movement of funds among these parts would follow the rule above. One example of this would be an auxiliary enterprise having a deficit that must be eliminated because of a provision in an agreement with bondholders. Another would be the lifting of a restriction by a donor, resulting in the movement of funds from a restricted to unrestricted category.

In some instances, legal provisions and government regulations pertaining to certain funds may require accounting and reporting practices that differ from generally accepted accounting principles. It is recognized that in these instances such legal and regulatory provisions must take precedence. However, such restrictions do not obviate the need for adhering to generally accepted accounting principles for the purpose of reporting financial position, changes in fund balances, and current funds revenues, expenditures, and other changes. An alternative that might be considered by an institution would be to prepare supplementary schedules that would disclose compliance with any restrictions while presenting the basic financial statements (see page 255) in accordance with generally accepted accounting principles. Such a presentation would make it unnecessary for the auditor to qualify the opinion on the basic financial statements absent other reservations concerning them. The auditor might be able to express a separate opinion on the supplementary schedules, for example, stating that they had been prepared in conformity with legal provisions, regulations, or other requirements.

BASIC FINANCIAL STATEMENTS

Colleges and universities generally use three basic statements: a balance sheet, a statement of changes in fund balances, and a statement of current funds revenues, expenditures, and other changes.

The balance sheet presents a series of fund groups, with each group having its own self-balancing assets, liabilities, and fund balances.

The statement of changes in fund balances portrays all the activity that changed the fund balances of the fund groups between the preceding and the current balance sheet dates. This statement includes all additions to, deductions from, and transfers among the fund groups.

The statement of current funds revenues, expenditures, and other changes supplements and presents in detail some of the information presented in summary form in the current funds section of the statement of changes in fund balances. It does not purport to match expenses with revenues to derive a net income—rather, it presents in detail the current funds revenues by source, the current funds expenditures by function, and other changes in current fund balances. Also, it does not report the total revenue and expenditure activity of the institution, but only that related to current funds. The reporting objectives achieved by this statement may be accomplished in other ways.

The emphasis in these basic financial statements is on the status of funds, the flow of resources through fund entities, and the financial operations of the institution. Consideration should be given to supplementary schedules that combine nonfinancial with financial information to assist in further evaluating the activity, achievements, and overall operations of the institution.

ACCRUAL ACCOUNTING

The accounts should be maintained and reports prepared on the accrual basis of accounting. Revenues should be reported when earned, and expenditures when materials or services are received. Expenses incurred at the balance sheet date should be accrued, and expenses applicable to future periods should be deferred. However, certain deferrals and accruals, such as investment income and interest on student loans, are often omitted. Nevertheless, the only basis for their omission should be that the omission does not have a material effect on the financial statements. Revenues and expenditures of an academic term, such as a summer session, which is conducted over a fiscal year end, should be reported totally within the fiscal year in which the program is predominantly conducted.

Encumbrances representing outstanding purchase orders and other commitments for materials or services not received as of the reporting date should not be reported as expenditures nor be included in liabilities in the balance sheet. Designations or allocations of fund balances or disclosure in the notes to the financial statements should be made where such commitments are material in amount. Failure to disclose the distinction between true liabilities and encumbrances that are not true liabilities could result in the presentation of misleading information to state authorities, regulatory bodies, budget commissions, and others.[2]

In the case of institutions that maintain their books on the cash basis, journal entries should be recorded, as necessary, to convert accounts to the accrual basis as of the end of a fiscal year.

ACCOUNTING FOR DEPRECIATION

Depreciation is an element of cost resulting from the service of long-lived assets in an economic organization. In business accounting, depreciation charges are recorded as an expense because they must be related to the revenue produced by the fixed assets in determining accurately the net profit or loss for a stated period of time. The correct determination of net profit or loss of a business operation is important for several reasons: (1) to gauge the value of the enterprise as a going concern; (2) to ascertain the value and earning power of its equity securities; (3) to provide a realistic basis for borrowing; (4) to determine earnings that may be available for distribution to owners in the form of dividends; and (5) to determine its tax liability under federal and state income tax laws.

Unlike businesses, colleges and universities are not faced with the same requirements for profit and loss determination. Rather, they exist to provide services, and the general expenditures incurred therefore have no causative relationship with and do not generate any general revenues. They do not pay taxes based on income; their fixed assets are not directly related to their general credit and debt-incurring capacity; they are not traded or sold as are businesses; and any excess of revenues over expenditures—for a single year or cumulatively—is not available for distribution

[2] American Institute of Certified Public Accountants, *Audits of Colleges and Universities* (New York: AICPA, 1973), p. 7.

in the manner that corporate profits are available for distribution to stock-holders.

Under these operating characteristics, which are devoid of profitability considerations, any recording of depreciation on capital assets in the current operating accounts would not only fail to serve any essential informational purpose in the financial statements and reports, but could actually be misleading to the users of such statements and reports—misleading because the charging of current operations with depreciation indicates a matching of costs with directly related revenues in the generally accepted business accounting sense when, in fact, no causative relationship between revenues and expenditures exists for colleges and universities.

That depreciation is not recorded does not, of course, deny its existence as an economic fact of life. Nor does it preclude the calculation and recording of depreciation in certain specialized accounting and managerial operations. For certain activities that are susceptible of accurate and definitive measurement, it may be desirable for management to know the unit costs of providing such activities on a continuing basis. Full costs are sometimes required as a basis for charging using departments for goods and services. In such cases, depreciation is an essential element in the development of unit costs.[3]

Thus, depreciation expense related to assets comprising the physical plant is reported neither in the statement of current funds revenues, expenditures, and other changes nor in the current funds section of the statement of changes in fund balances. Capital asset acquisitions financed from current funds are reported as expenditures of that group in the year of acquisition.

For purposes of statement presentation, depreciation allowance may be reported in the balance sheet and the provision for depreciation reported in the statement of changes in the balance of the Investment in Plant subgroup of the Plant Funds group. In the Endowment and Similar Funds groups, depreciation should be provided on depreciable assets held as investments in order to maintain the distinction between principal and income in those funds.

Depreciation should not be confused with the provision of funds for maintenance and replacement of buildings and equipment.

ACCOUNTING FOR INVESTMENTS

Investment purchases usually are reported at cost, and investments received as gifts usually are reported at the fair market or appraised value at the date of gift. As a permissible alternative, investments may be reported at current market or fair value, provided this basis is used for all investments

[3] Adapted from National Committee on Governmental Accounting, *Governmental Accounting, Auditing, and Financial Reporting* (Chicago: Municipal Finance Officers Association, 1968), p. 11.

in all funds. When using this alternative, unrealized gains and losses should be reported in the same manner as realized gains and losses under the cost basis.

Interfund sales of investments should be recorded by the purchasing fund at fair market or appraised value at date of sale. The differences between carrying value and fair market or appraised value should be accounted for in the selling fund as realized gains and losses.

Investments of the various funds may be pooled unless prohibited by statute or by terms of the gifts. Proper determination of equities and the basis of income distribution should be made by using current market values on a share or unit plan. This determination can be made through the use of memorandum records and does not require the recording of each investment at current market value in the accounts.

ACCOUNTING FOR INSTITUTIONS OPERATED BY RELIGIOUS GROUPS

Accounting and reporting records of an institution should be adequately segregated from the records of the sponsoring religious group so that the educational entity is in fact accounted for as a separate entity. Facilities made available to the educational entity by the religious group should be disclosed in the financial reports together with any related indebtedness.

The monetary value of services contributed by members of the religious group should be recorded in the accounts and reported in the financial statements. The gross value of such services should be determined by relating them to equivalent salaries and wages for similarly ranked personnel at the same or similar institutions, including the normal staff benefits such as group insurance and retirement provisions.

The amounts so determined should be recorded as expenditures by department or division, following the same classification as other expenditures, and a like amount should be recorded as gift revenue. The gift revenue should be reduced by the amount of maintenance, living costs, and personal expenses incurred, which are related to the contributing personnel and have no counterpart in a lay employee relationship.

In some cases, checks are drawn to the religious group and charged to expenditure accounts in the same manner as payroll checks. The religious group then makes a contribution to the institution, which records it as a gift. The determination of the contribution would rest with the religious group, since the latter is a separate entity.

In some cases these institutions inform the reader of the financial report as to the relative value of such contributed services by comparison with the average return on endowment fund investment. Such information should be limited to the notes to the financial statements, and the imputed capitalized value of such contributions should not be reflected in the balance sheet.

Appendix B: Principles of Accounting for Hospitals

1. For accounting purposes, the hospital is an entity capable of buying, selling, and taking other economic actions that are to be accounted for and summarized by means that segregate the affairs of the hospital from the personal affairs of those charged with its administration and operations.

2. Another basic accounting concept is that of continuity of activity—the hospital is a going concern.

3. Information produced by the accounting process should be based, to the extent possible, on objectively determined facts.

4. Although conservatism exerts less influence on accounting procedures that it once did, it is still one of the basic accounting concepts.

5. Consistency means that uniform procedures should be practiced continuously from one period to another.

6. The concept of full disclosure requires that all significant data be clearly and completely reflected in accounting reports.

7. Materiality is an elusive concept, for the dividing line between material and immaterial amounts cannot be readily determined. It is clear, however, that an amount is material if its exclusion from an accounting statement would cause misleading or incorrect conclusions.

8. Accounting records represent primarily events and facts that can be expressed in dollars and cents. Use of the monetary unit as the common

This material has been condensed and adapted by the author from *Chart of Accounts for Hospitals* (Chicago, IL: American Hospital Publishing, Inc., © 1976), pp. 5–13. Used by permission of the American Hospital Publishing, Inc., Chicago.

denominator in the accounting process enables summations to be made of different kinds of assets, liabilities, revenues, and expenses. Accounting is designed to measure every transaction according to the number of dollars involved, regardless of whether the value (purchasing power) of the dollars remains the same. The underlying assumption, of course, is that the general price level does remain reasonably stable; otherwise, the usefulness of the dollar as the standard of measurement would be impaired.

There is growing support for the practice of restating the historical costs of fixed assets and related depreciation charges to reflect general price-level changes. There is usually a significant difference between the historical costs and the restated historical costs reflecting changes in the general price level. For this reason, recovery of depreciation charges based on historical costs is inadequate to replace existing fixed assets. Historically, the price level rises; therefore, depreciation charges for a given period should be based on historical costs restated to reflect the current price level. In other words, it is not enough simply to recover the number of dollars invested in plant assets; accounting and financial policies should allow the hospital's productive capacity to be maintained substantially intact. The hospital's obligation is to preserve plant capital at the current price level.

The American Hospital Association endorses this method of depreciation and fixed asset accounting and recommends its use in financial recording and reporting, although it is not in accordance with the accounting principles promulgated by the AICPA. When depreciation charges are based on historical costs restated to reflect changes in the general price level, the following guidelines should be observed:

> Changes in the general price level should be determined by reference to an index of the general price level, not to an index of the price of a specific type of goods or service. The gross national product (GNP) Implicit Price Deflator is considered to be the most comprehensive indicator of the general price level in the United States and should normally be used.

> The general price-level increments should be formally recorded in the appropriate accounts. Depreciation should be computed on the basis of general price levels. Adjustments in the amount of depreciation recorded should be made for that portion of the assets currently being financed through debt.

> Full disclosure must be made in the financial statements on the basis of valuing fixed assets and of determining depreciation charges. The differences between those fixed assets and related depreciation charges that are based on historical cost and those fixed assets and related depreciation charges that are restated for general price-level changes must also be disclosed.

> Changes in the general price level should be determined and presented in terms of the general purchasing power of the dollar at the time the latest balance sheet is generated.

9. Cost is used in accounting as the basis for valuation of most assets and for recording of most expenses because it is considered to be a permanent and objective measurement that reflects the accountability of management for the utilization of funds. . . . When a hospital acquires property or services through donations there is no cost in the usual sense. Nevertheless, the acquired property or service should be entered in the accounting records at its fair market value when received.

An exception to the historical cost principle can be made in the valuation of long-term security investments. Traditionally these investments have been carried in hospital accounting records at the original cost, if purchased, and at the fair market value at the date of donation, if donated. However, periodic (quarterly, semiannual, or annual) adjustment of the investment accounts can be made to reflect current market values.

10. To ensure completeness, accuracy, and meaningfulness in accounting data, use of the accrual basis of accounting is required.

11. If a hospital uses accelerated depreciation for cost reimbursement purposes and a different method for financial statement purposes, the effect of such differences should be deferred.

12. In addition to funds that can be used for general operating purposes, hospitals also receive gifts, endowments, grants, and appropriations. . . . In fund accounting the hospital's resources, obligations, and capital balances should be segregated in the accounts into logical groups based on legal restrictions and administrative requirements. There are two basic fund groups: restricted funds and general funds.

Restricted funds can be categorized as follows: endowment funds, plant replacement and expansion fund, and specific purpose fund. The accounts for each restricted fund are self-balancing, as each fund constitutes a subordinate accounting entity.

The general fund or operating fund is used to account for the resources, obligations, and day-to-day activities that are not restricted by terms of grants, gifts, or other donations.

13. Various funds can be pooled for investment, unless this practice is prohibited by statute or by the terms of the donation or the grant.

14. All pledges should be included in the hospital's accounting records, and a provision made for amounts estimated to be uncollectible.

15. Some hospitals have endowment type funds held in trusts by outside parties. . . . These funds should not be included in the balance sheet, but their existence should be disclosed.

16. Hospital revenue consists mainly of the value—at the hospital's full established rates, regardless of the amounts actually paid to the hospital by or on behalf of patients—of all hospital services rendered to patients.

17. In many instances, the hospital receives less than its full established rates—sometimes even nothing—for the services it renders. It is essential that accounting information reflect both the potential gross revenue and the revenue "losses" resulting from the inability to collect payment at the established rates. These revenue "losses," called *deductions from revenues*, are of five basic types:

    (a) charity services
    (b) contractual adjustments
    (c) personnel adjustments
    (d) administrative and policy adjustments
    (e) provision for bad debts.

18. Expenses are expired costs; that is, costs that have been used or consumed in carrying on some activity and from which no benefit will extend beyond the present.

The objective of expense accounting is to accumulate, on an accrual basis, complete and meaningful records of expenses in a manner that clearly associates them with responsibility centers in the hospital.

19. Hospital revenue should be recorded in the period in which it is earned, that is, in the time period during which the services are rendered to patients. Once the revenue determination has been made, measurement should be made of the amount of expense incurred in rendering the service on which the revenue determination was based. Unless there is such a matching of accomplishment (revenue) and effort (expense), the reported excess of revenue over expenses of a period is a meaningless figure.

BIBLIOGRAPHY

Accounting Advisory Committee. *Report to the Commission on Private Philanthropy and Public Needs.* Washington, DC: The Commission on Private Philanthropy and Public Needs, 1974.

Adams, Bert K., Quentin M. Hill, Joseph A. Perkins, Jr., and Philip S. Shaw. *Principles of Public School Accounting.* State Educational Records and Reports Series, Handbook II B. Washington, DC: National Center for Educational Statistics, Department of Health, Education, and Welfare, U.S. Government Printing Office, 1967.

American Council on Education. *College and University Business Administration.* 4th ed. Washington, DC: American Council on Education, 1982.

_____. *American Universities and Colleges.* 12th ed. Washington, DC: American Council on Education, 1983.

American Hospital Association. *Chart of Accounts for Hospitals.* Chicago: American Hospital Association, 1983.

_____. *Guide to the Health Care Field.* Chicago: American Hospital Association, 1977.

American Institute of Certified Public Accountants. Accounting Standards Executive Committee *Exposure Draft.* "Proposed Statement of Position on Accounting Principles and Reporting Practices for Nonprofit Organizations Not Covered by Existing AICPA Audit Guides." New York: AICPA, 1978.

_____. APB Statement 4, *Basic Concepts and Accounting Principles Underlying Financial Statements of Business Enterprises.* New York: AICPA, 1970.

_____. Accounting Standards Division, Subcommittee on State and Local Governmental Auditing. "Statement of Position on Accrual of Revenues and Expenditures by State and Local Governmental Units." In *AICPA Industry Audit Guide on Audits of State and Local Governmental Units,* pp. 161–168. New York: AICPA, 1975.

_____. Committee on College and University Accounting and Auditing. *Audits of Colleges and Universities.* New York: AICPA, 1973.

_____. Committee on Health Care Institutions. *Hospital Audit Guide.* 3rd ed. New York: AICPA, 1980.

_____. Committee on Health Care Institutions. *Medicare Audit Guide.* New York: AICPA, 1969.

———. Committee on Voluntary Health and Welfare Organizations. *Audits of Voluntary Health and Welfare Organizations.* New York: AICPA, 1974.

———. Report of the Study Group on the Objectives of Financial Statements. *Objectives of Financial Statements.* New York: AICPA, 1973.

———. Statement of Position 74-8, *Financial Accounting and Reporting by Colleges and Universities.* New York: AICPA, 1974.

———. Statement of Position 78-1, *Accounting by Hospitals for Certain Marketable Equity Securities.* New York: AICPA, 1978.

———. Statement of Position 78-7, *Financial Accounting and Reporting by Hospitals Operated by a Governmental Unit.* New York: AICPA, 1978.

———. Statement of Position 78-10, *Accounting Principles and Reporting Practices for Certain Nonprofit Organizations.* New York: AICPA, 1978.

———. Statement of Position 80-2, *Accounting and Financial Reporting by Governmental Units.* New York: AICPA, 1980.

Andrews, F. Emerson. *Attitudes Toward Giving.* New York: Russell Sage Foundation, 1953.

Anthony, Robert N. *Financial Accounting in Nonbusiness Organizations: An Exploratory Study of Conceptual Issues.* Stamford, CT: Financial Accounting Standards Board, 1978.

Anthony, Robert N., and Regina Herzlinger. *Management Control in Nonprofit Organizations.* Homewood, IL: Richard D. Irwin, 1980.

Babunakis, Michael. *Budgets: An Analytical and Procedural Handbook for Government and Nonprofit Organizations.* Westport, CT: Greenwood Press, 1976.

Boyett, Arthur S., and Gary A. Giroux. "The Relevance of Municipal Financial Statements for Investor Decisions: An Empirical Study." Paper presented at American Accounting Association Southwest Regional Meeting, New Orleans, March 24, 1977.

Bruce, Paul K., Robert Elkin, Daniel D. Robinson, and Harold I. Steinberg. *Reporting of Service Efforts and Accomplishments.* Stamford, CT: Financial Accounting Standards Board, 1980.

Canadian Institute of Chartered Accountants. *Financial Reporting for Non-Profit Organizations.* Toronto: Canadian Institute of Chartered Accountants, 1980.

Cary, W. L., and C. B. Bright. *The Law and the Lore of Endowment Funds.* Rev. ed. New York: Ford Foundation, 1974.

Chan, James L., ed. *Research in Governmental and Non-Profit Accounting.* Vol. 1. Greenwich, CT; London, England: Auai Press, Inc., 1985.

Club Managers Association of America. *Uniform System of Accounts for Clubs.* 2nd rev. ed. Washington, DC: Club Managers Association of America, 1967.

College Blue Book. 19th ed. New York: Macmillan Information, 1983.

Committee on Accounting in the Public Sector, 1974–76. "Report of the Committee on Accounting in the Public Sector." *The Accounting Review* 52; Supplement: 33–52.

Committee on Concepts of Accounting Applicable to the Public Sector, 1970–71. "Report of the Committee on Concepts of Accounting Applicable to the Public Sector." *The Accounting Review* 47; Supplement: 77–108.

Committee on Nonprofit Organizations. "Report of the Committee on Accounting Practice for Not-for-Profit Organizations." *The Accounting Review* 46; Supplement: 81–163.

_____. "Report of the Committee on Not-for-Profit Organizations, 1972–73." *The Accounting Review* 49; Supplement: 225–249.

_____. "Report of the Committee on Not-for-Profit Organizations, 1973–74." *The Accounting Review* 50; Supplement: 1–39.

Comptroller General of the United States. *Standards for Audit of Governmental Organizations, Programs, Activities and Functions.* Washington, DC: U.S. General Accounting Office, 1972.

_____. "Accounting Principles and Standards for Federal Agencies." Title 2 to the *Government Accounting Office Manual for Guidance of Federal Agencies.* Washington, DC: U.S. General Accounting Office, 1972.

_____. *New York City's Efforts to Improve Its Accounting Systems.* GAO Report to the Congress, April 4, 1977. Washington, DC: U.S. General Accounting Office, 1977.

Coopers & Lybrand and the University of Michigan. *Financial Disclosure Practices of American Cities.* New York: Coopers & Lybrand, 1976.

Copeland, Ronald M., and Robert W. Ingram. *Municipal Financial Reporting and Disclosure Quality.* Reading, MA: Addison-Wesley Publishing Company, 1983.

David, Irvin T., C. Eugene Sturgeon, and Eula L. Adams. *How to Evaluate and Improve Internal Controls in Governmental Units.* Chicago: Municipal Finance Officers Association, 1981.

Davidson, Sidney, David O. Green, Walter Hellerstein, Albert Madansky, and Roman L. Weil. *Financial Reporting by State and Local Government Units.* Chicago: The Center for Management of Public and Nonprofit Enterprise of the Graduate School of Business, The University of Chicago, 1977.

Drebin, Allan R., James L. Chan, and Lorna C. Ferguson. *Objectives of Accounting and Financial Reporting for Governmental Units: A Research Study.* Vols. 1 and 2. Chicago: National Council on Governmental Accounting, 1981.

Englander, Louis. *Accounting Principles and Procedures of Philanthropic Institutions.* New York: New York Community Trust, 1959.

Financial Accounting Standards Board. *Discussion Memorandum,* "Conceptual Framework for Financial Accounting and Reporting: Elements of Financial Statements and Their Measurement." Stamford, CT: FASB, 1976.

_____. *Exposure Draft,* "Objectives of Financial Reporting and Elements of Financial Statements of Business Enterprises." Stamford, CT: FASB, 1977.

Ford Foundation Advisory Committee on Endowment Management. *Managing Educational Endowments.* New York: Ford Foundation, 1969.

Friedman, L. B. *Budgeting Municipal Expenditures: A Study in Comparative Policy Making.* New York: Praeger Publishers, 1975.

Gross, Malvern J., Jr. *Financial and Accounting Guide for Nonprofit Organizations.* 2nd ed. New York: The Ronald Press Company, 1974.

Hackett, R. P. "Trends in Governmental Accounting." In *Handbook of Modern Accounting Theory,* edited by Morton Backer, pp. 563–580. Englewood Cliffs, NJ: Prentice-Hall, Inc., 1955.

Hay, Leon, E. *Accounting for Governmental and Nonprofit Entities.* 6th ed. Homewood, IL: Richard D. Irwin, 1980.

Henke, Emerson O. "Accounting for Nonprofit Organizations: An Exploratory Study." *Indiana Business Information Bulletin No. 53.* Bloomington, IN: Bureau of Business Research, Graduate School of Business, Indiana University, 1965.

Holder, William W. *A Study of Selected Concepts for Government Financial Accounting and Reporting.* Chicago: National Council on Governmental Accounting, 1980.

Kerrigan, H. D. *Fund Accounting.* New York: McGraw-Hill, 1969.

Lehan, Edward A. *Simplified Governmental Budgeting.* Chicago: Municipal Finance Officers Association, 1981.

Lewin, Arie Y., and James H. Scheiner. *Requiring Municipal Performance Reporting: An Analysis Based Upon Users' Information Needs.* Durham, NC: Graduate School of Business Administration, Duke University, 1977.

Lynn, Edward S., and Robert J. Freeman. *Fund Accounting: Theory and Practice.* 2nd ed. Englewood Cliffs, NJ: Prentice-Hall, Inc., 1983.

Mosk, Lennox L. *Municipal Bonds–Planning, Sale, and Administration.* Chicago: Municipal Finance Officers Association, 1982.

Municipal Finance Officers Association (now Government Finance Officers Association). *Guidelines for Preparation of a Public Employee Retirement System: Illustrations of Notes to the Financial Statements of State and Local Governments.* Financial Reporting Series 1. Chicago: Municipal Finance Officers Association, 1983.

Municipal Finance Officers Association (now Government Finance Officers Association). *Guidelines for Preparations of a Public Employee Retirement*

System: Guide to Municipal Leasing, edited by A. John Vogt and Lisa Cole. Chicago: Municipal Finance Officers Association, 1983.

Municipal Finance Officers Association (now Government Finance Officers Association). *Guidelines for Preparation of a Public Employee Retirement System: Disclosure Guidelines for State and Local Governments.* Chicago: Municipal Finance Officers Association, 1979.

Municipal Finance Officers Association (now Government Finance Officers Association). *Guidelines for Preparation of a Public Employee Retirement System: Fiscal Almanac.* Chicago: Municipal Finance Officers Association, 1982.

Municipal Finance Officers Association (now Government Finance Officers Association). *Guidelines for Preparation of a Public Employee Retirement System: Developing a Financial Management Information System for Local Government.* Chicago: Municipal Finance Officers Association, 1980.

Municipal Finance Officers Association (now Government Finance Officers Association). *Guidelines for Preparation of a Public Employee Retirement System. Directory of Financial Services for State and Local Government.* Chicago: Municipal Finance Officers Association, 1982.

Municipal Finance Officers Association (now Government Finance Officers Association). *Disclosure Guidelines for Offerings of Securities by State and Local Governments.* Chicago: Municipal Finance Officers Association, 1976.

National Association of College and University Business Officers. *Planning, Budgeting and Accounting: Section II of a College Operating Manual.* Prepared by Peat, Marwick, Mitchell & Co. Washington, DC: National Association of College and University Business Officers, 1970.

National Association of Independent Schools. *Accounting for Independent Schools.* 2nd ed. Boston: National Association of Independent Schools, 1977.

National Committee on Governmental Accounting. *Governmental Accounting, Auditing, and Financial Reporting.* Chicago: Municipal Finance Officers Association, 1968.

National Council on Governmental Accounting. *GAAFR Restatement Principles: Exposure Draft.* Chicago: Municipal Finance Officers Association, 1978.

National Health Council, National Assembly of National Voluntary Health and Social Welfare Organizations, Inc., and United Way of America. *Standards of Accounting and Financial Reporting for Voluntary Health and Welfare Organizations.* New York: 1975.

Peterson, John E., and Wesley C. Hough. *Creative Capital Financing for State and Local Governments.* Chicago: Municipal Finance Officers Association, 1983.

Price Waterhouse & Co. *A Survey of Financial Reporting and Accounting Practices of Private Foundations.* New York: Price Waterhouse & Co., 1977.

_____. *Accounting Principles and Reporting Practices for Certain Nonprofit Organizations.* New York: Price Waterhouse & Co., 1978.

_____. *Understanding Local Government Financial Statements: A Citizen's Guide.* New York: Price Waterhouse & Co., 1976.

Reilly, Paul R. *Fixed Asset Accounting and Reporting.* Chicago: Municipal Finance Officers Association, 1978.

Sherwood, Hugh C. *How Corporate and Municipal Debt Is Rated.* New York: John Wiley & Sons, 1976.

Skousen, K. Fred, Jay M. Smith, and Leon W. Woodfield. *User Needs: An Empirical Study of College and University Financial Reporting.* Washington, DC: National Association of College and University Business Officers, 1975.

Taylor, P. J., and K. T. Granville. *Financial Management of Higher Education.* New York: Coopers & Lybrand, 1973.

Texas, University of, and the Municipal Finance Officers Association. *Municipal Accounting and Reporting: Issues for Research.* (Reporting a conference presented by the Department of Accounting of the University of Texas at Austin and the Municipal Finance Officers Association, at Joe C. Thompson Conference Center, University of Texas, on Nov. 11 and 12, 1976.) Chicago: Alexander Grant & Co., 1977.

Touche Ross & Co. *Issues and a Viewpoint: Public Financial Reporting by Local Government.* New York: Touche Ross & Co., 1977.

Traub, Jack. *Accounting and Reporting Practices of Private Foundations.* New York: Praeger Publishers, 1977.

United States Cost Accounting Standards Board. *Cost Accounting Standards.* As listed in *Federal Register.*

United States Department of Health, Education, and Welfare. *A Guide for Non-Profit Institutions: Cost Principles and Procedures for Establishing Indirect Cost and Other Rates for Grants and Contracts with the Department of Health, Education, and Welfare.* Washington, DC: Department of Health, Education, and Welfare Publication No. OASC-5, U.S. Government Printing Office, 1974.

United States General Service Administration. *Cost Principles for Educational Institutions.* Federal Management Circular 73-8. Washington, DC: Office of Management and Budget, 1973.

United Way of America. *Accounting and Financial Reporting: A Guide for United Ways and Not-for-Profit Human Service Organizations.* Alexandria, VA: United Way of America, 1974.

Vargo, R. J. *Readings in Governmental and Nonprofit Accounting.* Ann Arbor, MI: Wadsworth Publishing, Inc., 1977.

Vatter, William J. *The Fund Theory of Accounting and Its Implications for Financial Reports.* Chicago: The University of Chicago Press, 1974. Midway reprint, 1974.

Wildavsky, Aaron. *The Politics of the Budgetary Process.* 2nd ed. Boston: Little, Brown and Company, 1974.

Williamson, J. Peter. *Performance Measurement and Investment Objectives for Educational Endowment Funds.* New York: The Common Fund, 1972.

Wolfe, Harry B., Judith D. Bentkover, Helen H. Schauffler, and Ann Venable. *Health Cost Containment: Challenge to Industry.* New York: Financial Executives Research Foundation, 1980.

INDEX

329